W9-AEN-032

STORIES LIVES TELL

Narrative and Dialogue in Education

STORIES LIVES TELL

Narrative and Dialogue in Education

Edited by
CAROL WITHERELL & NEL NODDINGS

Foreword by Maxine Greene

 Teachers College, Columbia University
New York and London

Samford University Library

Published by Teachers College Press, 1234 Amsterdam Avenue
New York, NY 10027

Copyright © 1991 by Teachers College, Columbia University

All rights reserved. No part of this publication may be reproduced
or transmitted in any form or by any means, electronic or mechanical,
including photocopy, or any information storage and retrieval system,
without permission from the publisher.

Library of Congress Cataloging-in-Publication Data

Stories lives tell : narrative and dialogue in education / edited by
 Carol Witherell & Nel Noddings ; foreword by Maxine Greene.
  p. cm.
 Includes bibliographical references and index.
 ISBN 0-8077-3071-8. — ISBN 0-8077-3070-X (pbk.)
  1. Literature—Study and teaching. I. Witherell, Carol.
 II. Noddings, Nel.
 LB1575.S76 1991
 807—dc20   90-48120
                                                    CIP

ISBN 0-8077-3071-8
ISBN 0-8077-3070-X (pbk.)

Printed on acid-free paper
Manufactured in the United States of America

97 96 95 94 93 92 91   8 7 6 5 4 3 2 1

LB
1027.3
.S76
1991

*We dedicate this book
to our children and our students,
whose stories have been great gifts.*

Contents

Foreword

MAXINE GREENE

The sounds of storytelling are everywhere today. Narratives of many kinds are being opened and explored. Journal keeping goes on apace on all levels of learning; people write autobiographies, shape family histories, become authors of their own lives. There were intimations of this phenomenon in years past: Roquentin, in Sartre's *Nausea*, realizing that "everything changes when you tell about life" (1959, p. 57); Walter Benjamin writing about the task of the storyteller being one of fashioning "the raw material of existence, his own and that of others, in a solid, useful, and unique way" (1978, p. 108). Alfred Schutz, in "Making Music Together," spoke about the "flux of experiences in inner time and living through a vivid present in common" (1964, p. 173). This depended on the communication of attitudes, the binding together of disparate events — in effect, the telling of a story. Jerome Bruner (evoked by a number of the writers in the chapters to come) wrote that "narrative deals with the vicissitudes of human intentions" and identified storytelling as a human mode of thought (1986, pp. 16 ff). Alasdair MacIntyre has stressed the fact that actions become intelligible when human beings tell about their intentions; "narrative history," he said, "of a certain kind turns out to be the basic and essential genre for the characterization of human actions" (1981, p. 194). More recently, Charles Taylor has written that "because we cannot but orient ourselves to the good, and thus determine our place relative to it . . . , we must inescapably understand our lives in narrative form, as a 'quest'" (1989, pp. 51–52).

The rich and far-ranging chapters in the present text bring these various concerns to a kind of culmination, certainly where teaching and learning are concerned. Even as they do so, they suggest the ways in which persons, long inarticulate, are overcoming the silences by thinking and speaking in terms of story. Many of the sources lie in women's experiences of such overcoming. Tillie Olsen wrote about how unnatural were the silences: "the unnatural thwarting of what struggles to come into being, but cannot" (1978, p. 6); and the following pages glow with incidents of and possibilities for the articulation she had in mind. Indeed, for all the

fact that a few of the chapters are written by men, it is difficult not to have
the feeling that the passion evoked by the discovery of "voice" and the
moral and cognitive significance of the discovery have much to do with the
belated recognition of "women's ways of knowing" (Belenky, Clinchy,
Goldberger, & Tarule, 1986). The authors of the book by that name speak
of the integration of the inner voice and the voice of reason, of what Sara
Ruddick calls "passionate reason," connected and caring reason (1984, p.
142). It is evident in this book, as it was in *Women's Ways of Knowing*, that
the new interest in dialogue and narrative transfigures and renews what
has been learned from the great spokesmen of the recent past.

Not only are voices set free to speak to others and among others in live
classrooms and counseling centers; they resonate with the sense of seeking,
struggling to name, striving to find language for what was repressed and
suppressed over the years. Also, they are marvelously multiple. There is, as
will be realized, a common theme: the ways in which stories — and myths,
and diaries, and histories — give shape and expression to what would otherwise be untold about "our lives." But the chapters are distinctive, because
each writer writes in an authentic tone, with a particular style. The connection and the integration the reader will achieve will come not only as an
emergent from a dialogue. They will be marked by what Mikhail Bakhtin
called "heteroglossia" (1981): the sound of many discourses, many voices;
and the consciousness of a listener or reader affecting what is thought and
what is said. There is an openness about these texts; there is the likelihood
of inclusion, the inclusion of those of us who read.

This is the kind of book that provokes its readers to new modes of
thinking, as it offers them a variety of novel resources for use in classrooms.
We are challenged to choose among a spectrum of alternatives in the course
of our reconceiving what it is to teach and what it is to learn. As the
authors say, we are "invited" to enter a conversation, one not quite like any
we have participated in before. Some may try drama in the classroom;
others, expansions of journal writing; still others, the reading of autobiographies or the writing of multiperspectival histories. Ethics, critical reasoning, religion, ethnography; collaborative work in research or the gathering of teacher "lore" — readers will find their own centers, their own
fundamental concerns. As we do, however, we will find the old poses of
detachment and distance no longer tempting or acceptable. The separation between subject and object will no longer exist, nor will the comforting assurances of cool and shining certainties. Finding our way in this new
domain of possibilities, we will be engaged, and we will be in search.

The closing pages of Toni Morrison's *Beloved* come to mind. Paul D is
remembering his friend trying to describe a woman he knew: "She is a
friend of my mind. She gather me. . . . The pieces I am, she gather them

and give them back to me in all the right order. It's good, you know, when you got a woman who is a friend of your mind." After a moment, Paul D looks at Sethe and thinks that "he wants to put his story next to hers" (1987, pp. 272–73). It may be that education can only take place when we can be the friends of one another's minds. Surely, there will be much to discover if we put our stories next to the stories in this book.

REFERENCES

Bakhtin, Mikhail. (1981). *The dialogic imagination*. Austin: University of Texas Press.

Belenky, Mary; Clinchy, Blythe; Goldberger, Nancy; & Tarule, Jill. (1986). *Women's ways of knowing*. New York: Basic Books.

Benjamin, Walter. (1978). The storyteller. In *Illuminations*. New York: Schocken Books.

Bruner, Jerome. (1986). *Actual minds, possible worlds*. Cambridge, MA: Harvard University Press.

MacIntyre, Alasdair. (1981). *After virtue*. Notre Dame, IN: Notre Dame University Press.

Morrison, Toni. (1987). *Beloved*. New York: Alfred A. Knopf.

Olsen, Tillie. (1978). *Silences*. New York: Delacorte.

Ruddick, Sara. (1984). New combinations: Learning from Virginia Woolf. In C. Asher, L. De Salvor, & S. Ruddick, *Between women* (pp. 137–159). Boston: Beacon Press.

Sartre, Jean Paul. (1959). *Nausea*. New York: New Directions Press.

Schutz, Alfred. (1964). Making music together. In Arvid Brodersen (Ed.), *Collected papers: Vol. 2. Studies in social theory*. The Hague: Martinus Nijhoff.

Taylor, Charles. (1989). *Sources of the self*. Cambridge, MA: Harvard University Press.

Acknowledgments

Many individuals have contributed to this book. First and foremost, we wish to thank the contributors, who helped to create and nurture the text to its present form. *Stories Lives Tell* had its origins at a symposium at an annual meeting of the American Educational Research Association in which we, along with Jo Anne Pagano, were participants. The work presented here grew to include contributions from many other authors from different disciplines and regions of the country.

We wish to thank those who read and critiqued portions of the manuscript at various stages, including Earl Hanson, professor of biology at Wesleyan University; Thomas James, associate professor of education at Brown University; Virginia Shabatay and Andra Makler, two of our contributing authors; Elaine Smith; James Shipton; and students in the graduate core program at Lewis & Clark College.

Carole Saltz, Susan Liddicoat, Karen Altman, and especially the late Ron Galbraith at Teachers College Press were not only helpful but wonderful to work with throughout this project. Our thanks go to them and to others at Teachers College Press who helped with this book at various points of its production.

Finally, every writer knows of the contributions and sacrifices made by colleagues, friends, and family members during the creation of a manuscript. We extend our deep thanks to Jane Wassam for her assistance with typing and editing, and to Heidi Witherell and Jim Noddings for their very special care and support.

STORIES LIVES TELL

Narrative and Dialogue in Education

Storytelling, as every writer knows,
is a kind of magic act.

Cynthia Ozick
"Usurpation (Other People's Stories)"

PROLOGUE

An Invitation to Our Readers

CAROL WITHERELL and NEL NODDINGS

What is it that captures us in a good story? "Tell me a story," we beg as small children, in order to both know and imagine our world. "Can you give us an example?" our college students ask, looking for a story in which to ground a new theory or idea. A 92-year-old woman, recently moved into a nursing home, asks her 54-year-old daughter to tell her again and again what happened to her piano and her cat, calling one she loves to help her hold on to the story of her life. The stories we hear and the stories we tell shape the meaning and texture of our lives at every stage and juncture.

Stories and narrative, whether personal or fictional, provide meaning and belonging in our lives. They attach us to others and to our own histories by providing a tapestry rich with threads of time, place, character, and even advice on what we might do with our lives. The story fabric offers us images, myths, and metaphors that are morally resonant and contribute both to our knowing and our being known.

We live and invent our lives through our texts, Carolyn Heilbrun writes in *Writing a Woman's Life*. Decisions as to which stories will be told and which suppressed not only give definition to a life but serve as a form of power for the writer. The teacher, like the writer, knows of this power through the oral and written texts of classroom life, as the counselor or analyst recognizes it in the therapeutic dialogue, and the pastor, priest, or rabbi, in narratives of faith and loss.

This book is about the power of narrative in human lives — the stories lives tell — in educational practice and research. It has been shaped by the work and thought of many individuals. Carol Gilligan's work on women's identity and moral development; Nel Noddings's writings on the ethic of care and moral education; the work of Mary Belenky, Blythe Clinchy, Nancy Goldberger, and Jill Tarule on the development of "voice" and women's ways of knowing; the rich cultural portraits in the work of anthropologist Barbara Myerhoff; Lawrence Kohlberg's lifelong work in the area of moral development; the work of Mikhail Bakhtin, Martin Buber,

1

Paulo Freire and Ira Shor, Maxine Greene, and Nel Noddings on the topic of dialogue — all have informed our understanding of narrative and dialogue in education. The stories of writers such as Elie Wiesel, Toni Morrison, Eudora Welty, Tillie Olsen, Flannery O'Connor, and Albert Camus and stories from many oral traditions have also served as a wellspring for this book.

One of us, Nel Noddings, brings to this work her experience as a mathematics teacher and teacher educator, as well as her background in philosophy and ethics. Currently a professor at Stanford University, she is the author of *Awakening the Inner Eye: Intuition in Education* (with Paul Shore), *Caring: A Feminine Approach to Ethics and Moral Education*, and *Women and Evil*. Her commitment to the ethic of care has also been grounded in her experience over the past 35 years as a parent of "lots of children," three of them adopted international children.

Carol Witherell, an associate professor at Lewis & Clark College, draws on her experience as a teacher of primary grades and music, a teacher educator, a developmental psychologist, and a parent of two grown daughters. Her current areas of special interest are life-span development, moral development, and ethics in education. She is the author of several articles on moral development and education.

THEMES OF THE BOOK

We bring three major themes to the writing of this book: that story and narrative are primary tools in the work that educators and counselors do; that education means taking seriously both the quest for life's meaning and the call to care for persons; and that the use of narrative and dialogue can serve as a model for teaching and learning across the boundaries of disciplines, professions, and cultures.

The Role of Narrative In Teaching and Counseling

Our first theme — that story and narrative are central to the kind of work that those in the teaching and helping professions do — stems from our experiences in teaching, particularly in the preparation of teachers and counselors to carry out and reflect upon their practice. Although narrative has been with us since the beginning of human language, interest in narrative as literary and cultural conventions has been a hallmark of this century. Theories of the nature and function of narrative have occupied many writers in the humanities and social sciences during the past quarter century, reflecting a movement in the academic world (and perhaps in Western culture as well) from a predominantly logico-scientific mode of knowing about the world to one that once again acknowledges the drama and metaphor of good stories as an equally significant way of understanding human experience (Bruner, 1985).

Interest in narrative as a way of knowing and teaching has sparked interdisciplinary and international interest. Within the field of literary study, theories of narrative have emerged as a central concern over the past 20 years, shadowing interest in the theory of the novel (Martin, 1986).

Although this book is very much about uses of narrative in education, it is not a study of theories of narrative. Such studies can be found in works such as David Carr's *Time, Narrative, and History*; Barbara Hardy's *Tellers and Listeners: The Narrative Imagination*; Thomas Leitch's *What Stories Are*; Donald Polkinghorne's *Narrative Knowing and the Human Sciences*; and Wallace Martin's *Recent Theories of Narrative*. There are additional references to writings on theories of narrative cited throughout our book, especially in Chapter 7 by Kirin Narayan.

As Narayan and Witherell suggest in their chapters, narrative involves not only a sequence of events, but also a storyteller and an intended audience. Narrative structure contributes to our understanding of the meaningfulness of everyday life. Like many writers on narrative, we acknowledge the central role that narrative structure plays in the formation of the self and in the construction, transmission, and transformations of cultures.

Adults, like children, are natural storytellers, though they have often learned to suppress their urge to tell stories as a way of knowing because of the theory of knowledge based on "objectivity and generalizability" that is so dominant within the Western world. Jerome Bruner has characterized these two ways of knowing as the narrative mode and the paradigmatic, or logico-scientific, mode (1985). Bruner contrasts the paradigmatic mode, which leads to "good theory, tight analysis, logical proof, and empirical analysis," with the narrative mode, which "leads instead to good stories, gripping drama, believable historical accounts. It deals in human or human-like intention and action and the vicissitudes and consequence that mark their course" (p. 98).

Whether writer or teller, the narrator of a story provides further meaning — and even further text — to the story being told. The narrator too has a story, one that is embedded in his or her culture, language, gender, beliefs, and life history. This embeddedness lies at the core of the teaching-learning experience and is a central interest of ours in this book.

To educate is to take seriously both the quest for life's meaning and the meaning of individual lives. Through our accounts of uses of stories and personal narratives in educational practice, we will explore the centrality of narrative to the kind of work that teachers and counselors do. Through telling, writing, reading, and listening to life stories — one's own and others' — those engaged in this work can penetrate cultural barriers, discover the power of the self and the integrity of the other, and deepen their understanding of their respective histories and possibilities.

In *The Call of Stories: Teaching and the Moral Imagination*, Robert Coles claims that it is only through stories that he can fully enter another's life (1989). His recounting of the use of stories in his medical education, teaching, and psychiatric practice captures the power of the story in its immediacy and "the wonderful mimetic power a novel or story can have — its capacity to work its way into one's thinking life, yes, but also one's reveries or idle thoughts, even one's moods and dreams" (p. 204). We would add to this mimetic power the apprehension of narrative truth as a means of envisioning possibility in one's life.

As Coles's autobiographical accounts so vividly illustrate, stories represent a journey into the realm of practical ethics. Stories can join the worlds of thought and feeling, and they give special voice to the feminine side of human experience — to the power of emotion, intuition, and relationships in human lives. They frequently reveal dilemmas of human caring and conflict, illuminating with the rich, vibrant language of feeling the various landscapes in which we meet the other morally. Through the poignant grip of story and metaphor we meet ourselves and the other in our mutual quest for goodness and meaning. The power of such instruction has been captured by Cynthia Ozick in her essay "The Moral Necessity of Metaphor":

> Through metaphor, the past has the capacity to imagine us, and we it. . . . Those who have no pain can imagine those who suffer. Those at the center can imagine what it is to be outside. The strong can imagine what it is to be weak. Illuminated lives can imagine the borders of stellar fire. We strangers can imagine the familiar hearts of strangers. (1986, p. 65)

Several of our authors illuminate the power of myth and imagination for deepening our understanding of human action and relationship. In a story in Chapter 14, Ken Donald recounts the dramatic healing of his mother, a Native American Indian medicine woman, from a life-threatening condition. He captures in this story the power of the mythic narrative as a fable, a ritual, and a transformer of experience in ways often inaccessible to other forms of knowing. It is a kind of story that calls us to consider a radically different way of knowing. Paula Gunn Allen writes: "Myth is a kind of story that allows a holistic image to pervade and shape consciousness, thus providing a coherent and empowering matrix for action and relationship" (1986, pp. 104–105). In Donald's amazing story of his mother's healing, the particular and the universal are bridged, revealing the mythic and spiritual dimensions of one woman's experience, with its accompanying nonordinary knowledge — "an experience that all peoples, past, present, and to come, have in common" (Allen, 1986, p. 106). The story reminds us of Barry Lopez's tribute to the power of narrative:

> The power of narrative to nurture and heal, to repair a spirit in disarray, rests on two things: the skillful invocation of unimpeachable sources and a listener's knowledge that no hypocrisy or subterfuge is involved. (1989, p. 69)

The Primacy of Caring and Dialogue in Educational Practice

The second theme we bring to the book is our belief that to take seriously the quest for life's meaning and the meaning of individual lives is to understand the primacy of the caring relation and of dialogue in educational practice. Our use of the term *caring relation* assumes a relational, or connective, notion of the self, one that holds that the self is formed and given meaning in the context of its relations with others. The notion of the "self-in-relation" is reflected in the work of philosophers Martin Buber and John Macmurray and psychologist Daniel Stern, and in recent writings within the relational feminist tradition by Carol Gilligan, Nel Noddings, and Catherine Keller. Yet, with Keller, we believe that the concept of the relational self does not reflect a peculiarly feminine psychology, but rather a vision of an affinity with all beings: "We connect, all of us, spaciously, timefully" (1986, p. 248).

We further assume that the term *caring* connotes multiple levels of meaning, from the caring that is grounded in particular attachments that we form to a caring for the world — its past, present, and future inhabitants we have never met, its resources, its harmony. This obligation to care for the earth is addressed compellingly in Christopher Stone's *Earth and Other Ethics*. Although we typically focus on the first form of caring, it is not to the exclusion of these other forms of care; rather, they might all be viewed as part of an ever-widening, interconnected web of relations — one that defines the self in relation to particular others, to groups, to communities, to many cultures, including our emerging global culture.

Feminist theorists as well as their critics are giving considerable attention to the notion of caring these days (see Carol Gilligan, *In a Different Voice*; Nel Noddings, *Caring: A Feminine Approach to Ethics and Moral Education*; Jean Grimshaw, *Philosophy and Feminist Thinking*; Owen Flanagan and Kathryn Jackson, "Justice, Care, and Gender: The Kohlberg-Gilligan Debate Revisited"; Joan Tronto, "Beyond Gender Difference to a Theory of Care"; Karen Offen, "Defining Feminism: A Comparative Historical Approach"). The notion of caring is especially useful in education because it emphasizes the relational nature of human interaction and of all moral life. The word can be used to describe a virtue or constellation of virtues—as in, "She is a caring person"—but it is more powerfully used to characterize a special kind of relation. A *caring relation* requires contributions from both parties in the relation. The one-caring, or carer, comes with a certain attitude, and the cared-for recognizes and responds to this attitude. The relation provides a foundation of trust for teaching and counseling alike.

The first member of the relational dyad (the carer, or one-caring) responds to the needs, wants, and initiations of the second. Her mode of response is characterized by *engrossment* (nonselective attention or total presence to the other for the duration of the caring interval) and *displacement of motivation* (her motive energy flows in the direction of the other's needs and projects). She feels with the other and acts in his behalf. The second member (the one cared for) contributes to the relation by recognizing and responding to the caring. In the infant, this response may consist of smiles and wriggles; in the student, it may reveal itself in energetic pursuit of the student's own projects. A mature relationship may, of course, be mutual, and two parties may regularly exchange places in the relation, but the contributions of the carer (whichever person may hold the position momentarily) remain distinct from those of the cared-for. It is clear from this brief description why an ethic of caring is often characterized in terms of responsibility and response.

In relations that are necessarily often unequal—relations such as those formed in teaching and counseling—the teacher or counselor must nevertheless practice *inclusion*. Martin Buber describes inclusion this way:

> It is the extension of one's own concreteness, the fulfillment of the actual situation of life, the complete presence of the reality in which one participates. Its elements are, first, a relation, of no matter what kind, between two persons, second, an event experienced by them in common, in which at least one of them actively participates, and, third, the fact that this one person, without forfeiting the felt reality of his activity, at the same time lives through the common event from the standpoint of the other. (1965, p. 97)

The teacher's act of inclusion is one-sided, Buber says, because the teacher can experience the student's learning, but the student cannot experience the teacher's teaching. This contention sounds odd at first, but when we study it, we see that it contains a deep insight. The teacher or counselor can take the perspective of student or client—can set the student or client free to pursue his or her own legitimate projects—but the student cannot fully take the teacher's perspective. The event, the learning event, belongs to the student, and the teacher experiences it through inclusion. The teacher thus bears a tremendous responsibility. Striving always to see the learning event from the standpoint of the student, the teacher teaches by actively pursuing the student's objective, an objective that teacher and student have together constructed. In a caring relation, the student responds by engaging fully in the event. He or she grows, and the teacher seeing this knows that teaching has had a desirable effect. The reader will encounter many powerful examples of acts of inclusion in the chapters that follow.

A caring relation also requires dialogue. The material of dialogue is usually words, but touch, smiles, affectionate sounds and silences, and glances may also be part of it. True dialogue is open; that is, conclusions are not held to be absolute by any party at the outset. The search for enlightenment, responsible choice, perspective, or means to solve a problem is mutual and marked by appropriate signs of reciprocity. This does not mean that participants in dialogue must give up any principles they hold and succumb to relativism. If we firmly believe that an act one of our students has committed is wrong, we do not enter a dialogue with him on whether or not the act is wrong. Such a dialogue could not be genuine. We can, however, engage him in dialogue about the possible justification for our opposing positions, about the likely consequences of such acts to himself and others, about the personal history of our own belief. We can share our reflections with him, and he may exert considerable influence on us by pointing out that we have not suffered the sort of experience that led him to his act. Clearly, time is required for such dialogue. Teacher and student must know each other well enough for trust to develop.

It is dialogue that allows the negotiation of meanings through which the self in relation to other selves and to one's cultural communities is constituted. Dialogue enables us to decipher language by entering what Roland Barthes describes as the "kitchen of meaning," where we "struggle with a certain innocence of objects" (1988, p. 158), as we acknowledge the complexities of language and of that which we take for granted. It is here that we are frequently called to confront the fact that "what everybody knows" is all too often not what everybody knows.

Throughout this book, readers will find examples of genuine dialogue and failed attempts at dialogue. Voices longing for dialogue will be heard. Wonderful moments of connection are recorded, but so are episodes of heart-aching separation. For teachers and counselors, both sorts of episodes will ring true. From these moments of dialogue and inclusion we learn more about caring for ourselves, each other, and the professions to which we are committed.

Narrative and Dialogue as a Model for Teaching and Learning

Our third theme is the belief that narrative and dialogue can serve as a model for teaching and learning across the boundaries of disciplines, professions, and cultures. A growing body of literature in philosophy and psychology has acknowledged that narrative structure is at the core of the formation of the self (see, for example, Paul Brockelman, *Time and Self*; David Carr, *Time, Narrative, and History*; Karen Hanson, *The Self Imagined: Philosophical Reflections on the Social Character of Psyche*; Alasdair MacIntyre, *After Virtue*; Donald E. Polkinghorne, *Narrative Knowing and the Human Sciences*; Theodore Sarbin, editor, *Narrative Psychology: The Storied Nature of Human Conduct*). The self is construed here in the particular, relational sense, the sense in "which each of us is and comes to be" within the context of persons-in-relation, rather than in the universal sense of selfness. Paul Brockelman writes of the "thickness of personal identity" revealed through an emerging personal story, a story that has a narrative plot characterized by connections across time, by intentions, and by an attitude toward life (1985). This attitude toward life is a "preconceptual, passionate, and personal vision or interpretation of what life and reality is about *for me*, a focal vision which does not precede my actions and behavior as much as it pervades them as their very sense" (p. 54). The story does not end here, however, for our personal vision attains its real meaning in relation to another's vision, to the communal self, and to the social network that gives meaning and support to individual existence.

We take classroom discourse to be at the very heart of the teaching-learning process, as it represents the meaning systems mutually constructed by teachers and their students. Similarly, therapeutic discourse in the counseling session serves to represent the meanings constructed by counselors and their clients. These meaning systems do not occur in social or historical vacuums, but are rendered meaningful to participants according to both personal and cultural histories and contexts. The acknowledgment and sharing of these meaning systems and their contexts becomes a significant and always unfinished "text" in the teaching or counseling process.

The power of narrative and dialogue as contributors to reflective awareness in teachers and students is that they provide opportunities for deepened relations with others and serve as springboards for ethical action. Understanding the narrative and contextual dimensions of human actors can lead to new insights, compassionate judgment, and the creation of shared knowledge and meanings that can inform professional practice.

Those who educate must acknowledge several paradoxes. As with any paradox, what appears to be contradictory or oppositional is in some central sense compatible. Teaching is both a public and a private activity. It calls on both narrative and analytic ways of knowing. It invites a quest for both the general and the particular. Teaching can deepen our understanding of and respect for both persons and communities in ways that render the familiar strange and the strange familiar. It asks us to address the moral and aesthetic as well as the practical aspects of everyday experience. The act of teaching calls us to live in the worlds of actuality and of possibility and vision. It asks us to see clearly and attentively and at the same time acknowledge Edmund Burke's maxim that a particular way of seeing is also a way of not seeing. The use of narrative and dialogue in our professional practice is likely to deepen our sense of mystery, yet there are daily reminders in institutional life of Flannery O'Connor's observation that mystery is an embarrassment to the modern mind. Our understanding of the power of narrative and dialogue in teaching and counseling practice cannot help but expand our vision of our responsibilities as professionals within our professional communities, including the relationships that we nurture with our colleagues and students. We are thus faced with some very substantial challenges.

ORGANIZATION OF THE BOOK

While the three themes just elaborated appear throughout this book, we choose to organize the book into three parts based on the contributors' approach to narrative and dialogue. Part I, "Narrative and Ways of Knowing and Caring," includes chapters by Kim Stafford, Andra Makler, Anita Plath Helle, and Madeleine Grumet. Each of these authors explores the power of narrative as an epistemological tool — as a way of knowing about ourselves and other knowers. Their stories, and those of their students, convey some of the ways that stories can teach us about caring — for ourselves, for others, for our history, and for our future.

Part II, "Narrative and Notions of the Self and the Other," includes chapters by Carol Witherell, Joanne Cooper, Kirin Narayan, and Virginia Shabatay. These authors examine narrative and dialogue as they reflect and contribute to our understanding of the self and the other. Each author suggests that the self develops and can only be grasped within the context of its relation to other selves. Poignant examples of our human yearning for both individual fulfillment and inclusion are offered through vivid narratives from literature, personal biographies, and cultural lore.

Part III of our book, "Narrative and Dialogue as a Paradigm for Teaching and Learning," includes chapters by Nel Noddings, Mark Tappan and Lyn Mikel Brown, Jo Anne Pagano, William Schubert, Susan Florio-

Ruane, and Celeste Brody and Carol Witherell with Ken Donald and Ruth Lundblad. Each of these chapters offers examples of narrative and dialogue in actual classroom life as they reveal a model for educating and for researching human growth and learning. The model offered is grounded in several central notions: that we live and grow in interpretive, or meaning-making, communities; that stories help us find our place in the world; and that caring, respectful dialogue among all those engaged in educational settings — students, teachers, administrators — serves as the crucible for our coming to understand ourselves, others, and the possibilities life holds for us.

We found ourselves thinking of this book as something of a collection of memoirs on teaching that reach across disciplinary affiliations and cultural boundaries. Toni Morrison describes the writing of a memoir as a process of gaining access to interior life — "a kind of literary archeology: on the basis of some information and a little guesswork you journey to a site to see what remains were left behind and to reconstruct the world that these remains imply" (1987, p. 12). The metaphor seems an apt one for the kind of reflection that we have engaged in as we survey the landscapes of our discoveries in teaching, and imagine and invent the terrains that lie ahead. We welcome our readers on this journey.

REFERENCES

Allen, Paula Gunn. (1986). *The sacred hoop: Recovering the feminine in American Indian tradition*. Boston: Beacon Press.

Bakhtin, Mikhail. (1981). *The dialogic imagination*. Austin: University of Texas Press.

Barthes, Roland. (1988). *The semiotic challenge* (Richard Howard, Trans.). New York: Hill and Wang.

Belenky, Mary; Clinchy, Blythe; Goldberger, Nancy; and Tarule, Jill. (1986). *Women's ways of knowing*. New York: Basic Books.

Brockelman, Paul. (1985). *Time and self*. New York: Crossroads.

Bruner, Jerome. (1985). Narrative and paradigmatic modes of thought. In Elliot Eisner (Ed.), *Learning and teaching the ways of knowing* (pp. 97–115). Chicago: National Society for the Study of Education.

Buber, Martin. (1965). *Between man and man* (Ronald G. Smith & Maurice Friedman, Trans.). New York: Macmillan.

Buber, Martin. (1968). *I and thou* (Ronald G. Smith, Trans.). New York: Scribner's.

Carr, David. (1986). *Time, narrative, and history*. Bloomington: Indiana University Press.

Coles, Robert. (1989). *The call of stories: Teaching and the moral imagination*. Boston: Houghton Mifflin.

Flanagan, Owen, & Jackson, Kathryn. (1987). Justice, care, and gender: The Kohlberg-Gilligan debate revisited. *Ethics, 97*(3), 622–637.

Freire, Paulo, & Shor, Ira (1987). *A pedagogy for liberation: Dialogues on transforming education.* South Hadley, MA: Bergin & Garvey.

Gilligan, Carol. (1982). *In a different voice: Psychological theory and women's development.* Cambridge, MA: Harvard University Press.

Gilligan, Carol; Ward, Janie Victoria; & Taylor, Jill McLean. (1988). *Mapping the moral domain.* Cambridge, MA: Harvard University.

Greene, Maxine. (1988). *The dialectic of freedom.* New York: Teachers College Press.

Grimshaw, Jean. (1986). *Philosophy and feminist thinking.* Minneapolis: University of Minnesota Press.

Hanson, Karen. (1986). *The self imagined: Philosophical reflections on the social character of psyche.* London: Routledge and Kegan Paul.

Hardy, Barbara. (1975). *Tellers and listeners: The narrative imagination.* London: Athlone Press.

Heilbrun, Carolyn. (1988). *Writing a woman's life.* New York: W. W. Norton.

Keller, Catherine. (1986). *From a broken web: Separation, sexism, and self.* Boston: Beacon Press.

Kohlberg, Lawrence. (1981). *Essays on moral development: Vol. 1. The philosophy of moral development.* San Francisco: Harper & Row.

Kohlberg, Lawrence. (1984). *Essays on moral development: Vol. 2. The psychology of moral development.* San Francisco: Harper & Row.

Leitch, Thomas. (1986). *What stories are: Narrative theory and interpretation.* University Park, PA: Pennsylvania State University Press.

Lopez, Barry. (1989). *Crossing open ground.* New York: Vintage Books.

MacIntyre, Alasdair. (1981). *After virtue.* Notre Dame, IN: Notre Dame University Press.

Macmurray, John. (1961). *Persons in relation.* New York: Harper & Row. (Original work published 1954)

Martin, Wallace. (1986). *Recent theories of narrative.* Ithaca, NY: Cornell University Press.

Morrison, Toni. (1987). The site of memory. In William Zinsser (Ed.), *Inventing the truth: The art and craft of memoir* (pp. 101–124). Boston: Houghton Mifflin.

Myerhoff, Barbara. (1978). *Number our days.* New York: Simon & Schuster.

Noddings, Nel. (1984). *Caring: A feminine approach to ethics and moral education.* Berkeley: University of California Press.

Noddings, Nel. (1989). *Women and evil.* Berkeley: University of California Press.

Noddings, Nel, & Shore, Paul. (1984). *Awakening the inner eye: Intuition in education.* New York: Teachers College Press.

Offen, Karen. (1988, Autumn). Defining feminism: A comparative historical approach. *Signs, 14*(1), 119–157.

Ozick, Cynthia. (1983). Usurpation (Other People's Stories). In *Bloodshed and three novellas.* New York: E.P. Dutton/Obelisk. (Original work published 1976)

Ozick, Cynthia. (1986, May). The moral necessity of metaphor. *Harper's Magazine*, pp. 64–65.

Polkinghorne, Donald. (1988). *Narrative knowing and the human sciences.* Albany: State University of New York Press.

Sarbin, Theodore (Ed.). (1986). *Narrative psychology: The storied nature of human conduct.* New York: Praeger.

Stern, Daniel. (1985). *The interpersonal world of the infant.* New York: Basic Books.

Stone, Christopher. (1987). *Earth and other ethics.* New York: Harper & Row.

Tronto, Joan. (1987). Beyond gender difference to a theory of care. *Signs, 12*(4), 644–663.

PART I

Narrative and Ways of Knowing and Caring

Stories invite us to come to know the world and our place in it. Whether narratives of history or the imagination, stories call us to consider what we know, how we know, and what and whom we care about. The chapters in Part I explore the epistemological and moral power of narrative in the lives of teachers and learners, both in and out of classrooms.

Chapter 1, "The Story That Saved Life," was originally published by Kim Stafford in 1986 in a collection of personal essays on the natural history and Native American lore of the Northwest. Here it is accompanied by the author's reflections on the writing of the essay and the stories and characters that guided it. The essay conveys how stories save "life a little at a time by making us see and hear and taste our lives and dreams more deeply." The stories included to exemplify this idea arise from a particular region in northeastern Oregon and range from a Native American coyote tale to contemporary personal narrative. Within this series, the essay recounts how one particular story actually did save the author's life (by helping him turn away from a tainted stream), and how stories at large help us see each other, value place, and search for power in our lives.

Andra Makler, in Chapter 2, "Imagining History: A Good Story and a Well-Formed Argument," describes her experience teaching high school students and future high school teachers to write historical narratives based on their researching their own family history. She also describes how the assignment led her to understand better her personal history as she recounts the story of her own grandmother's life.

> I know from experience that high school students found the task of creating life histories engaging; that they invested this task with meaning; that they sought correspondences between their personal lives and the fictional histori-cal selves they created. I think the key to the power of this task lies in its relational qualities; adolescents are fashioning an identity for themselves as

they move through high school. I think they cared about this curriculum because it enabled them to sense the interdependence of individuals and to see in history what Nona Lyons (1988) has called "a narrative of relationships and motives with which to confirm or deny believability." (p. 32)

In Chapter 3, "Reading Women's Autobiographies: A Map of Reconstructed Knowing," Anita Plath Helle illustrates the practical and theoretical advantages of using women's autobiographical narratives to explore the relationship between gender and knowledge in the classroom. She includes in her discussion of autobiographies Audre Lorde's *Zami: A New Spelling of My Name*, Alice Koller's *An Unknown Woman*, and Gertrude Stein's *Autobiography of Alice B. Toklas*. Exploring the intersection between feminism and postmodernism in order to understand an important juncture in her own life and teaching, Helle uncovers ways that women's studies can both theorize women's oppression *and* offer alternative ways of transforming knowledge. Her essay includes a pedagogical narrative, a paradigmatic narrative of the autobiographical journey, and a narrative on reconstructed knowing that shows how autobiographies promote a dialogic awareness of the process of integrating voices.

In Chapter 4, "The Politics of Personal Knowledge," Madeleine Grumet offers an account of her work with teachers in a course Theatre in the Classroom as a means to understand the power of personal knowledge and narratives in the work of educators.

> If telling a story requires giving oneself away, then we are obligated to devise a method of receiving stories that mediates the space between the self that tells, the self that told, and the self that listens: a method that returns a story to the teller that is both hers and not hers, that contains her self in good company.

Through her reflections on three narratives written by one of the teachers, Grumet explores the power of multiple texts and multiple interpreters as ways of coming to know about ourselves within a public community of knowers.

1

The Story That Saved Life

KIM R. STAFFORD

Kim R. Stafford is director of the Northwest Writing Institute of Lewis & Clark College in Portland, Oregon. A poet and essayist, he is the author of Having Everything Right: Essays of Place, *which won a special citation for excellence from the Western States Book Awards in 1986. He has also published a collection of folklore,* Rendezvous: Stories, Songs & Opinions of the Idaho Country, *and several books of poetry. He is currently writing a book about old-growth forests and a second collection of essays.*

Memory is made as a quilt is made. From the whole cloth of time, frayed scraps of sensation are pulled apart and pieced together in a pattern that has a name: Grandmother's Garden, Drunkard's Path to Dublin, Double Wedding Ring. Call this, The Story That Saved Life.

On the way into Wallowa County in northeastern Oregon, just at the edge of the quilt, the hem of the story, you come over a rise. The wheat and haylot blocks of the farms look about the same, the hill-patch pines and long seam of the road dashing on into a swale. But there are signs. One sign warns that no potatoes, hay, or wheat is to be carried into the county. The place is disease-free. The ground is pure. Take a deep breath, and listen.

There is a town called Elgin. They say one night the door of the doctor's office jangled open. There was a woman full in her form, expecting. Behind her stood a thin rail of husband with a hard glint to his eye.

"Good evening. What can I do for you?" The doctor rose up from the rocking chair.

This chapter appeared in somewhat different form in *Having Everything Right: Essays of Place* by Kim R. Stafford, 1986, Lewiston, ID: Confluence Press. Copyright ©1986 by Kim R. Stafford. Adapted by permission.

"We're ready for the baby." The husband stepped around his woman. He wasn't from town. Mud stiffened his pants to the knees.

The doctor turned to the woman. "How long have you been in labor?"

"I'm not." She bobbed and rolled before him, trying to curtsy. "Not yet, sir."

"But we're ready for the baby." The husband moved behind her and nudged her forward, his boots nipping her heels.

The doctor stepped back. He should have turned on more light, but it had been almost time to close. The woman was a dim silhouette against the evening snowlight of the window.

"If you're not in labor yet, there's not much I can do. Can you stay with friends in town?"

Then from behind the woman a knife glittered in the husband's hand.

"I said we're ready, now." The husband came around his woman again and faced the doctor, the canopy of light from the desk lamp coming up only as far as his hand and its hunting knife. There was grease under his fingernails. "I got to leave for awhile — elk season. Don't want none of this happening while I'm gone." The woman whispered a long breath.

"Okay," said the doctor. "If it's that way, let me get my bag." Staying in the pool of light, he turned and snapped open the black case on the table beside. His hand went inside. When it came out, there was a pistol — not exactly aimed anywhere, but part of his gesture.

"You folks are just going to have to wait. Now go on home, or somewhere. Let me know again when it's really time. I'll be glad to help you then."

Old Joseph was born before anyone wanted to raise hay in the Wallowa Valley. When the first whites came, Old Joseph planted a row of poles along the divide where the signs about pure seed potatoes now stand. The poles were not a fence, but a mark of understanding. But only the Nez Perce understood.

After the Nez Perce were driven away, Old Joseph's grave at Wallowa Forks happened to coincide with a gravel quarry. The Indians came back, loaded his bones in a buckboard, and carried them south to Wallowa Lake. A bronze plaque there tells about it. At the lake is a mound of stone. At the Forks, where the bands used to gather, there is only the damp pit of the quarry.

Past Elgin, along the Minam Canyon rim is a place where people scan the far slope for elk. Some do strange things in elk season. Some do strange things all the time. The mountains let you be that way. Beyond the Minam Canyon into the canyon of the Wallowa, every curve in the river road has a story, and every straight run is the pause before a story. Story, story, story the map-quilt gets made, gets folded for the pocket of the mind: that house with the three little cabins strung out behind, where the Civil War colonel, fled from Louisiana to Oregon, planted his slaves. Story. That road out Bear Creek where a logger stole a cement highway bridge from the U.S. government, loaded it on his truck somehow, and disappeared. Story. That single grave of the Indian girl. Story. School children heard the story and built her grave a picket fence, painted it white. In the bluff over town a cave is carved with children's names. Dusk erased them. The cave was a stone telescope, and Wallowa glimmered far away. Measure that distance in years.

How many generations to work a story down to size, to rub away the burrs and sawdust of its making? You have to forget 90% of what happens if you want to tell the story right. So said Wilma, substitute teacher in residence at Wallowa School. She was a teacher by story, story alone. Something about the way her dress, softened by a lifetime of washings, hung down. Something about the spark her eyes kindled. Something about her hands held up to shape a face that's been long buried but burns in the air:

"My uncles, they all had handsome faces, but Earl was the darling — dark hair, chin like a pretty little axe, but he could talk blue. Those eyes. Had to leave West Virginia in a hurry. We never did know why. But he made the best white lightning you ever dreamed. He always kept a Mason jar full in the refrigerator. Liked his cold.

"Well, he comes home pretty looped one night, along in the spring, shouting about the cabbage maggots. We hear him slam the car door and shout, 'Damn you, maggots! I'll fix you!'

"We hear him fumbling around in the hall, stumbling around. I remember I figured he was just trying to make it to his bedroom. But no. I hear the snap of his shotgun action getting loaded.

"'You think just because you're little, you're safe!' That line wakes everybody up. I can hear Mama call out, 'Earl! I want you calm!' But then he starts for the back door, and I sit up in bed. It's just starting to get light. I pull the curtains back when I hear the screen door bang shut and the dogs whimper as they get out of Earl's way.

"'Your time's come, so stand up all of you and take it!'

"'Earl!' Mama's in the hall, but I can see she's too late. Earl's in the garden and raising the shotgun toward the east. And just as the sun's first rays flicker onto his face, he fires off both barrels level over the garden into the trees out east.

"BOOM! BARRROOOOM! He has a wild, satisfied grin on his face, and all of Mama's calling from the back porch can't make it go away.

"You know, we never did have trouble with cabbage maggots after that. I know it sounds crazy. It is crazy. Gardening is like that. And Earl's white lightning is too. We took it for a saying in the family, whenever things got so impossible we didn't have any logical thing to do, we'd say, 'Fire two shots toward the rising sun!' And after we said that, and thought about Earl standing there so happy his pants were about to fall down, nothing seemed quite so bad."

Before I came to Wallowa County, I was warned by a city-friend: "You've got to watch it out there. That's real gun country, you know. Did you read once there were these two Wallowa brothers bagged elk out of season, and when this cop went out to arrest them, they shot him? They had to call out the National Guard and surround the place. Sure enough, through binoculars they could see that cop car shot full of holes and dragged into the barn. Had a big shootout, before they finally nailed those two guys. That's still the real West out there. You better watch it!"

When I had been in Wallowa for a few weeks, I asked a friend, "What's this about the two brothers who did some poaching, then shot the cop, and the National Guard surrounded their place and shot them down?"

"Oh, sure. It's true, except it didn't happen quite like that. You see, there were these two brothers had some ground in wheat, and the elk got to grazing in there every day, just like it was their own private pasture. Brothers figured since they'd fattened that whole elk herd, they had the right to slaughter one, just like it was their own stock. So they bagged one and hung it up in the barn.

"Well, these two cops drove out there to arrest them, but it was kind of a joke. *Everybody* poaches. But the two cops go out to give them a warning or something, anyway, and one of the brothers gets so upset he hooks a chain to the rear axle on the cop car, drags it into the barn, locks the door, and the cops can't do a thing but walk back to town.

"There wasn't any shooting, though. This is the West, but it's not *that* wild."

When I had been in Wallowa several months, I asked an old timer, "What's this about the two brothers who did some poaching just like everybody does, but then they dragged a cop car into their barn with a tractor and locked the door, and the cops had to walk back to town?"

"Where'd you hear that? It's true, all except the part about the barn. There are these two brothers up on Alder Slope. They've got a nice little piece of wheat ground up there against the mountains, you know. Up where the elk will get you if the cold snap don't. It ain't hardly poaching. It's more like taking a cut off your own herd. But say, that reminds me about this hunter one time came out here from Portland—brand new squeaky hunting clothes he got out of some catalogue, some fancy spit and polish boots, and a new gun that didn't hardly have the sale tag cleaned off it.

"Well, this Portland hunter stops in at the market—you know that little market in Enterprise, on the left just before you head out toward Joseph? He stops in there to buy a little beer, and the clerk boy starts in admiring his outfit:

"'Mister, you look like you're about to get yourself an elk.'

"'I sure hope so,' says this Portland hunter. But then he lowers his voice and says, 'Only trouble is, I've never seen one.'

"'Golly, mister!' The clerk boy looks around, and then leans forward with his hands on the cash register. 'I'm really glad you mentioned that, mister, because there could be some real problems if you made a mistake.'

"'Anything you could tell me,' says this Portland hunter, 'I'd really appreciate it.' A line is forming up behind the hunter, and the boy has to lower his voice even more.

"'Well, here goes. You drive on out of town, you'll start to see herds of these elk in the pastures beside the road. They have big red and white patches on their sides, little bitty short horns that curve up like this by their ears, and when you stop your rig, they'll all turn around and look at you. That's a pretty good time to get off a shot.'

"'Hey, thanks for the tip,' says the hunter, wanting to shake the boy's hand. 'I really appreciate it.'

"So the hunter goes out, but the next morning he comes back in all excited, says to the boy still standing there at the cash register, 'I got my elk, thanks to you! Want to see it?'

"'Sure,' says the kid, jamming his dusting feathers into his back pocket. He gestures toward some men to leave their shopping carts and follow along.

"'I got him right out here in the pickup—nice rack on him, too.' The hunter leads them all out to the parking lot, where the kid looks over the side of the long box on that shiny new truck. Sure enough, there's a nice big steer lying there shot all to hell. And the kid's about ready to bust out laughing, when he notices his own daddy's brand burned into the hide.

"Yeah, the kid never bragged on that story too much, but everybody else sure loves to tell it."

"The hunter got the steer, but you got the story."

"Yeah, that's right. So these two brothers, they had their elk strung up in the barn when the cop car drives up. Those two cops did a little poaching on the side themselves. You have to, with the economy what it is. They'd just come out to razz their friends a little, you know. Well these two cops start reading them the statute about poaching, while the four of them have some beer, and them all laughing about it, and one of the brothers gets to horsing around on the tractor. Had the forklift rigged on the back, I guess. And he kind of accidentally pokes a hole in the radiator on the cop car. Just a little hole that looked like nothing. Didn't even hurt the grill.

"But the two cops, by the time they'd finished their beers and got halfway back to town, their radiator was dry. They had to hitchhike the rest of the way."

I was to visit the school at Joseph, and I would tell a story to the high school class. It was a strange thing to carry a book of Nez Perce tales into Wallowa County, where the latest census shows not one Nez Perce woman, man, or child. I carried the collection edited by Jarold Ramsey, *Coyote Was Going There: Indian Literature of the Oregon Country* (Seattle: University of Washington Press, 1977). I read with deep pleasure in the place. From my second-story apartment window, I looked up from the book at the hills: three trees huddled together on the horizon. A hundred years ago, the Nez Perce all were driven out. A twist of pride and guilt hangs in the air. Chief Joseph's image tops the masthead of the weekly *Chieftain*, but Nez Perce people only come for the rodeo. And lately, they've asked for money even to come to that, to wear their costumes and ride in the parade. Then they go back to their exile again at Lapwai or Colville.

It was a strange thing to leave my book of tales, and carry one of its stories in my head to the town called Joseph, to walk into an all-white class and unfold a narrative rooted to the place we stole. I decided to try a Nez Perce tale that had made me laugh when I read it silently to myself. Coyote is such a fool. He postures and hopes, makes all the predictable mistakes, then sits alone on a hill waiting for the world to change, waiting to see his foolish wish come true and the world forgive him. In my apartment I had laughed, and put the book down. Now I stood in front of the class. I could not remember the story just as it was, but it would have been too strange to read it, so I told it like this:

"Coyote had a wife, and his wife died, and he mourned her for a time. But then a shadow came to speak with him.

"'Coyote, if you do just as I tell you, your life will be as it was. Your wife will live with you as before.'

"'Tell me, and I will do as you say.'

"'Follow me five days,' said the shadow, 'and do as I do. Then you will see your wife. You may bring her back among the living, if you do right.'

"They had been traveling most of one day, when the shadow said, 'Look what fine horses are running there.' Coyote saw nothing, but he held his hand up over his eyes, nodding as the shadow did.

"'Look what fine horses are running there,' Coyote said. And they traveled.

"One day, the shadow said, 'Let us bend down these branches and gather serviceberries for our meal.' The shadow pulled at the air where nothing grew, and chewed.

"'Let us bend down these branches and gather serviceberries for our meal,' said Coyote, and he scooped the air with his hands and chewed.

"The fifth day, they came to a low hill.

"'Soon it will be dark,' the shadow said. 'Then we can enter the lodge of the dead. You will see your wife.' Coyote and the shadow sat down to wait. The sun moved not at all, then slowly, then it went down. The shadow stood up.

"'It is time to go inside.' The shadow's hands seemed to be lifting a door-flap. The shadow bent down and went through.

"'It is time to go inside,' said Coyote. He raised his hands, bent down, stepped forward. People were singing. They were gathered about a fire. Farther along was another fire, then another. Coyote walked from one fire to another, searching the faces of the dead. There was his wife.

"The shadow said, 'As you walk with her toward your home, you must not touch her. Remember that one thing.'

"The sun came up. The fires were gone, and the people, the lodge, and the shadow. Beside Coyote was something in the air. She followed him all day. That night, beside their fire, Coyote looked at her. He could begin to see her more. And they walked another day. He could see her more. The fifth night he could see her across the fire.

"He said, 'Tomorrow we shall be home.' She looked at him. It was his joy to reach out. She was gone.

"The shadow said, 'Coyote, could you not wait one more night? Now she will never be with you.'

"'I will go back,' said Coyote. 'Now I know the way.' The shadow was gone. The fire died down. Coyote slept.

"Coyote started out, and soon he said, 'Look what fine horses are running there.' He held his hand up over his eyes.

"Another day, he began to paw the air: 'Let us bend down these branches and gather serviceberries for our meal.' He chewed.

"The fifth afternoon of his travel alone, he stood on the low hill where the dead had danced, where he had stood among them. He sat down to wait. The sun stood still, then it moved slowly, then it went down. Coyote tried to lift a flap of darkness away, to step forward. Then he waited again. Soon he would hear the dead sing. He would see their fires, he would walk from one to another. He would see the face of his wife.

"He waited on the hill. It was dark. Nothing happened."

The students before me were very still. In my voice among them, Coyote was not a fool. The teacher looked at me hopefully. We did not know how to end the class.

Coyote did not play this story as Orpheus had, wandering the groves with a lyre and a faraway gaze. Coyote was both a master of beautiful seductions and a slapstick clown. And in the Wallowa Valley, where the Nez Perce people had been driven from their homes a century before, the Coyote story held a special tug: One of the real people of this place might come back searching, might stand on the moraine east from Wallowa Lake, waiting for the people, but no one would appear.

I left the car at the rim of Joseph Canyon, and started down. A snow squall ended in sunlight, where elk bedded across a meadow ignoring me, and I followed their trails where my people had made none, down through the pines that flavored the wind I sipped, rollicking through damp needle-duff with a swinging step all afternoon. Up on the rim, huge helicopters lifted whole trees from where the loggers had felled them—distant as dragonflies carrying twigs of grass. And I plunged down the slope.

The story is not what you do, but what fits. The story is not a sequence of actions, but a whole quilt unrolled in the story-maker's mind. My walk down Joseph Canyon was filled with sensation, with danger, meditation, discovery—pitch and smoke, rain down my back, a bed of rock at the top of Starvation Ridge. An owl called as I crossed the net of moonlight filtered through trees. I found a book of songs the mice had chewed. I fed on nettle and fern root, and wood ticks fed on me. And I was lost three hours in the snow, getting slowly chilled, afraid to sit down, tipsy with confusion, until I stepped abruptly out from the trees by the highway, and hitchhiked home.

None of that was the story. No incident had enough of the tight terror and swirl, the exhilaration of change. Pitch and dragonfly, owl and moonlight, a cabin where no one lived for years—those are all nice in their way, but when I told the children at Wallowa School, they all got righteously bored. I could tell by how they got polite. They folded their hands. One glanced at the clock. Another got interested in the boots I wore. So I asked them to tell me about what it was like when they were old. In the third grade, this is an easy task. They told me without fear. One paper I carried away told this:

I Was Old

God woke up and he herd a Dinusor but
he was old and he sed to myself how
come he am in The old day how come
he don't no why and then I died and
he died for a little while and then he
came out of my graveyard and he
went back to sleep and he died
again and he woke up and Then
he was young and he Loved to dy
young and The End.

Vicki was the quiet one. She could be Coyote's wife. And, the end. But there were seven minutes before the class was done. I remembered one more little thing from Joseph Canyon — the time I bent down to drink. It was the smallest moment, but Vicki's story about being old made me know something, and I started to tell it anyway. This time, the children forgot about me and listened to the story itself:

It was a hot day, and I was clear at the bottom of Joseph Canyon — hadn't taken enough water. But Joseph Creek, you know it's a big muddy torrent this time of year, with a couple of cow pies floating by every so often. I wasn't going to take a drink of that.

Well, pretty soon I came to a little stream flowing in from the side — clear little stream about a foot wide — and I bent down to fill my hat. Water was real cool on my hands as I dipped the hat in, but as I stood up, a whole story went through my head. You know how fast a story can flash past your mind? It's a story my parents told me, sitting on the couch at home, when I was just a little guy:

Once upon a time there was a king, and this king liked to hunt, liked to take his hawk on his arm and ride out looking for game. He would send that hawk up to circle around until it saw a little rabbit, or maybe a quail, and then the hawk would swoop down and grab that little critter and bring it back.

Well, this one day it was pretty hot, and they weren't doing too well. Hadn't caught a thing. So they were riding home, with the hawk on the king's arm, and the king on the horse's back, just trotting along through the dust and hot wind. And this king gets real thirsty. Comes to a cliff where the water is dripping down, sends the hawk up to circle around while he holds his silver cup — kings always carry a silver cup, even to the hunt — holds his silver cup up to the water that drips and drips and drips. And just when he brings the cup that's full of this cool water up to his lips, the hawk swoops down and knocks it out of his hand and spills the water.

Hawks get kind of wild sometimes, and the king, being a king, isn't the kind of guy who just gets mad over any little thing, so he waves off the hawk, picks up the silver cup, and holds it up to the dripping water again. Well, the hawk circles above, the man holds his cup — even though his arm's about to fall off, he's so tired — and the water drips, and drips, and drips, and drips. And he sort of looks up at the hawk and tries to bring the cup up to his lips real fast — but the hawk is faster, swooping down and knocking the cup out of his hand again and spilling that water.

This time the king gets real mad, and he whips out his sword. Holds his cup up to the water again, and it drips, and drips — and this time when it's only half full he thinks he can fool that hawk, and he brings the cup up to his lips. But the hawk's too fast — swoops down, knocks the cup out of his hand, spills the water, and he swings his sword and kills that hawk with one blow.

By now this king is so thirsty, he can't wait to let that water drip again. So he drops his sword and his cup by the hawk, and he climbs up that cliff, and there at the top, sure enough, is a little pool where the water comes from. And just as he bends down to drink, his eyes see past the reflection of his face in the pool to where a snake lies dead in the water, sort of turned over on its side — a poison snake his hawk, circling above, had seen. The hawk had saved his life.

Then the story gets very sad. The king climbs down the cliff, takes up his hawk and folds its wings, wraps it in his crimson cape lined with gold, and rides home slow . . .

But there I was with my hat in my hand just standing up to drink when that whole story goes through my head. And that story makes me hesitate just for a moment. I think about that story, and the water soaking out cool through my black felt hat and running down my elbows. And as I hesitate, the wind — which had been coming down the canyon behind me — shifts around to the side a little, and I smell this terrible smell. Just a little whiff, but awful. Just a little touch in my nose.

Instead of drinking, I dump the water out of my hat, shake it out, and walk up that little stream past a screen of pine saplings — and there, not 30 steps upstream, a dead elk lies across the water, hot and rotten, covered with flies. Been there for days. And now, when I look close at the water flowing in the little stream, I can see the rainbow sheen of some poison riding that water down toward where I dipped my hat.

And then I think to myself, if I had not remembered that story, I would have drunk the water, and never climbed out from Joseph Canyon.

In the classroom where I told this, the bell had rung, but the children sat still. The buses had pulled up outside to take us home. Remember your stories, I said. They can save your life a little at a time.

Grace lives too far from town to worry when the snow falls deep. Can't drive? Stay home. But today the road is clear. As we step from the car, the colt hangs back, but her three Appaloosa mares crowd the barbwire fence stapled from tree to tree — aspen leaves just coming out. Bending to step between the second and third strands of wire, Grace says, "I guess a man goes over a barbwire fence, a child under, and a woman through. Glad you came out. Tea?" She gestures toward a mobile home hunched low into the ground, with a drift of gray leaves piled around the door.

Inside, bookshelves cover the walls.

"I've read them many times." Her hand sweeps the room. "The kind of snow we get is good for the mind." She turns around once and sits down. Her chair used to be red. Now it's covered with a faded quilt. "I'm kind of the unofficial historian of this place. I've got the books and got the time. People trust me with things, and I take care of them. Been to the museum? Sure you have! That's when I asked you to stop by. Have a seat!" We face each other across a formica table. Through the window, tiny aspen leaves flicker in sunlight.

"You said there is a tribe of people living in Joseph Canyon."

"Oh yes, the hippies. Wanted to get away, I guess, and that's away! No one sees them, but everyone knows they're there. And you know, they found something. Got to digging around, disturbing one of the campsites, you know, and came up with a little stone carved to the shape of a buffalo. They kept it for awhile, then got to feeling guilty, I guess. Got to feeling bad about digging it up. So they took it back to where they'd found it. Tied a note to it. Left it there. My friend found that. He brought it to me.

"It was a buffalo carved out of basalt, a little one curled up asleep. It was a magic thing in your hand. You wanted to hold it forever. You wanted to hold it, and at the same time it didn't feel right to hold it. It belonged to the ground, to them, you know, to the people we drove away."

"I kept it for awhile, then I sent it to the State museum, with a note asking them to give me some information on it and send it back. I thought they might have something similar, or some book that could tell me about it. But you know, they never sent it back. They never even wrote back. I got the idea they didn't trust me with it. We're just the country people, you know. Left me bitter, I'm afraid. Left a bad taste in my mouth. I'd go bury it in the ground again, if I could."

The kettle boiled, and she got up to shut off the stove. Wind pushed wide the flimsy door, framed in aluminum, and sunlight burst across the rug covered with dog hair. Grace stood a moment with the kettle steaming in her hand.

"Things get lost, but then things get to be stories, I guess. And stories stick to people like cockleburrs." She left the door open, held up a cup. "You take it black?"

I finished this essay once with the story of Grace, and published this run of stories in a book called *Having Everything Right: Essays of Place*. The book did well, friends asked me if I had everything right yet, I said no, years passed, and I thought that chapter in my writing life was done. But then I made the lucky mistake of talking with a friend out in Wallowa County, 8 years after my time there.

"How did Grace like my portrait of her in 'The Story That Saved Life'?" I asked.

"I'm not sure she's seen it," my friend replied.

Several weeks later I found a letter from Grace in my mailbox: "Who is this 'Grace'?" Grace demanded. "I don't raise Appaloosas, I don't live in a trailer house, and I *certainly* don't have dog hair on my rug. You have some explaining to do!"

I was stunned. My memory of that glorious day visiting Grace is old but vivid. I admire her tremendously, and thought I had my memory of this day right. My admiration for her has not been dimmed, but my faith in my own mind falters. Thinking back, I know I see steam from the horses' nostrils as they nose the hay she has thrown to them. I can still feel the exhilaration I felt then to find all those books in that mobile home in the woods. And I can glory in the glitter of sun off the dog-fur fuzz of that rug on the threshold. Yet none of that happened, she says. What *did* happen, then, in my mind or to my mind? How did this story get made? How did Grace and Wallowa begin to enter my mind?

I think of two moments where the story started — one on the ground, and one in exile. The first scene has me driving alone into Wallowa County for the first time. It's the fall of 1977, and I have just left a life on the coast behind for a job in the interior. On the coast, in the little town of Florence, Oregon, I had been Oral Historian for the Pioneer Museum. I had spent 2 years recording stories from the likes of Forrest Francisco, Belle Dick, Bea

Williams, and Tubby Beers. That was history—carefully recorded and transcribed and filed away in the archives. But as I came over the divide into Wallowa County, crossing the ridge I have described at the beginning of this essay, a song started shouldering its way into my mouth. It came into my mouth before it came into my mind, and I felt right away it was drawing together the stories from the coast as that world closed behind me. The new story worked old learning into a shape that was portable over time, so new learning could begin:

> Sail away, oh sail away.
> Take your chance at sea,
> Where sailors dance and sailors sing—
> The roving life so free.

This beginning was a plain thing, but as I drove on, the song went deeper. Gypsy Davy hove into port from somewhere. Stella Martin was named into being, and asked her man Davy to give up the sea.

> Flood tide runs into the land.
> The salmon dart and play:
> Silver fins in moonlight dim.
> It's salmon in the bay.
>
> Stay by me, and stay by me.
> Foggy nights are cold.
> Stay by me, oh stay by me.
> Together we'll grow old.

But Gypsy Davy spoke in the words of Ed Tatom, one of the old salts I had interviewed:

> Have you seen the sails unfurl
> When at the mast you stand?
> Have you felt the ship catch wind
> And sail away from land?

The ship, Ed had said, yearned forward like a living thing under his feet when the wind caught her. And then it was the words of Fred Buss inhabiting my voice. "We found her, yes, after she drowned and drifted with the tide 3 days, and there was that gold engagement ring still hanging by the bone." And the song reached for those words and caught them. The storm rose, the ship went aground, Stella walked the beach, the old sailors sang.

And I sang—in a way you can only sing when you are alone, driving, and your life is about to change.

Something like 30 verses, in changing and then converging form, passed through my mouth. Verses flooded into being, and ebbed away. Sometimes I would have to pull over and write them down. Sometimes I would sing them over and over until they settled into memory for good. I couldn't shake off the song until it was done. But when it *was* done, I knew I could look around at this new place I was to live. The song about my old home wasn't exactly true about that place (where to my knowledge Gypsy and Stella never lived), but it was true about my experience of the place. When I pulled up in front of the school in the town of Wallowa, population 623, where I was to work as writer in residence for 12 weeks, the song was done and I had arrived.

The making of the song cleared the way for the new life. As I worked and rambled and listened in Wallowa, I enjoyed the stories I heard and the people I met. I sat in awe in Wilma's classroom, hunched at the bar in Baird's tavern, visited Grace, and hiked the canyon. But it wasn't until I was 5 years out of Wallowa that the writing of the essay began. Its making was invisible to me until it was essentially finished by springing whole to mind. Like topping the divide and starting the song, this happened suddenly. This time, I was riding a city bus in Portland, Oregon, about to begin my first steady teaching job at Lewis & Clark College. This time, I thought of the title first: "The Story That Saved Life." I wrote that phrase on an envelope pulled from my pocket.

I had told that particular story probably 20 times aloud by then: how the king with his hawk came winging to my mind as I stood with a hat full of water. It had a shape and a momentum. I can't remember how my thinking started, but as I jostled along on the bus, that story began to grab magnetically at others, and I jotted their names on the envelope: the doctor and the husband with the knife; Wilma and her uncle Earl; Acey; the poaching brothers; the Portland hunter; God woke up; Coyote; Grace. All these stories entered one idea together: A story saves life a little at a time by making us see and hear and taste our lives and dreams more deeply. A story does not rescue life at the end, heroically, but all along the road, continually. I do not make the story; the story makes me.

If I can live deeply enough, I will not feel the need to live this life again. Stories do stick to people like cockleburrs. I may be wrong about Grace, but I know that.

2

Imagining History
"A Good Story and a Well-Formed Argument"

ANDRA MAKLER

Andra Makler is assistant professor and coordinator of the Master of Arts in Teaching Intern Program at Lewis & Clark College in Portland, Oregon. She received the M.A.T. degree from Reed College in French and social studies and her Ed.D. degree from Harvard Graduate School of Education in administration, planning and social policy. An advocate of interdisciplinary studies, Dr. Makler teaches courses that combine sociological, historical, and critical perspectives on the relationship of teaching to curriculum and evaluation. Her research focuses on the intersection of academic and personal knowledge in the work of individual teachers. She recently completed a study of mentoring policy and practice in preservice teacher education.

Teachers and students are quintessentially interdependent knowers. I know this from having taught social studies in a white, working-class high school for 7 years. One of the courses I taught was a state-mandated U.S. history class for eleventh graders. Unfortunately for history teachers in high schools, most adolescents do not presume the existence of either story, motive, reason, or consequence in history. They come to class believing that history is dead certainty and/or meaningless lists of names, places, and dates. I took it as my project, with help from colleagues in the social studies department in which I taught, to fashion a curriculum that would help students to re-create the past through construction of personal narratives.

The curriculum we developed was a framework in the form of a set of open-ended scripts, different for each student, presented to students as an outline of the history of "their" fictional family; the scripts could be regarded as a kind of "story grammar" that provided an outline of vital statistics, such as the fictional persona's age, occupation, place of residence, family status, religion, and race (Makler, 1987). The students' task was to use this information to develop a personal life history connecting this character to the events and issues of the historical period under study.

Developing these narratives (entries in diaries, letters, expository essays) was a means for students quite literally to write themselves into the historical record. As textbooks are manifestations of the relationship between publishers and markets, female students, minority students, and students from "ordinary" homes often do not see themselves in the text; thus, the historical project we fashioned was the project of creating ourselves—of seeing ourselves as agents, acting upon and in the world, as we moved through the years from the fifteenth century to the present. To use the language of academics, students wrote tales of the past that they made believable by constructing webs of relationships between the facts of the real historical situation and the invented life of their persona. They did this through reason and invention, by exercising a "historical imagination" (an idea rooted in C. Wright Mills's notion of the "sociological imagination," 1959). By combining a tale with a well-formed argument, students made plausible claims about how their "character" behaved, thought, and felt about particular events and issues, based upon their "knowledge" of this fictional individual and the historical record. These narratives instantiated the projection of historical imagination.

Though I had many teaching objectives in mind, I will name only the most salient. I wanted students to understand the historian's work as that of deriving meaning from data. I wanted them to understand that the historian writes an interpretation of the past that is, in essence, a carefully constructed argument for plausibility rather than an exposition of dead certainty. I also wanted them to seek meaning in the history we were studying—to see events and occurrences (battles in Congress or at Gettysburg, migrations from Iowa and Oklahoma to California, state laws that forbade the teaching of reading to slaves, socioeconomic and legal conventions that prevented women from owning property, voting, or obtaining a divorce) as lived representations of relationships among human beings born into a particular set of social circumstances. Most of all, I wanted them to experience for themselves the historian's task of constructing "possible worlds" (Bruner, 1986).

After several months of practice writing historical narratives describing the lived realities of several of these "fictional" forebears in different time periods (e.g., 1789, 1850, 1903), students were asked to confront their own realities—to research the history by which members of their own families (or a family of their choice) had come to the United States and to the particular place in which they found themselves today. Students found this project interesting; they entered into dialogue with parents at home and telephoned and wrote to other relatives in distant states and foreign countries. They brought their stories to class and discussed their findings among themselves; they explored differences and similarities between their real family's history and that of friends. They marveled at correspondences that cropped up between real ancestors and their fictional historical selves, discovering in their past relatives who were Native Americans and immigrants, slaves and slave traders, Quakers, traveling preachers, chaplains to soldiers during the Civil War, pioneers on the Oregon Trail, schoolteachers on the frontier, illegitimate children of powerful men, grandparents who were the "first to . . . ," parents who had marched in civil rights demonstrations or fought in Vietnam. As they worked on this project, they were involved in a special kind of accounting: in developing their narratives, they were accounting for themselves.

I was surprised by the power of this curriculum, by the level of interest it generated among students and their families, by the change it provoked in the atmosphere of my classroom. It confirmed my suspicion that teachers and students are indeed interdependent knowers, learning to construct relationships to each other as much as to the subjects they study. Now I am engaged in a different project, that of teaching those who wish to be teachers. In order to be responsive to their concerns and confusions, to hear their stories as a narrative about their place at this time in their lives, I find that I must confront my own understandings and assumptions. These teachers are struggling to present their knowledge of history to their students. I struggle to present my achieved understandings about the power of learning tasks that engage students in constructing meaning, about the importance of encouraging their students to *imagine* the past instead of perceiving it as a kind of received truth.

Denis Shemilt (1987) has shown that adolescents have difficulty comprehending the concept of "historical time"—they do not easily grasp the historical notion of cause and effect, nor do they understand the historian's role in interpreting that relationship. They tend to have a rather static notion of time as that which is, rather than as a reality to be constructed. For many adolescents, the idea of choosing one's self through responsible action, and thereby fashioning a future, represents a risk; to commit oneself to a vision of what might be seems impractical. But to speculate on the choices that were open to those who now are dead is relatively safe. By adopting the narrative stance of a first-person storyteller, students learned to perceive the past as a series of choice points, of potential options for the future.

I know from experience that high school students found the task of creating life histories engaging; that they invested this task with meaning; that they sought correspondences between their personal lives and the fictional historical selves they created. I think the key to the power of this task lies in its relational qualities; adolescents are fashioning an identity for themselves as they move through high school. I think they cared about this curriculum because it enabled them to sense the interdependence of individuals and to see in history what Nona Lyons (1988) has called "a narrative of relationships and motives with which to confirm or deny believability" (p. 32).

Certainly that is what I seek to achieve in this essay, as I explore the difference between writing a personal history of my grandmother and writing the history I have been trained to write. I feel I know very little about my grandmother as a person, as a woman, that my knowledge of her is stuck in time. I see her still as I saw her as a child, the time in my life when we were most often together. I realize that the image I held of my grandmother was a constructed image, based upon family relationships. The way other members of my family saw and treated my grandmother influenced the way I related to her as I grew up. Nothing extraordinary in that, but in attempting to write her life history, I realized that although I lived in the same house with my grandmother from my fifth birthday until I went off to college the week following my eighteenth birthday (13 years of daily contact), I had no concept of my grandmother as a person. I saw her only as "my grandmother."

I found my lack of knowledge troubling, for it represented in a personal and powerful way the history of women in general; I knew my grandmother in terms of her role relationship to me, not as a person in her own right. I knew, however, when I stopped to consider it, that the phases of her life cycle included statuses other than that of grandmother, as my own life consisted of roles other than mother, wife, daughter, and teacher. And I noted that for myself, as well as for my grandmother, the primary identifiers were relationships to others, rather than personal accomplishments.

I resolved to try to uncover facets of my grandmother's existence that would reveal her self to me by using the tools I touted to my students: interviews with family members, reflections, my knowledge of the historical time in which she lived. I also wanted to explore the meaning of the sense of her that I held as a child. I decided to try to do two things: to write a narrative drawing only on my childhood knowledge of my grandmother, and then to juxtapose this image of her against the facts that I acquired from my research. I was trying to right a wrong, to alleviate my sense of guilt for not having shown her more care as we both grew older. I was seeking understanding of myself as much as I was seeking understanding of her self. I wanted to reestablish the thread of continuity between us, in order to gain a different perspective on my life in relation to the lives of women who preceded me in time, women to whom I see myself linked by gender and circumstance, quite apart from my will to have it so. And as a teacher, I wanted to experience the task I had set for my students as they experienced it, in order to develop a more acute sense of the power of narrative, the influence of perspective, and the impulse to devise a meaning for a life history by situating knowledge about that life in its own context as well as in relation to my own.

This story of my grandmother has three parts. First I present a remembrance of my grandmother as I knew her as a child. It is my attempt to retrieve memory, to explore the relationship we had as I experienced it then, by slipping back in time, much as Proust does when he stumbles on a cobblestone and in that moment reestablishes contact with his childhood self by remembering himself in another time, eating a madeleine. Next I attempt to locate my grandmother as a person, to understand the woman I did not know by unpeeling the layers of fact and story provided by other members of my family. Finally I explore some of the connections between personal family history and the history prepared for public presentation, whether as narrative, chronicle, or retelling of the tradition, to better delineate the meanings we choose to invest in these different forms of discourse.

MEMORIES IN SEARCH OF MY GRANDMOTHER

My grandmother had a bosom. She never wore a brassiere. She never wore makeup either, despite the combined onslaught of her husband (my Grandpa Jack, who died when I was 5, bringing Grandma Eva permanently into our household); her married daughters (my mother, Gloria, and her sister, my Aunt Helen); and me. My grandmother steadfastly refused to do either of these two things, although she rarely stood up to anyone about anything. Now I wonder why I did not ask her why she felt so strongly about these items, undergarments and makeup, instead of judging her hopelessly old-fashioned. Then I was so self-righteous about the proper appearance, behavior, and concerns of women. Now I am less sure what "proper" means. Then I was 15 years old, and she at least 65; now I am 46, physically and emotionally closer to her age then.

Grandma Eva saw many changes during her lifetime, but she rarely commented on those changes. She liked to talk about the old days, offering pictures of herself, climbing flights of stairs in New York City tenements to visit one of her many sisters. She was the thirteenth of 15 children, all of whose names I still do not know, for my mother cannot remember all of them and some of them I never heard uttered. It amazes me now that I never knew their names, let alone met them. I think they were all still alive when I was 5. How many died between my fifth and eleventh birthdays, when my father's father died? His death I remember, though I saw him rarely. But I have no memory of any funerals in my grandmother's life, though I saw her daily.

My grandmother wore black, in memory of her husband, Jack DeDuke, who still remains a mystery to me, a romantic figure with a gift for storytelling and a talent for painting. I remember being told that he left Russia in a barrel sometime around 1910, to escape conscription into the czar's army. In 1980, I learned that DeDuke was not his given name but rather a name that he took to repay the man who smuggled him across the border, a gesture intended to guarantee his benefactor that his name would be remembered. But oh! small irony of life: Jack had two daughters and no son to continue the name for posterity. "DeDuke" now exists only as a name traced in spidery hand or adolescent scrawl on yellowing pages of sheet music in my piano bench, and on identity documents for my aunt and mother, sandwiched between their married names and their given names.

My grandmother told me stories, sometimes they were stories about her family. "My brother," she would begin, as we sat in the kitchen on Saturday afternoons that were long for both of us. Her brother. My great-uncle. What was his name? My grandmother could say it, but I cannot; his was a Russian name I no longer remember.

Not Osip.

I knew Osip. I thought him a strange, cold, balding man, with a mustard tint to his skin. Osip always wears a beret and carries a brown cane when I think of him. Osip was married to Doritchka, and they were on the "outs" with my father, so Grandma only invited them to the house when my parents were out of town. They would sit together in the living room, speaking Russian, laughing, engaged with each other and unmindful of me. No, that Russian brother's name was not Osip. Nor was it Grecia.

I recalled Grecia as the name of the oldest of Grandma's brothers living in New York. I also saw him as the family villain, because his was a name not to be mentioned in our household. He was a doctor, and he had let my mother labor for too long with my older brother, the one who died just days after his birth. It was Grecia's fault that my mother had had so much pain, and that my brother, whose short existence was mentioned to me always only within this context, had not lived. Now I know that Grecia was actually the son of the brother whose name I still cannot recall; but in the memory, Grecia remains my Grandma's brother . . . and this is an attempt to recall a memory.

So we never saw Grecia. Grandma never spoke of him in my father's presence, and it was only when Osip and Doritchka visited that I heard snippets of gossip about him. In fact, it strikes me now that my grandmother rarely talked about her siblings, or any members of her family, in our house. Our house, not hers — for although she lived with us from 1947 until close to her death in 1963, I don't think she ever behaved as if she felt it was her home.

The Russian brother who appeared most often in my grandmother's stories was a court physician to the czar at the summer palace, where he knew Tolstoy. This was an important relationship, for at this point in the story, my grandmother would produce a metal ashtray bearing a representation of Leo Tolstoy's face and, I think, some quotation from his work. This, I knew instantly, was an Important Treasure, although I never understood why. Grandma sounded as if this was important; that was all I needed to know.

My grandmother never discussed her parents with me. I didn't even know their names; though they are my great-grandparents, I have no memory, no knowledge, of them. Although I have a photo album with pictures of people my mother names "Aunt Masha, Aunt Sasha," and so on, there seems to be no remaining family memory of my grandmother's parents.

Zollzein. So. *Zollzein* is what my grandmother used to say when there wasn't anything else to say; the English language equivalent is something like a resigned "so," said with just a trace of a sigh. So. My grandmother came to the United States when she was 4 years old. On a boat to New York City. She lived with her parents in Harlem, where there were many stairs. In her stories of her girlhood, there were always many stairs to climb.

In New York City, as a child and as a young woman, my grandmother worked. This is what I know about her. And this is a problem to me now, as it was a marvel to me as a child. How to reconcile the young woman of the stories with the white-haired, rather dumpy Grandma whom I loved but did not exactly respect, who offered her bedroom as a refuge when I was upset or when I was angry with my parents, who always had a piece of Dentyne gum tucked away in her purse. This Grandma, whom I could coax into talking once in a while in the kitchen, but who never sat with the family in the living room, unless there were other relatives ("company") in the house, scuttled visibly and symbolically out of sight as soon as my father came home (which upset him and made him yell things like, "Eva! Goddammit! Where are you going?!"). My brother and I always shared looks together over this behavior on the part of grown-ups. The answer to my father's question was obvious to us. She was going to her room (Goddammit!), to listen to one of her shows on her radio: the news, the Saturday opera broadcast from the Met, "Fibber McGee and Molly," or one of the all-night talk shows.

Occasionally Grandma took refuge in the kitchen to stand vigil over Rose (who was originally from Florida and understood "Mrs. D." because she had always worked for Jewish folk), to be sure that Rose didn't do something unspecified and dreadful to the kosher meat. We did not keep a kosher home (we even ate bacon on Sunday morning), but all our meat was purchased from the kosher butcher, Morris, with whom my grandmother had a long-standing love-hate relationship. She telephoned; he delivered. She called back to complain about the delivery. He replied, when he wasn't too busy to come to the phone, in phrases that drew forth an unvarying response. She hung up.

My grandmother plucked tail feathers and pin feathers from chickens and turkeys, kept the *pupik*, or "part that went over the fence last" (I *still* wonder what that actually meant), for my father, and put chicken feet in the soup. She made her own gefilte fish, which involved grinding fish heads and performing other odious rites in the kitchen; at such times my brother and I were barred from entry, though I never wanted to be in there anyway, then. She also cooked *pchav* — a calf's foot jelly that my mother claims to like (though I have never seen her eat it), vegetable soup, pot roast (which I dismissed as chewy and stringy), and applesauce.

Everything else Rose cooked, and my grandmother watched over. Rose had enough of a sense of humor to tolerate my flying tackles when she was making the beds, to joke with my brother when he teased her, and to tolerate the alternation between my grandmother's suspicion and her desire for conversation.

So. What I knew about my grandmother as a child was limited. What I knew about her background was scanter still. There was family still living in Russia. Mostly my grandmother's brothers, names unknown to me. My grandmother's family were from Russia, but they had a German name. They lived in Riga, which is the capital of Latvia, but they considered themselves Russians. My grandmother called herself a Russian, and she would rise consistently to my father's bait that because she was born in Latvia, she must be Litvak. That was one of the few times when she was angry enough to fight back. The catalogue of such moments is small: She would argue about wearing a bra, over lipstick, over the insinuation that she was not really a Russian, and about casting her vote for President Truman (instead of Henry Wallace) in the 1948 election.

This was my grandmother. This is how I saw her as a child. She was a tentative person, who literally hovered in the background. She waited on my younger brother and me at table in the kitchen, disappeared up the stairs at the sound of my father's voice, called my mother "Glory" — a nickname she loathed — and unloaded the dishwasher well before 7 A.M. on weekend mornings. She usually said goodbye to me on school mornings by asking the one question calculated to provoke my instant unbridled (and now shameful) adolescent wrath: "What do you want for dinner?" (Dinner! Who wants to leave for high school at 7 A.M. thinking about dinner!) "How should I know?" I would scream as I slammed out the door.

This was my grandmother, this person who had card games where she introduced me to her friends, who were always "Mrs." without first names, who sewed sheets into bandages and bed pads for cancer patients once a week as a volunteer at the Golden Age Canteen, and who otherwise sat by the venetian blinds in the den, peering into the street. This was my grandmother, a woman who had completed the eighth grade, who spoke three, perhaps four, languages, a person I watched read Isaac Bashevis Singer's book, *The Family Moskat* (1950), with a magnifying glass a half hour at a time. (Then I thought, how slowly she reads, how poor her education; now I know how determined she was to finish this book despite poor eyesight, and I think about how important reading this book must have been to her.)

I never saw her read another book, though she read the newspaper daily. This memory of her reading so slowly has such a profound hold upon me that *The Family Moskat* is the one book of Singer's that I cannot bring myself to open. It is too much a part of my sense of my grandmother and too little a book to be read. (Ghosts are not easily exorcised when the guilt is deserved.) But this woman was more than my grandmother. She had lived a whole life before I ever knew her. She had been a child, a young woman, a bride, a worker, and a mother before she became my grandmother. But I never thought much about that, until recently.

This person who scuttled around the house had once been a young woman, independent in a foreign land. She had worked for a newspaper, as a Spanish language stenographer (where had she learned Spanish, for God's sake, when she had only finished the eighth grade?), and had sold shoes in a large department store in New York City, and at G. Fox, in downtown Hartford.

What happened to this person? Where did she go?

Perhaps she was still there, in the house of my childhood, but I was too blinded by my own cultural framework and childishness to see her.

It was a family joke that my grandmother never did housework. My aunt and my mother both told me that Grandpa Jack used to vacuum or pick up for company, or in flusher times, the maid did this work. Grandma never denied or corroborated these stories; she simply sat silently through them.

Sometimes I heard whispers about Grandpa Jack as a "ladies' man" and about Eva, who had tolerated "all that" until . . . and the door would slam shut, leaving me to wonder, until what? In my memory, Grandpa Jack is tall, thin, and wears glasses; he is a "former" dancing teacher and violinist (now I know that he played the piano; so where did I get this idea about the violin?), a landscape painter who took annual vacations alone so that he could paint, a photographer who did colorized portraits of his clients, the inventor of the first cold-process permanent wave (I have the patent in my photo album), the owner of a successful chain of beauty salons, a casualty of the Depression, and my-grandfather-who-lived-in-Hartford-and-visited-me to tell stories about Nurse Jane Fuzzy-Wuzzy and Uncle Wiggly, as he padded around our apartment in slippers or leaned on his cane in the park in the sun. Grandpa Jack was a real person to me, even after he died, though I knew him for only the first 5 years of my childhood.

Grandma Eva, however, was not really a person to me, though we lived in the same household. She was a presence, a shadow, perpetually hovering on the edge of everyone's consciousness, part of our peripheral vision, a fixture in the house, always there.

Yet I know that she was not always there. Between 1947 and 1950, she flew alone to California to visit her relatives. She was gone for about 2 weeks, and I remember her return because I was in the bathtub and couldn't touch the red fireman's hat she brought me. She took me visiting, to see her sisters and her sister-in-law, my great-aunts. We went all over New York City, on trolleys, buses, and subways, and we never got lost. She always knew, miraculously it seemed, where to turn, which doorbell to push. But she never went "out" with friends, to the movies, to dinner, or just to visit. When I was little, I often came home from school to find she wasn't there; but I never thought to ask what she did with her time on those days. She must have gone somewhere, done something. I guess that since I never asked her, she had no reason to tell me.

My grandmother laughed and joked in Yiddish and what I assumed to be Russian, but only when my parents were gone and her circle of people was invited in. This was unusual at any time, and I was not much interested in the conversation, in a language that excluded me. Although my father and mother often urged her to stand up against her sisters "who walk all over you," I never remember her responding to their criticism. And when my favorite uncle died, and I thought the world would end, she offered me the comfort of her arms that my parents, who were too busy with their own grief and the funeral arrangements, had no time to provide.

Yet I did not go to her funeral.

I did not say goodbye, nor make a gesture of thankfulness for all that I received. I was pregnant and I chose not to hassle with the airlines and my doctor over the "advisability" of my making the trip, but I know that I did not want to go. It is only recently that I have begun to wonder about the wisdom of my choice. It is only recently that I have begun to wonder about the parts of my grandmother's life that she chose not to make visible, about the silences she chose not to break. In all the stories that she told me, there were no tales of her childhood, of friends, nor were there tales of my mother's childhood. There were no tales of her life with her parents, nor of her life with her husband. Only those stories about selling shoes and climbing stairs, and descriptions of milk wagons and trolley cars. Now there is no way to fill these gaps, for there is no one left to tell. Her sisters are dead, and my mother is not able to fill in the missing parts, for she knows no more than I. Now that it is too late, I wonder why I did not ask.

FACTS IN SEARCH OF MY GRANDMOTHER

In writing this piece of family history, a memory of my grandmother embedded within, and wrapped around, memories involving other family members, I have become aware of the way we use stories to make sense of our selves. I recognize that in my quest to know my grandmother differently, as an "other" woman, as a person apart from me, I am seeking to account for inadequacies in my relationship to her. In this attempt to make the familiar strange, I seek the general within the particular. I am trying to understand one woman in relation to her time; to tease out the meaning in the ambiguities her "case" presents to me to see whether I learn something more, or better, from this analytical search for trends, patterns, to place her in categories, to see her as a member of a particular cohort. What am I to make of the lack of information all the women in the family possess about her life? What can I learn about her from using traditional historical sources and methods of analysis? If I approach her life as a text to be disclosed, will this change my sense of her, my relationship to her? Can I construct a new narrative and a new sense of my grandmother as a person?

I asked my mother and brother to tell me what they knew of Eva. After all, my mother had shared a household with her mother for approximately 42 years of her childhood, adolescence, and marriage—except for the first 6 years of her marriage, when my parents shared their apartment with my father's brother and father. I discovered to my amazement that my mother actually knew very little about her own mother. (But wait, how much more do I know about my mother?) The information she made available did not substantially alter the biographical information my brother and I were able to piece together, by sharing our separate childhood remembrances of our grandmother, but it did enable me to situate what I knew of my grandmother's life within a larger historical picture.

I sought information about my grandmother's "times" in the historical experience of Russian Jewish immigrant women in America. In doing so, I discovered that my grandmother's personal history deviates from the general group experience depicted by historians such as Rudolph Glanz (1976), Abraham Karp (1969), and Mary Ryan (1979). In so doing, I realized that my family experience is also an exemplar of a particular set of relationships, shaped by socioeconomic and political considerations as much as by personal affiliation and affection. Of course I understand that this is so. How could it not be? But it is oddly unsettling to think of myself in these terms.

Here then is my grandmother's biography, based upon information provided by my mother and corroborated by her sister, my grandmother's other daughter.

Eva Altschuler was born about 1885 in Riga, the capital of Latvia, then part of White Russia. Her parents were Ida Sarah (maiden name not remembered) and Nathan Altschuler. Nathan and Ida died before my mother was born, which "explains" her lack of relationship to them. She knows Ida's name only because her younger sister, Helen, was given Ida Sarah's Hebrew name, consistent with the Jewish religious practice of perpetuating the memory of a recently deceased close family member through continuation of the name.

Nathan Altschuler was a grain merchant on the Riga exchange. He evidently was well-to-do, as my grandmother's older brothers and sisters were all educated abroad. (She was the thirteenth of 15 children and the last child born in Russia.) Her brother Isai was the court physician whose name I did not know. Isai remained in Russia and came to America between 1938 and 1940, with his son, Grecia, the physician my father disliked.

Abraham Karp (1969) writes that it was very difficult for Jews to gain entrance into university or technical schools in Russia, as only 10% of the places could be filled by Jews. Anti-Semitism was a national policy institutionalized most violently in centuries of pogroms. A new law of 1772 restricted Jewish residence solely to those areas in which they then were living. This original restricted area, or Pale of Jewish Settlement, encompassing Russia, the Ukraine, Lithuania, and Poland was further constricted by czarist decrees during the nineteenth century. Increased legal repression beginning with the "May Laws" of 1882, three pogroms of increasing violence between 1892 and 1910, and a policy of often forced emigration culminated in a mass migration of Jews from Russia. Emigration from Riga peaked between 1880 and 1910.

According to my mother, Nathan Altschuler decided to emigrate because of business reversals on the grain exchange, not because of anti-

Semitism. He booked passage for his family (from a port no longer remembered), leaving behind several adult children, and disembarked at Ellis Island, with his wife, daughter Eva, and at least four other daughters — Sasha, Masha, Fanny, and Vera. My mother is certain that one daughter remained in Russia. My mother thinks that Eva was 4 years old when the family arrived in New York City and established residence in Harlem, where Nathan and Ida operated a cigar-store-cum-newspaper-stand.

Eva worked with her parents as a young child, selling newspapers at least until she left school upon graduation from eighth grade. Thus, her life circumstances were very different from those in which the four other sisters who came to America with her grew up, for all the older siblings had finished their education in Russia. This fact, and the difference in their ages (when the family came to New York, the next youngest sister had already completed high school), probably accounted for the odd relationship I noticed as a child visiting my great-aunts with my grandmother.

I thought Eva's sisters treated her with a kind of contempt. Her role appeared to be to serve them. When we came to visit them at their apartments, she brought them their coffee, ran errands, listened to their complaints and admonishments, and generally took orders. When I was a child, the relationship among the three sisters made me uncomfortable; I felt that my father was somehow right when he told my grandmother to stop "being a doormat" to her sisters, which she of course resented.

My grandmother was thus "different" within her own family, for she was the only daughter whose education ended with completion of grammar school, who worked as a child, and who continued to work upon completing school. Eva sold newspapers as a child and then went to work as an office clerk of some sort for the Hearst newspaper chain. Her work pattern was atypical for females in her own family as well as for females of her immigrant generation.

In his study of Jewish women in America, Rudolph Glanz (1976) notes a sharp cultural division between the German Jews in New York City, who had both education and money, and the Yiddish-speaking Russian Jews, who arrived later and were ill-educated and poor. Glanz comments that "a real class of Jewish female wage earners appeared only with the Russian Jewish catastrophe — immigration" when "a youthful generation of women arrived with their families" and were "immediately forced onto the labor market" (p. 324). The majority of these women found jobs in factories, particularly in the garment industry. Glanz suggests that socioeconomic factors were important determinants of self-identity for these immigrant women: "In this initial phase of her life, the Russian Jewish girl had to find herself in her own cultural milieu, of which the Socialist movement was the strongest factor" (p. 324).

This was clearly not Eva's cultural milieu. In Russia, the family had belonged to the professional class, and despite her limited formal schooling, Eva found employment as a white-collar clerk. My brother and I both recall our grandmother telling us that she was a Spanish language stenographer. My mother accepts this as fact and believes that "she probably went to night school." What strikes me as curious here are several anomalies in my grandmother's life. For example, she was fascinated by Tolstoy on a personal level, because he was a celebrity with whom her family had had contact in Russia, not because of his connections with the ideology of socialism. Although her sisters were born into and grew up in an upper-middle-class family, she grew up in an upper-lower-class family. She worked as a child, and then, after marrying at the relatively late age of 29, she continued to work with her husband in his photography studio, until the birth of their first child, my mother.

At this point, Eva evidently changed her life pattern. As soon as her husband's income permitted, the family employed a maid and a chauffeur, both in Newark, New Jersey, and after moving to Los Angeles, California. Eva did not clean house; she did not like to cook or to bake, although she evidently enjoyed canning and preserving, and she stopped going to work. My mother says that she had many women friends, Jewish and non-Jewish, with whom she played cards (usually bridge and whist), and visited, and that she was "always helping her sisters, especially Vera, who was not too well-off." She did not belong to any organizations or clubs and was not active in religious groups or the synagogue. No member of the family presently living can explain exactly what she did all day every day.

IN SEARCH OF UNDERSTANDING:
SELF IN RELATION TO OTHERS

In some ways, then, my grandmother's life history appears more typical of American-born females of her generation than of immigrant Russian Jewish females of her age cohort. She was a white-collar worker, part of a sociological shift. According to historian Mary Ryan, prior to 1940, "the major transformation in the pattern of female employment" in the United States in general was the shift from manual labor to the more prestigious white collar jobs (1979, p. 187). It is well to resist the temptation to overgeneralize and to recognize that individual women made particular choices. As Ryan reminds us, "The actual position of women in any sex/gender system is too complex and variable to justify such mechanical theories of causation and is more contingent upon female cooperation, participation and even invention" (p. xviii).

In Eva's case, it is questions about her cooperation and participation in the roles assigned to her that most interest me, along with the concurrent question raised by my memory that she chose not to cooperate in these roles on specific and rare occasions. The common immigrant system of pooling wages to survive hard times was part of Eva's experience within her family unit. But some element of personal choice was involved because, although Eva worked, her sister Fanny did not; nor did Fanny contribute to the family's finances after her marriage, as Eva did.

Although my grandmother certainly seems to have demonstrated a commitment to what researchers Carol Gilligan (1979) and Nona Lyons (1983) call an "ethic of care," she does not appear to have regarded this as an important part of her social role. Historian Ryan (1979) posits the existence of a "maternal principle of social benevolence" that women internalize as part of their socialization to the cultural role of tender to the sick and needy. Thus Ryan sees connections between women's work, women's clubs, and social reform; she asserts that the avowed goals of most women's organizations (especially those formed by women of my grandmother's generation) were to serve the needy and weak rather than to conquer wealth and power. Although this may be true of American women's groups in general, immigrant Russian Jewish women of my grandmother's generation often made of themselves powerful public political figures, as labor organizers, radical tract writers, and even poets. (Take, for example, the lives of Emma Goldman, Golda Meier, or Anzia Yezierska.)

The anomaly here is that Eva was apparently content to tend her immediate family (including her older sisters) and to play cards, until the last 10 years of her life, when she joined the Golden Age Canteen and sewed bandages for cancer patients at the local Catholic hospital. Eva's reasons for joining the canteen appear to have been purely social. She was alone in a house in a suburb of New York City. There was little for her to do in the house, as my parents, who both worked, employed a maid to cook and clean. Her oldest sister, who lived in New York City with her daughter, was sick and cared for by a woman companion. Eva's involvement in the sewing of bandages appears to have been a by-product of a chance association with the only senior citizen's group in the city, rather than the implementation of a strong desire to do good or a political expression of some sort of "social conscience." Although she did take pride in this endeavor because it was useful work, I believe this was, for her, a secondary gain. I must also conclude that she was probably very lonely; as she grew older and less able to seek company outside the house, my brother and I were less often at home.

Another element of personal choice that interests me is Eva's resistance to what Ryan calls the seductive message of the "sexy saleslady" myth. Eva was a saleslady in two large department stores, but she never internalized the notion that she ought to be sexy. As I have noted, she determinedly refused to use cosmetics or to exchange her corsets for a brassiere. Obviously, my grandmother had a sense of her own womanhood and identity, but I never heard her talk about this with anyone. Despite the fact that the sisters to whom she usually deferred used cosmetics and urged her to do likewise, she resisted them and the culture's many subliminal and overt messages about the "proper" expression of femininity. I do not know what her reasons were, although I suspect that the idea of using cosmetics conflicted with her sense of morality.

My mother's stories about my grandmother revealed an unsuspected ability to display a kind of erratic independence, seen by the family as stubbornness. Eva and Jack moved their family to Los Angeles, where Eva obtained a driver's license in 1934. My mother remembers that her father steadfastly maintained that Eva was incapable of learning how to drive. Eva obtained a driver's license, which she showed to the family; but no one ever saw her drive a car.

It seems to me that despite general family consensus about the type of person Eva DeDuke was, none of us really knew her well. Perhaps the consensus that Eva was not independent, assertive, or even "interesting" permitted us to take less account of her, to be less responsive to her, to separate from her. Perhaps, however, Eva preferred to keep some inner core of her personality from our view. As there is no honest way to assess Eva's motives, the "remembrance" that I have written does not truly represent Eva DeDuke. It does honestly portray my childhood perceptions of my grandmother, and my adult sense that something of her self is missing from my memories. It also depicts my struggle to find a way to relate my adult self to her adult self; when I find myself giving in to family pressures, I see myself "behaving like my grandmother." And then I think about my reasons for choosing to "give in" or to argue my point, and I realize she must have weighed such considerations too. I frequently have a sense that my children, much as they love me, do not adequately understand my reasons for adopting certain courses of behavior; then I stop and wonder how often the members of my family chose to explain my grandmother's behavior in ways that suited our constructions of her, and did not reflect her motives at all.

Why does this matter? Well, it matters to me that I cannot do justice to my grandmother's memory because I do not know her well enough to create a portrait that I believe she would recognize as true to her sense of herself. This is the historian's, or the biographer's, task, is it not, to situate the person in time, in context, in a way that would be recognizable to the person herself, and to those who knew her? I can do this for strangers, but I cannot do this for my grandmother. Is this because I do not know those strangers, and thus believe what I find of them in the "public" record of others' recollections, writings, stories to be true? Or is it because I did not really know my grandmother?

All this reflection leads to questions about the narratives we accept as history. Granted that these narratives are constructed representations of a reality we choose to consider as valid, granted that we make such judgments based on the weight of evidence; still, there is this nagging sense that our relationship to history is a function of distance more than a function of chronology, that the weight we give to evidence is easier to decide the further removed we are from the subject of our study. It is easier, somehow, to speak of strangers than to talk of those we love. For we are joined to those we love, and we wish not to harm them. Even in the telling here, I have chosen to excise portions of my memory, not to recount certain events because they seemed to add little to the narrative and had the potential to cause discomfort. Would I be as circumspect about the life of a stranger? Am I as circumspect about the ascription of motives to those who have "made" history, in recounting my understanding to my students?

How I feel about my grandmother is related to what I know of her, about her, and from her. It is my relation to her that is in question: did I fulfill my obligations, did she know that I loved her? These are personal questions, to be addressed in a personal journal, in private correspondence, through the medium of fiction, poetry, art. They are questions about intimacy, about personal knowledge and personal meaning.

So, too, the narratives that I asked my students to write were responses to questions about intimacy, personal knowledge, and personal meaning. To situate oneself in time means to make a personal connection to that which has come before, to be willing to develop a relationship, to see the common thread that binds us now to those who long since died. How else to understand the past, other than by attempting to develop a sense of what made life meaningful for those who lived it? How else to understand the demographics of mass migrations, if not in terms of the personal sacrifices entailed by those who made the trip, and in terms of the quality of existence that they both experienced and sought?

History is an attempt to make the strange familiar — to know not just what happened, but why. There is a grammar and syntax to history, a set of relationships that shapes our expectations for how to recount the past appropriately. And these expectations are culturally defined, as Native American historian Lawanna Trout (1982) argues forcefully. It is common now to say that in retelling the past, we bespeak a perspective, we expose our own values, we seek meaning — to know why, and how, this came to pass (and not that). This search is a search for a story to tell; it presumes the existence of a story, of motive or reason, of consequence. If we did not presume these to exist, we would not seek to find them. And therein lives the tale. To recount the past is to reclaim it, to reevaluate our selves in relation to others.

In *Actual Minds, Possible Worlds,* Jerome Bruner (1986) asserts the separateness of different ways of knowing:

> Each of the ways of knowing . . . has operating principles of its own and its own criteria of well formedness. They differ radically in their procedures for verification. A good story and a well-formed argument are different natural kinds. . . . The epistemological question . . . [is] how to know truth . . . the broader question . . . [is] how we come to endow experience with meaning. (pp. 11, 120)

Although I accept the logic of Bruner's assertion, I also wish to contend that the historian must fuse these ways of knowing, if history is to be more than mere record keeping. We read history partly to find ourselves reflected in Tuchman's (1978) "distant mirror," to learn a lesson about the conduct of our affairs and our lives.

C. Wright Mills (1959) practiced a method of engaging the world that he named the "sociological imagination." Surely there also is a form of engaging the world that is expressed as "historical imagination"—a capacity to create empathy between one's self and the lived experience of those in other times and places. It seems to me that imagining a narrative context to support the events, actions, decisions, and artifacts recorded as part of history is an act of knowing that seeks to understand the experience of others both on their terms and ours. It is a way of acknowledging the common dimensions of shared humanity across the chasm of passed time and the cultural separations of place, language, custom, belief, social class, and gender. The power of writing a narrative lies in the ordering of the experience of others, in tracing connections between cause and consequences, continuity and change. In creating the narrative, the writer discovers that the attraction of history is the power in the act of disclosing a possible world.

REFERENCES

Bruner, Jerome. (1986). *Actual minds, possible worlds.* Cambridge, MA: Harvard
    University Press.
Gilligan, Carol. (1979). Woman's place in man's life cycle. *Harvard Educational
    Review.* Reprinted in Sharon L. Rich & Ariel Phillips (Eds.), *Women's experi-*

ence and education (pp. 224–239). Harvard Educational Review Reprint Series #17, Cambridge, 1985.

Glanz, Rudolph. (1976). *The Jewish woman in America: Two female immigrant generations, 1820–1929.* New York: Ktav Publishing House.

Karp, Abraham. (Ed.). (1969). *The Jewish experience in America: Selected studies from the publications of the American Jewish Historical Society.* Waltham, MA: AJHS.

Lyons, Nona. (1983). On self, relationships, and morality. *Harvard Educational Review, 53*(2), 124–145.

Lyons, Nona. (1988, May 25). Commentary: Learning from new research about women. *Education Week*, p. 32.

Makler, Andra. (1987). Recounting the narrative. *Social Education, 51*(3), 180–185.

Mills, C. Wright. (1959). *The sociological imagination.* New York: Oxford University Press.

Ryan, Mary P. (1979). *Womanhood in America: From colonial times to the present* (2nd ed.). New York: Franklin Watts.

Shemilt, Denis. (1987). Adolescent ideas about evidence and methodology in history. In Christopher Portal (Ed.), *The history curriculum for teachers* (pp. 39–61). London: Falmer Press.

Singer, Isaac B. (1950). *The family Moskat.* New York: Farrar Straus.

Trout, Lawanna. (1982). Native American history: New images and ideas. In Matthew Downey (Ed.), *Teaching American history: New directions* (NCSS Bulletin No. 62, pp. 91–115). Washington, DC: National Council for the Social Studies.

Tuchman, Barbara. (1978). *A distant mirror: The calamitous fourteenth century.* New York: Knopf.

3

Reading Women's Autobiographies
A Map of Reconstructed Knowing

ANITA PLATH HELLE

Anita Plath Helle is assistant professor of English at Iowa State University and an affiliate member of the Center for the Study of Women in Society. She has published essays and reviews on twentieth century women writers in Modern Fiction Studies, Northwest Review, *and the* National Women's Studies Association Journal *and is currently working on a collection of essays on feminist pedagogy and literary theory. She wrote this essay while on leave as a visiting professor of English at the University of Oregon.*

> Along with the sense of personal authority arises a sense of voice—in its earliest form, a "still small voice" to which a woman begins to attend rather than the long-familiar external voices that have directed her life. This interior voice has become, for us, the hallmark of women's emergent sense of agency and control. (Mary Belenky, Blythe Clinchy, Nancy Goldberger, & Jill Tarule, *Women's Ways of Knowing*, p. 68)

> If the imagination is to transcend and transform experience it has to question, to challenge, to conceive of alternatives, perhaps to the very life you are living at the moment. You have to be free to play around with the notion that day might be night, love might be hate, nothing can be too sacred for the imagination . . . to call experimentally by another name. For writing is re-naming. (Adrienne Rich, *On Lies, Secrets, and Silence*, p. 43)

I teach courses in feminist critical theory from an interdisciplinary base in literature and women's studies. Often, I find it inspiring to recall from Adrienne Rich's now-classic essay, "When We Dead Awaken: Writing as

Re-Vision" (1979), a passage that links the reality of change in women's lives to narrative power. Rich assumes that certain spectacular effects are possible: putting the personal and the particular into perspective may turn day into night, night into day, enabling us to envision "alternatives to the very life we may be living at the moment" (p. 43). But how, exactly, is this to be accomplished? Writing at a different historical moment, and viewing life from within the walls of an academic institution, I also recognize that transformation is not all magic: it requires critique as well as vision. Listening in on the complex and myriad ways language defines our relationship to knowledge and power, I find it important to recognize that narrative is also a language whose palpable effects can be analyzed and described. This essay offers two such related applications: an application of narrative to feminist thought, and an application of narrative to pedagogy. I honor the spirit of Rich's vision by exploring transformation and connections as themes in women's autobiographies and feminist philosophy. I also use literary criticism to analyze narrative as an alternative procedural language, a way of critiquing separate knowing and valuing dialogic processes.

FEMINIST THEORY AND PEDAGOGY: ISSUES AND PRACTICES

Although it has become commonplace to consider the spoken and written narratives of women's lives as "texts" to be analyzed, considerable debate remains over the relevance of the personal narrative to feminist theory and pedagogy. As a matter of pedagogical practice, radical feminists frequently advocate bolstering the "self" and revaluing "experience" without exactly defining what these terms mean, or why and how they produce change (Bunch, 1983). Feminists in the liberal tradition, historically more committed to reason and autonomy as a standpoint for knowing, typically mistrust self-reflective procedures and may even view them as reactionary. As one political theorist put it, "Theory must distance itself from the world to determine where the key to it can be found" (Cocks, 1985, p. 176). Profoundly at issue is what might be meant by a narrative sense of self, and why and how it contributes to feminism. My own answer to this question is that the reevaluation and redefinition of narrative procedures for knowing has special urgency in the current climate of feminist theory. Narrative ways of knowing function collectively to affirm the values of multiplicity and connection, desirable alternatives in a feminist climate threatened by division and fragmentation. Furthermore, narrative processes function as a connected *medium* for knowing — an embodiment of an intimate relation between the knower and the known.

Using narrative to teach feminist theory requires more than an interest in themes and transitions in feminist thought; it also requires a recognition of how the parameters of knowledge are being altered by the questions feminism raises. In my course on Feminist Theories of Gender and Knowledge we work by deconstructing and reconstructing, unmaking and remaking. Such strategies are necessary, I believe, if the transformation of knowledge is to remain pluralistic and open-ended, available to defining the realities of women's experience and to the ongoing struggle to determine how we must act even as history acts upon us.

Initially, our reading offers a critique of masculinist epistemologies through the lens of women's oppression. Evelyn Fox Keller (1985) and Sandra Harding (1986) help demystify the broad-based rationalist and empiricist traditions of Cartesian subjectivity. Essays by Catharine MacKinnon (1982), Nancy Hartsock (1981), Hilary Rose (1982), Helene Cixous (1986), and Stephen Heath (1982) mark points of convergence and divergence within the epistemologies of feminist thought. Elizabeth Flynn and Patrocinio Schweickart (1986), Michel Foucault (1972), Paulo Freire (1970), and Adrienne Rich (1979) extend this critique to include alternative notions of truth and representation. Mary Belenky, Blythe Clinchy, Nancy Goldberger, and Jill Tarule (1986) offer a critical apparatus for what I term reconstructive readings of women's autobiographies, readings that enable us to trace patterns of epistemological development. Autobiographical narratives such as those by Gertrude Stein (1933), Marion Milner (pseud. Joanna Field) (1981), Alice Koller (1983), and Audre Lorde provide some representative examples of how oppositions between self and other, subject and object are broken down to shape more inclusive definitions of knowledge and truth.

We discover that the structures of autobiography and epistemology invite certain comparisons. In constructing knowledge and in reading autobiography, an "I" renders itself both subject and object and represents a concrete world of past and future predicated upon this relation. The various textual strategies writers may employ "fit" the selves we may become in and through the processes of reading. By making sense of the text, we participated in an intersubjective dialogue. In what follows, I outline first some reasons for paying particular attention to the language and epistemology of narrative. Second, by way of illustration, I offer some representative readings of autobiographies whose experimental forms and themes put into practice what Nel Noddings has described as a "caring relation" — that is, one grounded in an attitude of "receptivity, relatedness, and responsiveness" (1984, p. 61).

NARRATIVE AND DIALOGUE IN FEMINIST THEORY

In the current sociopolitical climate, feminist theory is challenged to define ever more inclusive, multiplistic, and heterogeneous orientations toward knowledge and truth. As historically sensitive definitions of feminism bring to light the richness and diversity of women's efforts to combat male privilege, the Anglo-American tradition of the past 200 years, with its insistence on equal rights and a feminism formed around an individualistic ethic, appears increasingly to offer an exclusive and therefore limited focus. As Karen Offen has urged (1988), the range of effective strategies that constitute definitions of feminism must be "revisioned" to include arguments that have at their core a relational as well as an individualistic concern. A historically enriched and fully comparativist vision of the history of feminist theory thus must be

> capacious enough to include the concerns of women who are married as well as women who are single, women who are mothers, as well as women who do not choose motherhood, and women whose most important relationships are with other women. It must speak to poor women as well as to wealthy women and to women of various ethnic backgrounds and religious persuasions. It must also include men whose self-concept is not rooted in domination over women. (p. 157)

To be sure, even currently well-informed efforts to justify feminist theory by defining a single objective standpoint for feminism appear to have reached an impasse. Alison Jaggar's influential proposal for "theoretical desiderata" organized around an "impartial" and "comprehensive" account of the data of women's experience (1983, pp. 354, 384) constitutes one such example of the difficulty — and indeed the dangers — of couching such desiderata in empiricist terms. Not only have the diverse strands of feminist thought failed to produce a clear consensus about what constitutes an impartial and comprehensive view, but we are also frequently reminded, notably by women of color, that all women are not equally oppressed or oppressed in similar ways (Hooks, 1984). In addition, the urgency of defining feminism *globally* demands interpretive schemes for viewing women's collective action *responsively* — in terms of the cultural contexts that produced them, including recognition of political and socioeconomic agendas that often take precedence over claims to self-sovereignty. A standpoint that attempts to place itself out of the range of dialogue is more likely to constrain than to enhance opportunities for meaningful thought and action.

Problems that arise from current issues in defining feminist theory are further complicated by the need to discover appropriate applications of theoretical frameworks in the classroom — applications, that is, that enable us to see that both gender and knowledge operate in traditional contexts by sacrificing the "still, small voice" to the dominant social order. The current feminist critique of knowledge describes this silencing as a denial of otherness (Felman, 1982; Keller, 1985). And whether the other is a different voice, a different way of reasoning, a different procedural language, feminist revisions of knowledge emphasize that alterity is to be positively valued as *part of* rather than *apart from* the structures of insight. Concretely, in teaching, I recognize the crucial importance of acknowledging the other by noting the difference between teaching by syllogism and teaching by narrative. Syllogism and narrative each in its own way tells me something about facets of my being, but the two forms imply different orientations toward self and other. Teaching syllogistically, I communicate far different social and verbal intentions than I do when offering a narrative case — for example, an account of the perils, hopes, and frustrations of my life or the lives of others. Syllogism models the world of the class according to a self-contained definition of knowledge as the system already in place: the virtues of such explanations are taken to be those of ready-made transmission, complete and self-contained. Teaching from narrative, on the other hand, models the process of recognizing the other. The other is within me, consciously and unconsciously, when I seismographically test the truth of an idea against the variable pulse of experience, for experience makes leaps and digressions that move beyond the insight arrived at through the model of self-containment and control. In narrative, the intentions of the other are also present *in* language: not only does the social context determine the presentation of any given incident, but the meaning of any given utterance will be interpreted differently from the standpoint of any reader or listener. A broadly informed rationale for using narrative to teach theory calls attention to and invests trust in the fact of irreducible otherness as part of shared reality.

Creating a verbal climate that fosters dialogue and values otherness is also important as an authentic standpoint for critiquing dominant paradigms of knowledge and authority. In the large public universities where I have most often taught, the makeup of courses in women's studies is increasingly diverse. Women and men who sign up for topics in feminism and critical theory are most likely to resemble what Barbara Hillyer Davis (1985) has described as a multilayered subject with multilayered agendas for education. Very few of my students now fit the 1970s profile of women seeking new role definitions in their emergence from the household, though many describe themselves as "in transition" in other ways. The majority have already set some professional directions or are changing professions. Many have grown up in environments where the third wave of the women's movement has been more or less taken for granted. These students may now expect from feminist theory a systematic logic and value system comparable to that of the master theories of other disciplines. Others are searching for practical ways of converting women's traditional strengths to a competitive job market. Still others have come to view gendered perspectives through the prism of other differences such as race, age, class, and disability.

With remarkable frequency, however, I find that many women and some men count among their list of feminist concerns the manner in which disciplinary structure, academic procedures, pedagogical styles — the entire educational apparatus — have shaped the selves they have become. I was made aware of this most recently in a graduate seminar on feminist theories of knowledge. At the introductory meeting, even before the design of the syllabus had been explained, students who by conventional standards were successes at the education game introduced themselves by telling stories about gaining or losing a sense of authentic voice. Participants seemed to be searching for alternative standpoints from which to question and to deconstruct the dominance of impersonal and authoritarian procedures for knowing, while maintaining a feeling of control of their lives. As one member, whose class project eventually turned out to be an autobiography of her struggle to claim an authentic voice after years of community college teaching, observed, "You can think you have gained a voice in the sense of mastery of a discipline and a semblance of authority, and then you can turn around and find that you have also lost a voice, in the sense of being disconnected from yourself." Another student and former teacher, who associated the onset of a near-fatal disease with the stresses of defining her professional life in terms of other people's expectations, offered what came to be a central metaphor for integrating voices, the metaphor of *bridging*: "I guess I am searching for a bridge between what I now see as the built-in demands of my profession and my own awakening desire to place these demands on a par with my own sense of self-definition."

SEPARATE AND CONNECTED KNOWING

Such messages of aspiration and painful self-division define a hidden state of emergency in women's sense of agency, control, and ways of knowing. Procedural knowledge is in a sense unavoidable: its codes confer membership in professional communities, institutions, disciplines. But as Belenky and her coauthors (1986) suggest in their groundbreaking research on female epistemology and development, authentically radical and transforming critiques of a patriarchal world would necessarily mean that women make the leap "outside the frame authorities provide and create their own frames" (p. 133). Such transformation requires overcoming epistemic dualisms conditioned by procedural knowledge and assuming the power to construct knowledge. Language and representation in the context of constructed knowing do not signify an authoritative replica of an external reality; rather, language is a way of fostering cooperation and common endeavor, "a kind of compliment we pay to beliefs that are successful in helping us do what we want to do" (Hare-Mustin & Marecek, 1988, p. 133).

The research of Belenky and her coauthors (1986) also offers a compelling explanation for the conflicts women face as procedural knowers in terms that make sense for feminist theory. Although procedural knowledge typically privileges the "voice of reason," it also places a premium on what the authors, building on Carol Gilligan's studies (1982) on moral and psychological development, have termed "separate knowing." We recognize the voice of separate knowing because it conforms to expectations of what external authority sounds like, and this is frequently what masculine authority sounds like. Analyzing the effects of such procedures, Belenky and her coauthors point to an impoverishment of relational concerns:

> Separate knowers speak a public language. They exhibit their knowledge in a series of public performances, and they address their messages not to themselves or to intimate friends, but to an audience of relative strangers. Often the primary purpose of their words is not to express personally meaningful ideas, but to manipulate the listener's reactions, and they see the listener not as an ally in conversation, but as a potentially hostile judge. (p. 108)

In the case of "connected knowing," as Belenky and her coauthors discovered, we have a less rigidly codified procedure in which truth emerges through care, mutuality, and reciprocity. The voice of connected knowing carries with it an intimacy that presumes a sharing of self and other, a felt relation between knower and known. The voice of connected knowing is attuned to creating continuity between the so-called private language of self-reflection and the formal designs of public speech. We can recognize this voice by certain stylistic markers — it includes references to the self; it may include the vocabulary of feeling; it recognizes temporal flux and change; it is a voice in which there are echoes of internal dialogue brought out into the open. Belenky and her coauthors assure us that the apparent polarity between separate and connected knowing is neither historically inevitable nor gender-closed. Connected knowing, for example, is not an exclusively feminine approach. But current data suggest that at present, the two modes appear gender-related: "more women than men tip toward connected knowing, and more men than women toward separate knowing" (pp. 102–103).

If separate and connected knowing are not essentially gender-closed orientations, there are still plenty of reasons to think that the procedural norms of many disciplines favor separate over connected knowing. The example of discursive boundaries separating and excluding personal narrative from other types of discourse readily makes this point. Philosophical writing has often been suspicious of the truth claims of metaphor and narrative. And although philosophical parables have a place within the philosophical tradition, certain methods of doing philosophy negotiate their truth claims by expunging the ambiguity that the problem of the subject in language creates (Culler, 1982; Derrida, 1978). Within the literary canon, the status of women's life writing also has been particularly disadvantageous. Feminist literary criticism of women's autobiographical narratives has been neglected because women's autobiographies assume diverse, nontraditional patterns that are not easily assimilable to generic norms or to masculine notions of the authoritative self (Brodzki & Schenck, 1988; Jelinek, 1986; Smith, 1987).

The findings and methodologies employed by Belenky and her co-authors (1986) attend closely to the relationship between language and epistemology in the narratives of women's lives. Thus these findings and approaches open up ways of *revaluing* feminist research on personal narrative and also suggest *ways of reading* the conflict over "separate" and "connected" knowing as a dimension of the rhetorical forms and themes, paradoxes and plots of women's autobiographies. Applications of these strategies of interpretation have yet to be developed, but I demonstrate some possible directions in the next section. As we reflect upon our own epistemological journeys in the framework of reading women's autobiographies, my students and I recognize that in the course of our lives we have assumed a variety of epistemological stances and, indeed, that we may occupy many of these orientations toward knowing simultaneously, especially as the possibility of a more fluid integration of voices becomes a reality. Discovering the ways in which narratives help us rename ourselves helps us view the debate among competing theories of knowledge from a developmental perspective. The question becomes not what is the "right" standpoint for knowing, but how we can come to understand, individually and collectively, the forces that nourish greater inclusiveness, change, and growth over time.

THE NARRATIVE SENSE OF SELF
IN READING WOMEN'S AUTOBIOGRAPHIES

Men *create* the world from their own point of view, which then becomes the
truth as described. The male epistemological stance, which corresponds to
the world it creates is objectivity. . . . What is objectively known corresponds
to the world and can be verified by pointing to it (as science often does)
because the world itself is controlled from the same point of view. (MacKinnon, 1982, pp. 23–24)

About six weeks ago Gertrude Stein said, it does not look to me as if you were
ever going to write that autobiography. You know what I am going to do. I am
going to write it for you. I am going to write it as simply as Defoe did the
autobiography of Robinson Crusoe. And she has and this is it. (Stein, 1933,
p. 232)

Belenky and her coauthors (1986) correlate the development of a
"heightened consciousness and sense of choice" (p. 136) with the assumption of a narrative sense of self. A combination of textual analysis and
reader response can be used to illustrate the ways in which different forms
of discourse may place relatively different demands on our procedures for
knowing. To demonstrate, the epigraphs above juxtapose two passages.
Both could be said to make a similar argument: there is nothing necessary
or universal about a fixed and impartial standpoint as a criterion for truth.
But there is what Evelyn Fox Keller (1985) would describe as a "world of
difference" (p. 158) in the standpoints for knowing that the two passages
assume in their reading effects. The contrast lies in the difference of "fit"
between textual strategies and the range of appropriate responses they
regulate and control. In each case, textual strategies prescribe the *kind* of
subject I am asked to become in and through the act of reading.

The cultural codes that determine the activity of meaning making in
the passage from Catharine MacKinnon (1982) may be described as text-
based, in that they require exclusive focus on syntactic and syntagmatic
links, positioning the reading subject as a detached observer. When I read
the passage appropriately, I am engrossed to the extent that I can consciously exclude a broader range of awareness—personal associations, non-
linear shifts in time, connotative values, immediate awareness of my surroundings. It is equally irrelevant to my comprehension or judgment of the
value of this argument that I imagine myself *in relation* to one who is
writing—that is, to the voice of another subject with an interiority akin to
mine. The text effects the semblance of standing "outside" ordinary patterns of self-reflection, full of meaning and complete in itself. The self I
assume for the purpose of reading it conventionally—that is, in terms of its

procedural codes — is thus more likely to narrow to a bounded, autonomous core than to expand responsively in relation to another.

How different, by contrast, is the positioning of the reading subject in Gertrude Stein's narrative (1933). The narrative "turn" at the close of Stein's autobiography demonstrates ways in which dialogue can be said to be one of the *effects* of narrative — that is, narrative sets up in the reader a reflective awareness of the appropriateness of a relational response. In this autobiography, we arrive at such a recognition when we discover that Alice's Gertrude is in fact Gertrude Stein's invention after all — Stein has written the autobiography, Alice has conspired, and this fact has been disguised all along. We are thus witness to the paradox of a turning point that requires the positioning of a new set of relations: formerly, we had thought Alice was the author — now, of course, it's Gertrude. In order to make sense of this ending, we must reconstruct and reassemble narrative elements. In this way the reader participates in an active dialogue — reflecting, judging, and composing. One manifestation of this reading effect is finally a delight that attends the transformation of separate authorship to a notion of shared identity. I liken this pleasure of sudden recognition to the sensation of "joy" described by Nel Noddings (1984) as the recognition of the reality of relationship in our intellectual work. Rooted in an earlier consciousness of relation to another who listens and responds appropriately, the narrative closure affectively and cognitively gratifies expectations created in and through its form.

The process of reading I have just described is generalizable to other examples of narrative. Pivotal to the constructed self of the reader is the relation of events in time, linking narrative processes to the processes of human development, growth, and change. The reader is a subject-in-process, holding the meaning of prior events in abeyance, deferring them in anticipation of later events. Through what Paul Ricoeur (1981) has described as *refigurations* of the text, we recollect partial meanings and place them in a reconstructed strand. One reason rational and separate knowing occupies such a privileged position in relation to other procedures is that we are accustomed to thinking of truth as knowledge that is not subject to change (Martin, 1986). But in its temporal and reflective interdependencies, especially in experimental forms, narrative implies a dialogue in which the paradoxes of change and meaning function interdependently.

SPECULATIVE DISCOURSE IN AUTOBIOGRAPHY

We may also note the appearance in women's autobiographical storytelling of certain narrative forms that perform the role of critical inquiry often reserved for theory, but in a more fully connected mode. Literary critic Rachel DuPlessis (1985) has described such narratives as types of "speculative discourse" (pp. 178–179). Central to their form and content is an intrinsic interest in narrative procedures of inquiry — ways of knowing dependent on temporal and relational contexts. Though DuPlessis has been concerned primarily with speculative discourse in women's fiction, her analysis also helps to identify a similarly speculative mode of self-representation in women's autobiographies, where the question of who "I" will become in relation to self and others is an explicit theme.

Autobiographies of this kind perform a speculative role in several senses. First, they travel through time and into the future, challenging the complacency of static endings with affirmations of growth and change in human development. Their mission is to teach, and as teaching stories they assist the reader in reflecting upon and confronting feelings and beliefs in a dialogic fashion. In DuPlessis' terms, they "establish a dialogue with habitual structures of satisfaction, ranges of feeling, and response" (1985, p. 179). Finally, they are likely to be highly innovative verbal structures, experimental in form, and implicitly calling into question the role of any single form of discourse as dominant or universal.

The autobiographical narrative of Marion Milner (the pseudonym of Joanna Field, 1981) serves as one example of autobiography in a speculative mode, criss-crossing generic boundaries and offering a heuristic for relational procedures of knowing. The work itself is experimental in form and content: Milner's purpose is the discovery of a means of setting up "a standard of values that is truly one's own" (p. 12). She does so through diverse means, incorporating journal writing, list making, stream-of-consciousness experiments, dreamwork, and mythology as elements of experience through which a set of unique procedures evolve. All the more fascinating, then, that the narrative is constructed so that her readers experience the quest for a procedural language as a series of epistemological shifts from received knowledge through subjective knowing and, finally, toward a more fluid and open-ended multiplicity.

The political framework of the narrative is set by allusions to the ethos of rational skepticism in Bloomsbury circles of the 1920s, an atmosphere that in Milner's terms "had made a cult of the 'male' intellect" (p. 15). We begin the narrative sharing her state of doubt: "so I had for years struggled to talk an intellectual language which was for me barren, struggled to force the feeling of my relation to the universe in terms that would not fit" (pp. 15–16). At the same time, Milner is acutely conscious of living in a time of unprecedented change for women, and of struggling to discover which of the conflicting exhortations of a changing civilization are appropriate to her own goals. Like many caught up in changing cultural expectations, she is often numbed and silenced by internal conflict. Listening to the authorities, her first thoughts are ruled by awkward pretense. As she begins to direct her own inquiry into daily habits of reflection, however, she discovers she has aimed at living exclusively for what was expected of her:

> Pleasing, being popular, not missing things, doing what's expected . . . swayed by standards uncritically accepted from my friends, my family, my countrymen, my ancestors. Were these reliable guides for my own life? I could not assume they were, for everywhere around me I saw the old ways of doing things breaking down and proving inadequate. (pp. 22–24)

We sense Milner's preliminary efforts at self-reflection as a narrative of estrangement. Having taken a first-class honors degree in psychology, she seeks initially to investigate her own state of mind through empirical methods. So meager is her self-understanding at this stage of her journey, so impoverished is her own capacity for self-reflection, that a week's list of moments of satisfaction produces only one example of pleasure—a half hour in the bathtub! All the more remarkable, given her rigid training, are Milner's gradual abandonment of the self-help books of the 1920s by "mental training experts" and her plunge into language experiments of a more adventuresome and fluid nature.

In "The Coming and Going of Delight," Milner comes across a method of confronting directly the problem of cognitive dualism by "placing" her attention. Through this process she extends the core of what she had labeled "I-ness" to encounter more receptively the world of nature and art. The organic metaphors used to describe this widening of experience recall earlier stages of development in which, according to object-relations theorists, the boundaries of the self are shared rather than rigidly differentiated (Keller, 1985). Milner writes of her own discovery:

> I was reminded of that little one-celled animal which can spread parts of its own essence to flow round and envelop within itself whatever it wants for food. This spreading of some vital essence of myself was a new gesture . . . . it was more like a spreading of invisible sentient feelers, as a sea anemone spreads wide its feathery fingers. Also I saw now that my usual attitude to the world was a contracted one, like the sea anemone when disturbed by a rough touch, like an amoeba shut within protective walls of its own making. (Field, 1981, pp. 75–76)

A result of Milner's discovery of a more fluid and relational sense of self, eventually, is a more relaxed attitude toward her own narrative writing. At the heart of this epistemological journey is the insight that procedures and procedural languages can evolve *from* and *through* relational contexts. One of the themes of the autobiography is the struggle to overcome purposeless drift and fears of inadequacy as a helping professional. In her professional life, Milner is driven by the image of an internal "drill-sergeant" of thought, perpetually whipping the plodding initiate, herself, into shape. Consistent with her experience of an inner world rigidly poised between oppositional forces are perceptions of clients and coworkers as aggressive authoritarian figures, parents and judges waiting to "catch me out in some critical situation" (p. 116). Falling back into personal preoccupations, silence, or passivity (a subjectivist extreme) or adjusting her ordinary habits of speech to preconceived formalities are the strategies she has routinely used to cope with conflict. The turning point in Milner's professional life coincides with the discovery of what she terms an "aesthetic of emotional relations" (p. 192) that enables her to redefine the professional role. The discovery parallels the earlier recognition of a way to surmount inner doubt by widening perception; here it is applied to relationships with others in which she "feels the necessities of [another] being" (p. 193) without losing herself. The best example of this "aesthetic of relation" comes from an anecdote about her work in a residential treatment center:

> I was one day helping a very old lady from her chair to her bed. She was so old that she was past the age of reasonable understanding, and was like a child in most things, including the disinclination to go to bed. She was so heavy that I did not know how to deal with the situation at all and felt embarrassed, tightly withdrawn, wishing it were all over. Then I caught sight of her helplessly obstinate feet and something in them threw me out of myself into her problem so it became my problem too, and at once all her obstinacy vanished and she yielded easily to my help. (p. 193)

Here, the standoffish, paternalistic posture of the helper who gains professional dignity by doing "right" for someone else and therefore rising to a superior position over the other is transformed. Instead, the helper moves to include an "unvoiced relationship" as part of her concerns and enters into an authentic dialogue of shared experience and empathy, now grounded in a newly discovered capacity to listen to the self and the other at the same time. The recognition in this passage—that what is *not* said is also part of the context of meaning—is significant. Feminist theorists have often argued that the forms of expression relevant to women's experiences have been missing from the "legal" norms of representation, and that their exclusion is one of the ways in which power and dominance are reinforced (Gilbert & Gubar, 1979). Milner's renaming of silence as part of the "emotional aesthetic" richly attests to the power and relevance to *relationship* of discourses that point beyond words.

MULTICULTURAL REPRESENTATION
IN SPECULATIVE DISCOURSE

Speculative autobiographies by women such as Stein and Milner encode within their structures a relation to knowledge privileged to white women. Their problematic dualities of experience are primarily limited to a bifurcation along the lines of gender, the difference that separates maternal and paternal inheritance. Reading autobiographies by women writing from the margins of multicultural representation requires an analysis even more subtly attuned to multiple differences. A number of postmodern autobiographies from the margins may illustrate this point, but Audre Lorde's *Zami: A New Spelling of My Name* (1982) makes especially good use of narrative complexity by engaging the reader in a dynamic dialogue with multiple stories, multiple interpretations, multiple standpoints. Like the other autobiographies I have considered here, Lorde's challenges the ideology of separate knowing as well as the ideologies of gender and race. What makes her autobiographical strategy unique is the manner in which she negotiates self-representation in relation to the storytelling voices of several generations of black women. In her prologue, Lorde writes:

> I have felt the age-old triangle of mother father and child, with the "I" at its eternal core, elongate and flatten out into the elegantly strong triad of grandmother mother daughter, with the "I" moving back and forth flowing in either or both directions as needed. (p. 7)

Since Lorde's "I" is a communal figure, the reader must reconstruct and — eventually — invent points that connect life stories from several cultural discourses: the legendary matrifocal discourse of West Indian women, the racist and sexist discourse of Harlem in the 1930s, and the working-class lesbian culture Lorde encounters on her own. As in Milner's autobiography, Lorde's journal begins with the problem of received knowledge, the world as represented by parental injunction. Denying their own histories of injury in order to protect their children, Lorde's parents pass on contradictory messages about the meaning of self-pride and self-preservation:

> Both my parents gave us to believe that they had the whole world in the palm of their hands for the most part, and if we three girls acted correctly — meaning working hard and doing as we were told — we could have the whole world in the palm of our hands also. It was a very confusing way to grow up. (p. 18)

Part of the message of "behaving correctly" is the requirement to assimilate by adopting the procedural languages of the dominant culture, ways that are often at odds with ethnic and familial subcultures. In school, Lorde is admonished for printing her name at a slant and for refusing to write in crayons, which had been forbidden at home. On another occasion, her mother pulls her out of public school and into a more restrictive parochial environment because she believed that the "function of a school was to make me learn how to do what I was told to do" (p. 227).

Such injunctions are particularly troubling because they are at odds with what Lorde has learned about female strength and possibility from her West Indian inheritance. Her mother's wisdom is revealed through tales of spiritual power, healing, and communal ritual—"root truths" (p. 13) that implicitly attest to alternative, more connected ways of knowing. In her mother's native patois, the language spoken at home, Lorde learns what she terms a "secret relation" to words and a different vocabulary. The name *Zami*, which she eventually adopts for herself, for instance, is a term drawn from Carriacou culture for women who work together as friends and lovers (p. 14). The tone and texture of the autobiography are permeated with maternal presence—the ritual of food preparation, the sensuality of the maternal body, the mother's uncanny knowledge of care giving of which others seem ignorant. But male dominance in Harlem imposes its own harsh interdictions on black women, and Lorde picks up these messages, too, from her mother. Self-representation thus entails an uneasy appropriation and renegotiation of the boundaries between self and other:

> When the strongest words for what I have to offer come out of me sounding like words I remember from my mother's mouth, then I either have to reassess the meaning of everything I have to say or re-examine the worth of her old words. (p. 13)

The renegotiation of these boundaries toward a more fluid integration of voices requires renaming the ethic of care and connection and freeing it from repressive connotations. The intermediate terrain in which this recognition takes place is the body, source, and metaphor of a desire that begins and ends in relation to another woman. In the stifling Harlem summer, the mother's special attentiveness to her daughter's needs opens her up to the possibility of self-nurture through a storehouse of sensuous memories of the Grenadian homeland.

> Once home was a far way off, a place I had never been to but know well out of my mother's mouth. She breathed exuded hummed the fruit smell of Noel Hill morning fresh and noon hot, and I spun visions of spadilla and mango as a net over my Harlem tenement cot in the snoring darkness rank with nightmare sweat. Made bearable because it was not all. (p. 13)

Inhabiting her mother's words, however, is a conflicting desire, a conflicting narrative intention. In her cautionary tales about sexuality and in veiled and derogatory allusion to the "lower parts" of the body, the mother inculcates the norms of traditional femininity, the experience of bodily shame. As a child of her mother, Lorde acknowledges the problem of separate knowing in the guilt and estrangement she feels about her own awakening sexuality and the trepidation attached to giving a voice to her body.

Lorde eventually achieves her own education in constructed knowledge beyond the oppositions of gender and race learned through family and community. She regains access to the powerful storehouse of her mother's past by writing another story, a transgressive narrative of menstruation that challenges patriarchal interdictions. Pleasure and self-nurturance are metaphorically conjoined when, on the day of her first period, she takes her mother's wooden mortar bowl from the shelf and blends the spices into a mixture of her own making. Mortar and pestle, mother and child, past and present, masculine and feminine — these become a savory blend of differences: "It [mortar and pestle] conjured up from all the many different flavors pounded into the inside wall, visions of delicious feasts both once enjoyed and still to come" (p. 72).

CONCLUSION

I like to think Lorde's image of a blend of differences is also a potent metaphor for a feminist pedagogy grounded in two pivotal ideas: multiplicity and connection. Historically, feminism has continued to spawn many feminisms, and such diversity may be taken as a healthy sign. At the same time, women's studies in the academy faces unprecedented conditions of increasing formalization as a discipline and ideological struggle among competing standpoints. Collective thought and action require the continued critique of the exclusive reliance on separate knowing that has presented epistemic barriers to women and, ongoingly, active reimagining, renaming, reintegrating our voices. To this end, women's traditional valuing of a relational sense of self and connected knowing offers some distinctive strengths. Where narrative's power of specifying combines with theory's power of generalizing, ever more inclusive and multiplistic standpoints for knowing become possible. The risks of *not* mixing the languages of our inquiry are clear. Theoretical discourse has typically been language held by those in power, and it has often structured our reality by pointing to fixed and impartial frames of reference — hallmarks of the exclusive reliance on separate knowing. Once such references become part of a cultural code, they operate unconsciously to constrain rather than to liberate the construction of alternative standpoints (Eagleton, 1983). I cannot conceive of a world organized around the violent contradictions of women's lives transformed unviolently overnight. What I can imagine, however, are the expanding horizons of classrooms in which the activity of theorizing and the power of imagining are seen as complementary facets of women's education. To mix languages, to blend differences, is thus to struggle to produce change from within *and* outside procedures that constrain us.

I also take Lorde's image of the savory blend as a figure for the salutary reading-effects of the kind of autobiographical storytelling I have been describing. Lorde's text pursues oppressive cycles of representation toward a heightened sense of responsibility toward self and others. In the stirring of the political imagination, the moral sense, too, is reawakened. The bond that is forged between the writer and the reader through metaphor is also an extended boundary, acknowledging and celebrating our common dependence on conditions necessary for maintaining life — Lorde's "feasts once enjoyed and still to come." The freedom of constructed knowing is thus captured here in one of its paradoxical moments: my feminist reading of this passage, the position I construct, extends and reclaims a traditional feminine context. First, we have the seasoning and preparation of food; now, from a different perspective, I understand this gesture as a way of making greater sense of my life. Renaming in this sense does not spring from an autonomous notion of power and control but from a dialogue across generations and differences, inviting reading from several directions at once. In teaching, I have suggested, such interpretive acts are not the equivalent of hermeneutic closure, or of a theory that makes itself imposing by excluding or suppressing other standpoints. Rather, narrative procedures include the reading subject as well as intersubjective, connected ways of knowing. In feminist studies, where disciplines converge and comingle, there are abundant opportunities to draw upon such alternative languages and procedures, often from the margins, to illustrative that women have not been simply victims but, collectively, agents and forces in the active shaping of relational paradigms. In an era of unprecedented challenge for feminism, such stories keep history moving, even as it moves in and through us.

REFERENCES

Belenky, Mary; Clinchy, Blythe; Goldberger, Nancy; Tarule, Jill. (1986). *Women's ways of knowing*. New York: Basic Books.

Brodzki, Bella, & Schenck, Celeste. (Eds.). (1988). *Life/lines: Theorizing women's autobiography*. Ithaca, NY: Cornell University Press.

Bunch, C. (1983). Not by degrees: Feminist theory and education. In C. Bunch & S. Pollack (Eds.), *Learning our way: Essays in feminist education* (pp. 248–260). Trumansburg, NY: Crossing Press.

Cixous, Helene. (1986). *The newly-born.* (Catherine Clement, Trans.). Minneapolis: University of Minnesota Press.

Cocks, Joan. (1985). Suspicious pleasures: On teaching feminist theory. In M. Culley & C. Portuges (Eds.), *Gendered subjects: The dynamics of feminist teaching* (pp. 171–182). Boston: Routledge and Kegan Paul.

Culler, Jonathan. (1982). *On deconstruction: Theory and criticism after structuralism.* Ithaca, NY: Cornell University Press.

Davis, Barbara Hillyer. (1985). Teaching the feminist minority. In M. Culley & C. Portuges (Eds.), *Gendered subjects: The dynamics of feminist teaching* (pp. 245–252). Boston: Routledge and Kegan Paul.

Derrida, Jacque. (1978). *Writing and difference* (Alan Bass, Trans.). Chicago: University of Chicago Press.

DuPlessis, Rachel Blau. (1985). *Writing beyond the ending: Narrative strategies on twentieth century women writers.* Bloomington: Indiana University Press.

Eagleton, Terry. (1983). *Literary theory: An introduction.* Minneapolis: University of Minnesota Press.

Felman, Shoshana. (1982). Psychoanalysis and education: Teaching terminable and interminable. *Yale French Studies, 63,* 21–44.

Field, Joanna. (1981). *A life of one's own.* Los Angeles: J. P. Tarcher.

Flynn, E., & Schweickart, P. (1986). *Gender and reading: Essays on readers, texts and contexts.* Baltimore: Johns Hopkins University Press.

Freire, Paulo. (1970). *Pedagogy of the oppressed.* New York: Herder & Herder.

Foucault, Michel. (1972). *The archeology of knowledge.* New York: Harper & Row.

Gilbert, Sandra, & Gubar, Susan. (1979). *The madwoman in the attic: The woman writer and the nineteenth century literary imagination.* New Haven, CT: Yale University Press.

Gilligan, Carol. (1982). *In a different voice: Psychological theory and women's development.* Cambridge, MA: Harvard University Press.

Harding, Sandra. (1986). *The science question in feminism.* Ithaca, NY: Cornell University Press.

Hare-Mustin, Rachel T., & Marecek, Jeanne. (1988). The meaning of difference. *American Psychologist, 43,* 455–464.

Hartsock, Nancy. (1981). Fundamental feminism: Process and perspective. In *Quest* Staff (Eds.), *Building feminist theory: Essays from Quest.* New York: Longman.

Heath, Stephen. (1982). *The sexual fix.* New York: Schocken Books.

Hooks, Bell. (1984). *Feminist theory: From margin to center.* Boston: South End Press.

Jaggar, Alison M. (1983). *Feminist politics and human nature.* Totowa, NJ: Rowman and Allanheld.

Jelinek, Estelle. (1986). *The tradition of women's autobiography: From antiquity to the present.* Boston: Twayne.

Keller, Evelyn Fox. (1985). *Reflections on gender and science.* New Haven and London: Yale University Press.

Koller, Alice. (1983). *An unknown woman.* New York: Bantam.

Lorde, Audre. (1982). *Zami: A new spelling of my name.* Trumansburg, NY: Crossing Press.

MacKinnon, Catharine. (1982). Feminism, Marxism, method, and the state: An agenda for theory. In N. Keohane, M. Rosaldo & B. Gelpi (Eds.), *Feminist theory: A critique of ideology* (pp. 1–30). Chicago: University of Chicago Press.

Martin, Wallace. (1986). *Theories of narrative.* Ithaca, NY: Cornell University Press.

Noddings, Nel. (1984). *Caring: A feminine approach to ethics and moral education.* Berkeley: University of California Press.

Offen, Karen. (1988). Defining feminism: A comparative historical approach. *Signs, 14,* 119–157.

Rich, Adrienne. (1979). *On lies, secrets and silence: Selected prose 1966–1978.* New York: W. W. Norton.

Ricoeur, Paul. (1981). Narrative time. *Critical Inquiry, 7,* 165–186.

Rose, Hilary. (1982). Hand, brain, and heart: A feminist epistemology for the natural sciences. *Signs, 9,* 73–90.

Stein, Gertrude. (1933). *The autobiography of Alice B. Toklas.* New York: Harcourt, Brace.

Smith, Sidonie. (1987). *A poetics of women's autobiography: Marginality and the fictions of self-representation.* Bloomington: Indiana University Press.

4

The Politics of Personal Knowledge

MADELEINE R. GRUMET

Madeleine R. Grumet is currently dean of the School of Education at Brooklyn College. Formerly a professor of education at Hobart and William Smith Colleges, she is an active scholar in the area of feminist theory and education. Dr. Grumet serves as editor of the SUNY Press series on this topic and is the author of Bitter Milk: Women and Teaching, *an exploration of the contradictions that women teachers confront as they seek to bridge the private and public domains of their lives.*

It is a great relief to meet with colleagues who, like myself, have been working to devise forms for research in education that honor the spontaneity, complexity, and ambiguity of human experience. When I first started working with narrative in the early 1970s, I was busy justifying it to the psychometricians (Pinar and Grumet, 1976). That defense mounted, I turned to answer the Marxists who identified autobiography with bourgeois individualism, a retreat to interiority by those unwilling to don their leather jackets and storm the barricades, or at least picket General Dynamics (Grumet, 1981). But finally the querulous visitors have left, and at last we are alone. And so in the safety and security of your company I want to take this opportunity to raise the questions about this work that its defense has forced me to postpone.

Now before I began to think of narratives as forms for educational research and criticism, I thought of them as literature. I didn't necessarily expect my own journal scribblings as memoirs to be read along with Mon-

This chapter was originally presented at the Symposium on Classroom Studies of Teachers' Personal Knowledge, Ontario Institute for Studies in Education, Toronto, on December 10, 1985. It was subsequently published as "The Politics of Personal Knowledge," by Madeleine R. Grumet, *Curriculum Inquiry*, Vol. 17 (1987), pp. 319–329. Copyright © 1987 by the Ontario Institute for Studies in Education. Reprinted by permission of John Wiley & Sons, Inc.

taigne, Henry James, or Virginia Woolf. But I did see their writings and mine as part of the tradition of the aesthetic form, a resymbolization of experience distinguished from other markings, account books, shopping lists, even letters, by its freedom from instrumentalism. Finding form for knowledge about feeling, as Langer (1953) says, will and must suffice.

A Marxist perspective invites us to see this tradition of art split off from the business and events of everyday life as the separation of feeling from action, a process of alienation that divides what was hitherto integrated in the experience of the citizen and of the community. Why not tell a dream to decide whether it is safe to go fishing, paint your memory of spring on the school bus, and then park it and dance all the way there? Pastoral fantasies arrive as soon as aesthetics and community meet in my imagination. I collapse into another time that neither I nor anyone else has ever lived, and if I continued this indulgence, there would probably be shepherds with straw hats and flutes stumbling through these pages.

Somewhat less romantic, but still inclined to be sentimental, is the ethnographic perspective, which sees the narrative as a cultural symbolization that contributes to the continuity and shaping of the life of a community. Although the ethnographer, unlike the aesthete, celebrates the story's function, he joins his literary colleague in respecting the form of the telling as being bonded to its meaning. More possessive than the writer who relinquishes his text to an anonymous reader to make of it what she will, the anthropologist requires that those who participate in the process of interpretation share a history of community membership and experience with the narrator.

Each of these discourse traditions, aesthetics and anthropology, understands storytelling as a negotiation of power. The aesthetic remove is designed to protect story from having to accommodate to the forms and expectations of the ideological present that it addresses; the anthropological stipulations on interpretation acknowledge the power of the act that designates meaning.

So where does that leave us, we who read other people's stories in order to improve communities we do not really share with them? Probably only a little less alienated than the storyteller herself. Viewed against the background of bureaucratic, depersonalized institutions, storytelling seems pretty authentic, or at least expressive. It seems natural to assume that the first person is closer to us than the third, an intimacy that Sartre repudiates emphatically in *The Transcendence of the Ego* (1972), arguing that we do not know ourselves any better than we know others, and reminding us not to confuse familiarity with knowledge. As the counterculture moved our consciousness counterclockwise, we turned from the written to the oral tradition, imagining the story told and held, if preserved at all, in the memories of kith and kin to be the real thing.

And yet, even telling a story to a friend is a risky business; the better the friend, the riskier the business. How many of you would like to get your own story back from a certain person? Do you remember how her eyes were glazed, how she didn't really listen, only waited for you to finish so her own turn to tell would come? Do you remember how she asked the wrong questions, appropriating only those parts of the story that she could use, ignoring the part that really mattered to you? Do you remember how she finished that story when you tried to tell it again, forgetting whose it was in the first place, or the time she collapsed your story of the hurricane into her sister's account of being snowed in at O'Hare, revealing the disaster file that conflated both accounts and printed out only generic, if hyperbolic, distress?

And those are our good friends, our confidantes.

Please don't take my use of the female pronoun to suggest that women are less trustworthy receivers of tales than men. Just the opposite, my friends: It is because women can still imagine, if not remember, fidelity, that we continue to take the risks that our brothers, isolated and defended, rarely take.

Every telling is a partial prevarication, for, as Earle (1972) argues, autobiographical consciousness and autobiography never coincide. That voice inside our heads has no gray hair, no social security number, no dependents. We borrow it to answer the telephone, write a paper, respond when the kids call. It is that part of subjectivity that is never encapsulated in any act of consciousness but always escapes to come and see and speak again: what Sartre calls the "for-itself" (1966); Husserl, the transcendental ego (1960); Schafer, self-as-agent (1976). We must come to form in order to be in touch and so we speak. Our stories are the masks through which we can be seen, and with every telling we stop the flood and swirl of thought so someone can get a glimpse of us, and maybe catch us if they can.

Crafty tellers try to avoid getting caught. They wriggle out of their stories like a snake shedding old skins, Sartre says, celebrating negation as the foundation of human consciousness (1966). Settling into our stories is bad faith, he warns us; it is capitulating, forgetting that there is always a face beneath the mask. The politics of narrative is not, then, merely a social struggle but an ontological one as well. We are, at least partially, constituted by the stories we tell to others and to ourselves about experience. As Schutz tells us,

> Meaning does not lie *in* experience. Rather, those experiences are meaningful which are grasped reflectively. The meaning is the way in which the Ego

regards its experience. The meaning lies in the attitude of the Ego toward that
part of its stream of consciousness which has already flowed by. (cited in
Chamberlin, 1974, p. 131)

The stories we tell to others may be finally less dangerous than the ones
that we tell to ourselves.

Story, then, is the form many of us have chosen for our work. Maybe
there's still time to go back to statistics. After all, I preferred the report
card that said that my kid was getting an 83 in geometry to the one that
said he was working up to his ability, had some difficulty with abstract
concepts, but was an independent thinker and a good citizen. I suspect
that the difference between personal and impersonal knowledge, or practical and impractical knowledge, is not a difference in what it is we know
but in how we tell it and whom we tell it to. Personal knowledge in this
scheme is constituted by the stories about experience we usually keep to
ourselves, and practical knowledge by the stories that are never, or rarely,
related, but provide, nevertheless, the structure for the improvisations that
we call coping, problem solving, action. The politics of personal knowledge demand that we acknowledge that telling is an alienation, that telling
diminishes the teller, and that we who invite teachers to tell us their stories
develop an ethic for that work.

I usually don't like the word *ethic*. It always suggests rules for conduct, a way of behaving that has been displaced from the intimate relations where it belongs to a commodified exchange. The so-called professionals who need one are, indeed, impostors, and so we do need an ethic.
For we are not the imagined and anonymous reader of the writer's tales.
The aesthetic reference of a text that does not point specifically to the
author's or the reader's world but to an imagined place that gathers up yet
surpasses both places (Ricoeur, 1976) is not the space where curriculum
happens. The ethnographic eavesdropping that disclaims its own intervention as well as the legitimacy of the observer's interpretation does not suit
us who watch and listen and advise. And we are not protected by the
expectation of reciprocity that good friends share over time as they can
with good reason expect to misunderstand, misrepresent, and violate each
other's confidence as they themselves have been misunderstood, misrepresented, and violated.

Mary O'Brien reminds me that Hegel understood alienation to be the
moment that initiates a process of mediation rather than an end in itself.[1]
So if telling a story requires giving oneself away, then we are obligated to
devise a method of receiving stories that mediates the space between the
self that tells, the self that told, and the self that listens: a method that
returns a story to the teller that is both hers and not hers, that contains her
self in good company.

Let me describe my use of narrative as I work with teachers. I will not say that these methods of telling, listening, responding, all assuage the anxieties that I have been confessing. The only claim that I will make for them is that they inform abstention as well as action, and I hope that they provide some assurance that the teachers who work with me will not go away grimly humming, "Look what they've done to my song, Mom."

I am not sure that I want to call what I do research. The *Oxford English Dictionary* (1971) provides a disquieting history for the word *search*. I am comfortable with the circularity of it, for it is derived from the Old French *cherchier*, which in turn is related to *circus*, circle in Latin, and *circare*, to go round. Add the *re* and we have the temporal dialectic of intentionality and reflexivity, a hermeneutic circle of the soul, ever enlarging its self-story. Nevertheless, from the 1400s on, *search* takes on a public, intrusive, and corrective function. Searchers are described as examiners responsible for ascertaining contraband at customs, blasphemy in convents, and the cause of death in corpses. Our current reliance on the term as a knowledge-producing process is undermined with this history of public scrutiny. It reinforces Foucault's (1979) argument that in the history of the modern state the disciplines of knowledge evolved along with the disciplines of militarism, medicine, and punishment as the look replaced the blow and examination provided the rule, the order, and the subordination that had previously been accomplished by the display of force.

If my work permits the teachers I work with to examine their own work with a seeing that is more inclusive, that surveys an ever widening surround, that is a search I would gladly join. But if my work certifies me as an agent of the state to peer into what is hidden from public view, if it is my look that discovers and appraises, then I might as well approach the classroom with bloodhound as well as briefcase, and they ought to demand to see my warrant before they let me in.

An interrogation tactic of the police state is the refusal to tell the one who is questioned what the questioner is looking for. Kafka aside, even the criminal is entitled to know what she is being charged with doing. In a research paradigm that denies the agency of the subject, researchers are often afraid to announce what they are looking for because they are afraid of prejudicing the subject's responses. In this case, the question and ultimately the answer both belong to the researcher, and the subject of the research is merely the medium through which the question finds the answer. The process through which I induce you to feel or act out my own disclaimed intentions or impulses we call sadism, and even though some have named that process pedagogy, I prefer teaching, where the sadism is up front, to research where it is equally present but disclaimed.[2]

During a recent summer I worked with teachers in a course at the University of Rochester, Theatre in the Classroom. We worked with theatre in ways that were foreign to most school settings; we explored theatre as a way of knowing, a way of investigating and performing our understanding of texts. If I had asked these people to write about theatre at the outset of the course, they would have protested that they knew little about it, disclaiming their experience for someone else's world, their language for someone else's words. From the more philosophically focused inquiry into teachers' accounts of educational experience that I have been pursuing for the last decade, I have learned to ask for three separate narratives rather than a longer, continuous account. In William Pinar's (1976) approach to educational autobiography, *currere* entailed a triple telling as reflection was sorted into past experience, present situation, and future images. Multiple accounts splinter the dogmatism of a single tale. If they undermine the authority of the teller, they also free her from being captured by the reflection provided in a single narrative.

So I asked the teachers to write three accounts of moments in their lives that they considered "theatrical." I asked them to abstain from categorical impulses, to let the general definitions trail after the anecdotes, if they had to appear at all. This invitation to bracket restrictive assumptions is usually accepted eagerly, and just as accounts of educational experience are rarely situated in schools, accounts of theatrical experience hardly ever make it to the stage.

Most important, however, is the relation of multiplicity to interpretations. When there is one story, it becomes *the* story, *my* story, and when it is delivered to another, it arrives gift wrapped in transference. After all, teachers are supposed to be interested in other people's ideas and other people's children and only the very old and the very young, Didion tells us (1961), are allowed to recount their dreams at breakfast. If they are not very old, teachers who are asked for their story may feel very young, for that may have been the last time anyone asked them to tell it. If sentimentality and infantilization accompany the single narrative, so does eros. If work is the place where the self disappears, the increasing privatization of feeling and expression relegates the communication of experience to intimate relationships. "What does this mean to you?" becomes a very seductive question, and transference is reinforced when an interpretation is received as telling more about the narrative than its narrator knew.

Multiplicity is a wedge against what Janet Gunn (1982) calls the "success" of autobiography:

> It is the success of autobiography, not its failure, that becomes the problem — one of over-orientation rather than alienation, of completing not losing the self, or regressing to what Frank Kermode has called "paradigmatic rigidity."
>
> In other words, the problem of autobiography lies in the threat of ideology which dogs all narrative in its compulsion toward wholes. The pull toward

ideology is all the more difficult for autobiography to resist because the ideological impulse has so much in common with the autobiographical impulse.
Both arise from a simultaneous groundedness and a need for acknowledging a
meaningful orientation in a world; both are responses to the finitude and
vulnerability that characterize the human condition; and both represent an
effort to take hold of something in the process of vanishing or disintegrating.
Moreover, both impulses function toward the end that Clifford Geertz as-
cribes to ideology: "to render otherwise incomprehensive . . . situations
meaningful, to so construe them as to make it possible to act purposefully
within them." (p. 119)

When we work with life history, the autobiographical act is not complete until the writer of the story becomes its reader and the temporal
fissure that has opened between the writing and the reading invites negation as well as affirmation. But in this case I am trying to elicit, not
accounts that will reveal the psycho-logic of the self, but narratives that
will display what Freire calls the object to be known in the profiles it
assumes in the writer's consciousness.

Tom writes three stories of theatrical experience (T. Beeson, unpublished manuscript, July 1985). In the first he is a witness. From the passenger seat in a car he observes a street scene. There has been a fight. Kids are
huddled around

> a small skinny boy with red cheeks and teary eyes, lying on the side-
> walk. His boney right arm held his shoulders off the ground while his
> left hand held the side of his face, gently covering the injured area.
> . . . The most notable thing I remember of this boy was the way his
> lips were pushed together so firmly that you could see slightly the
> tensed muscles around it.

Walking away from the scene is the conqueror:

> Her head turned around hesitantly to look at the boy who was start-
> ing feebly to stand up. Her head turned back to her hands while her
> swagger resumed, this time more steady. Her right hand was now
> wrapping each finger of her left hand into a tight fist.

If this were the only scene it would be truly obscene, pointing away
from itself to something beyond it, hidden and unspeakable.[3] The politics
of its interpretation would require going behind the scene. If I participate
in the interpretation of this single story, I participate in what Freud called
the linguistic approach. Davis explains: "This kind of interpretation, in

other words, takes place through the substitution of one element for another according to certain narrative codes" (1976, p. 85). The politics of this hermeneutic invest me, the theorist whose cranium is lined with codes, with the vision to interpret what is displayed by substituting its elements with others from my collection. Metonymy becomes the trope, and in the process, Tom, the speaking subject, evaporates.

Fortunately, there are other tales to tell, and it is in the spaces between them, the interstitial residence of metaphor, that Tom survives. His second narrative is a scene from a movie he saw when he was 7. It is a horrific image of a vendor:

> A high-pitched, sing-song voice came from his sharp cornered mouth, offering his delights, "Children, I've got lollipops, bon-bons, licorice, peppermint sticks, chocolate, fudge and ice cream. All for free." . . .
> As he spoke his list, his black eyes darted from side to side. He hopped swiftly around the perimeter of the square, hunching low as his nose kept pointing to a new direction. His nose stopped at a basement window just above the cobblestones of the square. The right corner of his mouth pulled straight upward as if trying to reach the sharp corner of his right eye. Peering into the dirty, grimy window, he spoke his list again, his long tongue slowly pushing out each syllable.

If gesture was the only source of information in the first narrative, here it remains the prevailing semiotic, making the words that accompany it false.

In Tom's last narrative, he is more active, visiting his grandfather who is recovering from a stroke in a nursing home in England. Gesture decomposes in this place:

> In some of the beds were some old men. One demanded to know who we were here to see. Another kept wiping his left eyebrow with his thumb as if a robot in an unending program. But these ones who were in bed all had eyes that stiffly gazed forward, they said things but only the mouth would move.

Tom's grandfather squeezes his fingers when they meet.

> His body was like his hand in what it lacked and how the skin was loosely draped upon the bones. His face had one side where the skin just drooped as if tugged too hard once too often. But the left side of this face had an eye and a corner of the mouth darting around to give expression. Both turned downward as the nurse rhetorically asked, "Isn't it nice to see your grandson?" But corners of both eye and

mouth moved upward as I replied, "I'm hoping you'll say yes." At that moment, a familiar trace of Grandad had appeared, with his smile, even though really half of it; I knew he was deep within his own body struggling to control an uncooperative shell.

During the movement from the first narrative to the last, the authority of gesture becomes undermined. In the first story, the way things look is the way they are. Appearance will suffice. In the second, appearance is still compelling but contested by language. In the third, gesture and appearance are both truth and lie, and Tom must act in order to find his grandfather; observation will not suffice.

This hermeneutic, composed from the juxtaposition of disparate elements, is what Freud called pictographic, emphasizing what Davis (1976) calls combinatory possibilities:

> While in Freud's pictographic approach particular dream elements are meaningful (or lacking in meaning) as they are locked in a particular pattern, in the linguistic approach dream elements lack inherent meaning but can stand in for (be replaced by) other elements within a certain structure or set of possibilities. . . . Lacan chooses to go the second way of interpretation, that of language and linguistics — of, as Lacan says, "writing rather than of mime." (p. 85)

Although Davis goes on to challenge the absolute distinctions between these methods, his discussion reinforces the contribution made by multiplicity to the subject's participation in the hermeneutic process.

The questions that we draw from these texts may be clothed in those codes that I draw from the closet in my head, but their sources are inscribed in Tom's text and even if their inclusion is a preconscious rather than a deliberated act, it is his act to claim or disclaim as he chooses. Multiple narratives make it possible for us to go beyond and around the text, to research it without accusing it of false consciousness, on one hand, or succumbing to its rationale, on the other. It permits Tom and me to construct a question about the theatre work that we will do together. We will work with a method I call scoring — a process of designing improvisations that re-present interesting issues in the text in movement and performance situations that require participants to both explore situations and make choices within them (Grumet, 1978). The process relies on the knowledge of the body-subject, what Merleau-Ponty (1962) called knowledge in the hands and knowledge in the feet, but it also invites reflection and choice.

Tom's stories locate human freedom at the center of expression even as they celebrate gesture and bring the body to its proper place in drama. That is not the only issue about this work that these narratives reveal. Others in the seminar will read his texts differently, and with them he will develop different questions that he will bring to this work. Multiple texts and multiple interpreters bring the presentation of personal knowledge out of the whispered confidences of the analytic dyad, complicit couple, sado-masochistic duo, and into a community of people who share a world.

NOTES

1. I am grateful to Professor O'Brien for this point for it is essential to the process of response to autobiographical writing. Personal communication following the presentation of this paper, December 10, 1985.

2. The politics of desire are acknowledged in the study of teaching as revealed in texts by contributors to *The Pedagogical Imperative: Teaching as Literary Genre* (Johnson, 1982). See especially the section, "What Does a Teacher Want?"

3. The relation of the scene and the *obscene* is explored by Blau (1977).

REFERENCES

Blau, Herbert. (1977). Letting be be finale of seem. In Michel Benamou and Charles Caramello (Eds.), *Performance in post-modern culture*. Madison, WI: Coda Press.

Chamberlin, J. Gordon. (1974). Phenomenological methodology and understanding education. In David Denton (Ed.), *Existentialism and phenomenology in education: Collected essays* (pp. 119–138). New York: Teachers College Press.

Davis, Robert Con. (1976). Introduction: Lacan and narration. In Robert Con Davis (Ed.), *Lacan and narration: The psychoanalytic difference in narrative theory*. Baltimore: Johns Hopkins University Press.

Didion, Joan. (1961). On keeping a notebook. In *Slouching towards Bethlehem*. New York: Dell.

Earle, William. (1972). *Autobiographical consciousness*. Chicago: Quadrangle Books.

Foucault, Michel. (1979). *Discipline and punish* (Alan Sheriden, Trans.). New York: Vintage Books.

Freire, Paulo. (1970). *Pedagogy of the oppressed* (Myra Bergman Ramos, Trans.). New York: Herder & Herder.

Grumet, Madeleine R. (1978). Curriculum as theater: Merely players. *Curriculum Inquiry*, 8(1), 37–68.

Grumet, Madeleine R. (1981). Restitution and reconstruction of educational experience: An autobiographical method for curriculum theory. In Martin Lawn & Len Barton (Eds.), *Rethinking curriculum studies*. New York: John Wiley.

Gunn, Janet. (1982). *Autobiography: Toward a poetics of experience.* Philadelphia: University of Pennsylvania Press.

Husserl, Edmund. (1960). *Cartesian meditations* (Dorian Cairns, Trans.). The Hague: Martinus Nijhoff.

Johnson, Barbara. (Ed.). (1982). The pedagogical imperative: Teaching as a literary genre [Special issue]. *Yale French Studies, 63.*

Langer, Suzanne. (1953). *Feeling and form.* New York: Charles Scribner's Sons.

Merleau-Ponty, Maurice. (1962). *The phenomenology of perception* (Colin Wilson, Trans.). New York: Humanities Press.

Oxford English Dictionary, compact edition. (1971). Oxford: Oxford University Press.

Pinar, William. (1976). The method. In William Pinar & Madeleine Grumet (Eds.), *Toward a poor curriculum* (pp. 51–65). Dubuque, IA: Kendall/Hunt.

Pinar, William, & Grumet, Madeleine. (1976). *Toward a poor curriculum.* Dubuque, IA: Kendall/Hunt.

Ricoeur, Paul. (1976). *Interpretation theory.* Fort Worth, TX: Texas Christian University.

Sartre, Jean Paul. (1966). *Being and nothingness* (Hazel Barnes, Trans.). New York: Washington Square Press.

Sartre, Jean Paul. (1972). *The transcendence of the ego* (Forrest Williams & Robert Kirkpatrick, Trans.). New York: Octagon Books.

Schafer, Roy. (1976). *A new language for psychoanalysis.* New Haven, CT: Yale University Press.

PART II

Narrative and Notions of the Self and the Other

If the notion of the self can only be grasped within a relational context, the narratives of diverse cultures and biographies can contribute in poignant ways to our understanding of the self in relation to the other. We consider such understanding to be at the heart of education, healing, and social change. Buber's themes of dialogue and inclusion provide a conceptual landscape for the authors of these chapters as they explore the nature of the self-in-relation, revealed in cultural and personal narratives.

In Chapter 5, "The Self in Narrative: A Journey into Paradox," Carol Witherell explores conceptions of the self from psychological and philosophical perspectives, illuminating some of the paradoxes we confront in considering the self in relation to the other. The power of narrative as a means to understand this relation and to uncover possibilities for ethical action is discussed in the context of teaching approaches that make use of personal narratives.

> The creative use of story and dialogue lends power to educational and therapeutic experiences because of their capacity to expand our horizons of understanding and provide rich contextual information about human actors, intentions, and experiences. . . . The individual achieves personhood through caring relation with the other, yet the story of a life is always, in every moment, distinctive from the stories of other lives.

In Chapter 6, "Telling Our Own Stories: The Reading and Writing of Journals or Diaries," Joanne Cooper describes with vivid examples from her students' writings her use of journals and diaries in teaching college students. She suggests that telling stories and hearing others' stories is a way to nourish and sustain ourselves, individually and collectively, as we incorporate our own future and reconstruct our past.

As chroniclers of our own stories, we write to create ourselves, to give voice to our experiences, to learn who we are and who we have been. Our diaries become the stories of our journeys through life, stories that are both instructive and transforming in the telling and the listening. These stories, these myriad voices, then serve to instruct and transform society, to add to the collective voice we call culture. Diarists, then, both as researchers and research subjects, begin to heal themselves and the split society has created between subject and object. Thus diaries, these small, insignificant objects filled with the simple words of our lives, can serve to make us whole.

Kirin Narayan, in Chapter 7, "'According to Their Feelings': Teaching and Healing with Stories," describes how narrative assists in the formation of a coherent self out of "the flux and welter of experience." This self may be a personal self or a collective self, and these are given different weighting in different cultural contexts. Through her depiction of one storytelling event recorded in India, the country of her birth, she reveals the possibility for dialogue and mutual engagement between teller and listener. Although many have written on the power of symbolic analogies that narrative provides, Narayan suggests that a further power of folk narrative lies within its interactive, imaginative, emotional, and religious contexts. Whether the teller is an old holy man (*sādhu*), a patient in psychoanalysis, or a teacher in a classroom, the construction and telling of a story is an experience grounded in interpretive communities, both actual and potential.

We shape the stories we tell and hear according to our feelings, constructing possible futures and even possible selves. The storyteller Narayan describes most intimately, Swamiji, is a Guru, an indigenous teacher. From the author's recounting of Swamiji's stories, one can appreciate that storytelling in the Hindu tradition has ancient roots as a form of instruction and even as "a conduit for divine grace."

In the last chapter of this part, "The Stranger's Story: Who Calls and Who Answers?" Virginia Shabatay asks us to consider that the experience of being a stranger must be a primary concern for educators, writers, and social scientists. The stranger asks of us respect for her heritage or condition. This requires that those who encounter her enter into a dialogical relationship with her, where the uniqueness of the other can be brought forth. Such openness to difference characterizes the caring relation in the activity of teaching or counseling. Among the poignant questions we are asked to confront are, "What makes strangers and how do we treat strangers? . . . What problems are exposed by the stranger? Why are strangers a problem for our world?"

The community that allows for diversity is, as we have seen, a strong vital organization. Perhaps it is the stranger who teaches us how to treat strangers. The ability to appreciate otherness in individuals and communities is a way of redeeming the stranger and of redeeming the world. It is not up to human-kind alone to bring redemption, but redemption will not come until we make way for it through doing our share in perfecting the world. Is it not perhaps the stranger who calls us to account and who shows us the way?

5

The Self in Narrative
A Journey into Paradox

CAROL WITHERELL

*Carol Witherell is associate professor of education and director of teacher educa-
tion at Lewis & Clark College in Portland, Oregon. A former teacher of primary
grades, she received her Ph.D. degree in educational psychology from the University of Minnesota. Dr. Witherell has served on the faculties of Santa Clara University, Colgate University, the College of William and Mary, and Wesleyan University, teaching in the areas of moral development, life-span development, and
educational psychology. She recently delivered the final lecture in the GTE Foundation Public Lecture Series on "The Story of the Moral: Narrative, Ethics, and
Education" at Saint Benedict College in St. Joseph, Minnesota. Dr. Witherell
serves on the editorial board and as the North American book review editor for
the* Journal of Moral Education.

I have a vision of the Songlines stretching across the continents and
ages; that wherever men have trodden they have left a trail of song (of
which we may, now and then, catch an echo); and that these trails
must reach back, in time and space, to an isolated pocket in the
African savannah, where the First Man opening his mouth in defi-
ance of the terrors that surrounded him, shouted the opening stanza
of the World Song, "I AM!" (Bruce Chatwin, *The Songlines*, p. 282)

It is our inward journey that leads us through time—forward or back,
seldom in a straight line, most often spiraling. Each of us is moving,
changing, with respect to others. As we discover, we remember, remembering, we discover; and most intensely do we experience this
when our separate journeys converge. Our living experience at those
meeting points is one of the charged dramatic fields of fiction.
(Eudora Welty, *One Writer's Beginnings*, p. 102)

Two perspectives on the nature and formation of the self: one from the anthropologist-novelist Bruce Chatwin's story of the Australian aboriginals' ancient "Dreaming-tracks" (1987), the other from the autobiography of one of our country's finest southern storywriters, Eudora Welty (1984). Together they capture the narrative structure of the self that is woven within an intricate tapestry. The tapestry is composed of interlocking patterns of cultural-historical, individual-biographical, and interpersonal-relational threads.

In this chapter I will explore different views of the self from several philosophical and psychological perspectives and illuminate some of the paradoxes one confronts in addressing the nature of the self and the other. I will describe uses of narrative and dialogue to understand the self in relation to the other within teaching and counseling. Finally, I will show how the creative use of story and dialogue lends power to educational and therapeutic experiences because of their capacity to expand our horizons of understanding and provide rich contextual information about human actors, intentions, and experiences.

My interest in exploring the nature of the self grew out of my conviction that neither teaching nor counseling can be considered an ethically neutral activity. Each is based on identifiable assumptions regarding the nature of the self, the relation of self to other and to culture, and conceptions of knowing, meaning, and purpose. Some of these assumptions are known to the teacher or counselor; others are not. Both teaching and counseling involve forms of self-questioning, social criticism, empathy, imagination, and ethical motivation. Each activity, ideally, furthers another's capacity to find meaning and integrity through one's "living experience at those meeting points." And, whether or not it is acknowledged by the practitioner, each is designed to change or guide human lives.

When conceptions of the person, self, and community are not continually called into question in professional practice, reified and reductionist concepts emerge as common practice, creating new forms of "common sense" within the profession. Examples of such practices include excessive reliance on normative measures of aptitude, intelligence, psychopathology, values, or developmental stages for educational or psychological assessment. Although assessment in each of these domains can be useful in making clinical and pedagogical decisions, too often diagnostic instruments take the place of the attention and dialogue that the practitioner needs in order to understand individuals in the context of their personal and cultural environments. Jerome Bruner reminds us that it is these very contexts that provide the symbolic, linguistic, and conceptual systems that we use "to carve up and interpret the world around us" (1979, p. 169).

ON THE NATURE OF THE SELF

The formation of the self involves two major processes. One process is that of social formation, or the ways we define and are defined by our social and cultural contexts. These contexts include the collective norms, mores, values, prejudices, and preconceptions that have evolved over time and are sustained with minimal consciousness on our part. The other process involves our relations with other persons — our sense of self in connection with other selves and the meaning systems that evolve from our mutual predicaments and possibilities. Together these processes give structure to our daily lives in the ways that we learn, what we perceive, what we value, and how we relate to each other. They create, to return to Eudora Welty's metaphor, the "charged dramatic fields" in which we interpret, act, and grow. René Girard has suggested that in our twentieth-century drive to demystify daily life, we create the greatest myth of all — that of our own detachment (Bruner, 1983). Within teaching, counseling, and learning activities, it is a commitment to genuine dialogue, imagination, and ethical concern that guards against our detachment.

A central concern in discussions of the nature of the self during this century has been the legacy of the mind-body dualism posed by Descartes in the seventeenth century. The notion that there are two distinct realms of reality — one of matter "out there," without consciousness or purpose; the other of mind "in here," the realm of consciousness and selfhood — has left its legacy in debates about the relationships between subject and object, self and other, knower and known, intellect and feeling, masculine and feminine, and, always, the mind-body problem. These dualisms characterize the psychological theories of Freud and most of the early psychoanalysts, and, as well, much of nineteenth- and twentieth-century philosophy. Kathleen Nott, in *Philosophy and Human Nature* (1971), illuminates the central problem in the Cartesian cleavage:

> Wishing to leave us reassured about the real existence of the world outside us and of ourselves inside that world, Descartes succeeded in cleaving them apart. Thus cleft, never the twain have been able to meet. A knower or thinker who has to assume that there is possibly nothing to know, and a world which is unknowable, since there is none to know it, are complementary absurdities. (pp. 229–230)

Nott develops a case for what she terms a "Third Force" in philosophy — a way of questioning that rejects both the atomism and the separation of the Cartesian cleavage and instead acknowledges, with the early pragmatists, that "we are beings practising certain relations and expecting certain responses from the world that we meet and that happens to us" (p. 228). This view of the world acknowledges both our continuity with our environments and our distinctness from them.

The problems we confront in describing the nature of the self are located in the apparent contradictions between subjectivity and objectivity, between self and other, between individual and culture, and between necessity and possibility. For some these remain irreconcilable contradictions; others view them as different but complementary facets of the human experience.

THE SELF IN RELATION

Although Freud and many of his followers viewed the self as a unity of instincts and psychic structures and sought to objectify knowledge of the self through the analytic method (Wright, 1982), others have broken from this tradition in significant ways. Among these individuals are psychologists such as Erik Erikson (1975), Carl Jung (1963), and Carol Gilligan (1982) and philosophers such as George Herbert Mead (1934), John Macmurray (1961), Karen Hanson (1986), and Nel Noddings (1984). These individuals have viewed the self in its subjective and relational contexts, acknowledging the interdependence of body, mind, and spirit and the connectedness of self and other. Each has sought to break through and transcend the bonds of the subject-object dichotomy.

The Jewish philosopher Martin Buber offered a means of transcending the subject-object division through his notion of the "I-thou relation" (1966), where the other can never be treated as a means only and where subject and object are joined in an irreducible mutuality of growth and meaning.

> For the inmost growth of the self is not accomplished, as people like to suppose today, in man's relation to himself, but in the relation between the one and the other, between men, that is, pre-eminently in the mutuality of the making present — in the making present of another self and in the knowledge that one is made present in his own self by the other — together with the mutuality of acceptance, of affirmation, and confirmation. (p. 71)

This bond, paradoxically, presupposes an initial distancing. Distance provides the human situation; relation provides one's becoming in that situation.

The movements of distance and relation pose tensions in the human situation. In certain instances of extreme tension, one can achieve unity through its overcoming, as in moments of deep insight and even grace. Reading these passages led me to recall such an experience of unity reported by Jacob Needleman in *The Heart of Philosophy* (1982). Needleman was listening to Elias, one of his students, describe what he had learned about the illness that had taken over his body.

> "I've been reading up on leukemia," he said. And then he proceeded to relate everything he now knew about the process of the disease. My heart contracted as I listened to him explaining, with cool precision, how production of normal red cells in the bone marrow is displaced by the production of lymphosarcoma cells. . . . As Elias went on speaking . . . I became more and more fascinated by the subject itself and was soon no longer even thinking about Elias! I was just sitting there gobbling candy and discussing the functions of the various types of blood cells.
>
> Suddenly, I saw tears coming out of Elias's eyes. He fell silent and turned his head away from me, toward the garden. I also became silent. I thought that perhaps he was in pain and I started to get up to call his mother. Squinting into the sun, I saw that his whole face seemed to have gotten bigger and looser, as though it were melting. In a startling deep voice that came from far down in his chest, he shouted, angrily, "I'll never be able to *learn* about everything!"
>
> His words, and the strangely powerful sound of his voice, went right through me. Fighting back my own tears, I heard myself saying, also in an abnormally deep voice, "I'll learn for both of us!"
>
> Elias looked at me as though I were a fool. In the same loud voice, he said, "How do you know? Maybe you'll die soon, too!"
>
> My whole body shivered. In that moment, my own death was again real for me. I no longer felt sorry for Elias. I, too, was going to die. An extraordinary vibration appeared inside me; I felt solid as a rock at the same time that the awareness of my own eventual death poured through me and terrified me. We remained looking at each other for what seemed a very long time. I did not feel higher or lower than Elias. We were equals. I broke the silence.
>
> "Even if you weren't going to die," I said, "even if you lived to be a hundred years old, do you think you would ever solve the mystery of death?"
>
> Elias turned his head toward the ceiling. Suddenly he seemed calm again. His voice became soft. "Maybe," he said. (pp. 194–195)

Erikson acknowledged the integration of subjective and objective knowledge in his notion of "disciplined subjectivity," or the analyst's attempt to relate the deeply personal and irrational aspects of the therapeutic relationship to established theory and concepts without reifying them. Through his devotion to the narrative mode, to the search for truth through impressions, observations, word sketches, and illustrations, Erik-

son joined the landscapes of action and consciousness, a synthesis that leads
to believability through effective story rather than proof through logical
analysis (cited in Wright, 1982). Erikson (1964) also noted the "Cartesian
straitjacket [of rationality] . . . we have imposed on our model of man."
The way out of the straitjacket, he felt, is to understand the relationship
between reality and actuality, where actuality is defined as "the world
verified in immediate immersion and interaction" (pp. 163–164).

THE ROLE OF IMAGINATION
IN THE FORMATION OF THE SELF

Imagination plays a central role in the formation of the self, including its
narrative structure. It is imagination that enables us to ask the "what if"
and "as if" questions that can guide our explorations of human events and
actions of the past and our sense of possibilities for the present and future.
Karen Hanson, in *The Self Imagined* (1986), develops her notion of self as
grounded in imagination and in one's interest in the past, present, and
future, including their continuities. Hanson builds on Mead's notion of the
social self as essentially reflexive, although for her it is imagination, not the
vocal gesture, that serves as the mechanism of reflection. Although Hanson
accepts Mead's (1934) assertion that our perceptions are enmeshed with
our imaginings, she discards the notion of the generalized self and its
accompanying claim that the "whole of the self must be caught in reflection" (p. 103).

> Unification of the self need not be an inevitable theoretical problem, if only
> we do not first think of the human body as a collection of parts; and if only we
> admit that we do not need a unitary object to produce a unified object, that a
> variety of forces can work toward a single shape; and if only we remember
> that habits integrate vast regions of our lives. (p. 103)

I can't help but note how similar these thoughts are to this passage from
Eudora Welty (1984):

> Writing a story or a novel is one way of discovering *sequence* in experience, of
> stumbling upon cause and effect in the happenings of a writer's own life.
> . . . Connections slowly emerge. Like distant landmarks you are approach-
> ing, cause and effect begin to align themselves, draw closer together. Experi-
> ences too indefinite of outline in themselves to be recognized for themselves
> connect and are identified as a larger shape. And suddenly a light is thrown
> back, as when your train makes a curve, showing that there has been a
> mountain of meaning rising behind you on the way you've come, is rising
> there still, proven now through retrospect. (p. 90)

These lines capture quite dramatically Hanson's idea of the self's interest in the continuities between past, present, and future. They also speak to the variety of forces that compose an individual life. Our sense of our lives is embedded in what we make and remake of what happens to us.

Hanson (1986) explores a number of problems of the self as an imagining being. She accepts Mead's contention that *self-deception* does not represent an internal discontinuity so much as it represents a breakdown in the organization of perspectives, especially between those of an individual and a community. Hence, self-deception is not located wholly, or even primarily, within the individual or between the individual and an "objective world." Self-deception, within this rubric, is not viewed as necessarily blameworthy or dysfunctional. It strikes me that certain forms and levels of self-deception may serve to fuel the creative process. (Mozart and Byron come to mind!) "The idea that the self depends on imagination grants the complexity of persons and thus both acknowledges and helps to account for the difficulty and the instability of individual and community alignment" (p. 112).

On a topic of particular interest to those of us in the teaching and helping professions, Hanson describes self-knowledge as an activity rather than an entity. The act of imagining is actually grounded in self-knowledge: "I want to suggest that the ongoing enterprise of the production of images—or pictures or interpretations—of the self is the mirror of the activity of self-knowledge" (p. 124). She goes on to suggest that having a self is "inextricably bound with knowing that self. . . . One both makes and suffers one's self-interpretations" (p. 125).

Hanson devotes the closing section of *The Self Imagined* to a discussion of self-interest and the practical problem of egocentricity. Paradoxically, to have any self-interest, Hanson argues that one must assume the viewpoint or attitude of the other, a projection that is accomplished through sympathetic imagination. It is this sympathy that constitutes the basis of one's sense of self. "Just as imagination can take us to our selves, it can carry us out of and beyond ourselves—if we are interested, if we see some object as dearer to us than ourselves" (p. 133).

The ideas that there is something in each of us that is irreducibly private—"one's own unique story," as described so vividly by Carl Jung (1963) — and that the self is relational in its construction are not incompatible notions. The individual achieves personhood through caring relation with the other, yet the story of a life is always, in every moment, distinctive from the stories of other lives. Kierkegaard understood this fundamental paradox of human existence when he suggested that it was in the experience of its deepest solitude that the choosing self reveals "both a continuity and relationship with all other beings" (Manheimer, 1977). Nel Noddings identifies this paradox when she describes the "total conveyance of self to other, a continual transformation of individual to duality to new individual to new duality" that characterizes the caring relation (1984, p. 61).

THE ETHICAL SELF AND THE CARING RELATION

In her introduction to *Caring*, Noddings describes her approach to the ethical self as "feminine in the deep classical sense — rooted in receptivity, relatedness, and responsiveness" (1984, p. 2). The foundation of ethical caring, Noddings maintains, is our memory of caring and our longing for goodness, rather than our moral reasoning capacity, which philosophers from Immanuel Kant to Lawrence Kohlberg have claimed to be the springboard for ethical action. "Taking *relation* as ontologically basic simply means that we recognize human encounter and affective response as a basic fact of human existence" (p. 4).

Noddings views the ethical self as an active relation between a person's actual self and her vision of her ideal self in the capacity of the one-caring (or carer) and the cared-for. Differing from the cognitive constructivist philosophers, Noddings discusses her notion of receptivity in the context of a teacher-student relation:

> The teacher who encourages receptivity wants the child to look, to listen, to touch, and, perhaps, to receive a vision of reality. When we speak of receiving reality, we do not deny that each human consciousness participates in the construction of reality, but we give proper emphasis to the relatedness that must be perceived and accepted before any coherent picture can be constructed. The other is received, his reality is apprehended as possibility for oneself. (p. 60)

A hundred years ago Wilhelm Dilthey (1894/1977) wrote of the importance of developing an empathic understanding of human action through examining one's actions, intentions, and history within the culture, language, and meaning systems in which one exists. Extending this tradition, many contemporary psychologists and other observers of human nature have illuminated the importance of the subjective, imaginative, and metaphorical ways of knowing. Included in this company are Paula Gunn Allen (1986); Jerome Bruner (1983, 1986); Mary Belenky, Blythe Clinchy, Nancy Goldberger, and Jill Tarule (1986); Joanna Field (1981); Carol Gilligan (1982); Lyn Lifshin (1982); Jean Mandler (1984); Daniel Stern (1985); Robert Stone (1988); and Brian Sutton-Smith (1988). The work of these individuals (and many others) suggests that the self develops and finds meaning in the context of relationship — between self and other selves, subject and object, individual and culture, and between aspects of the self, both across and within the time dimension. Further, each emphasizes the central importance of story and dialogue within the process of human development, especially as they pertain to the development of one's sense of self.

Bruner claims in *Actual Minds, Possible Worlds* (1986) that the notions of sympathy, empathy, and phenomenology are all insufficient to explain "the easy access we have into each other's minds" (p. 57). He chides mainstream developmental psychology for its allegiance to essentially nontransactional theories of the self. Such theories may be characterized by four assumptions: that each stage of development has its unique egocentric perspective that sets the individual self apart from other selves; that the individual self is essentially a private self that achieves its definition with minimum cultural or public influence; that conceptual development is an activity of the individual, essentially unmediated by the other and by culture; and that cognition, affect, and action are viewed as separate systems in the developing self. The difficulty with these assumptions, Bruner claims, is that they are true under some circumstances and in some cultures, and clearly not true under others.

> One could argue against the tenet of privacy, for example (inspired by anthropologists), that the distinction between "private self" and "public self" is a function of the culture's conventions about when one talks and negotiates the meanings of events and when one keeps silent, and of the ontological status given to that which is kept silent and that which is made public. Cultures and subcultures differ in this regard; so even do families. (pp. 61–62)

Bruner emphasizes in this and other work the importance of stories in understanding both self and culture. Stories provide the tapestries of cultural and familial drama that map the territory of possible roles and possible worlds that an individual may enter. He contrasts the use of the narrative mode, which leads to gripping drama and believable historical accounts — with the mode of logic, mathematics, and science, the paradigmatic mode. While the logical mode is concerned with cause and effect in a linear, analytic sense, "narrative deals with the vicissitudes of human intentions" (p. 16). Yet it is the paradigmatic mode that has guided mainstream developmental psychology. I will return to this topic in a discussion of uses of narrative in the activities of teaching and the helping professions.

Belenky and her associates, in *Women's Ways of Knowing* (1986), and Gilligan, in *In a Different Voice* (1982), identify the themes of connection and care as central to women's psychological development and learning. Further, Gilligan argues for an ethical theory for both women and men that pays as much attention to considerations of care and responsibility as to considerations of justice. These authors propose, along with Noddings

(1984), an educational system that emphasizes dialogue and connectedness in order to promote healthy development and learning in all domains of the human experience.

The initial experience of attachment that an infant has during the first months of life may be of inestimable importance in laying the groundwork for the child's memory of caring as well as the capacity for reciprocity and mutuality in future relationships. In *The Interpersonal World of the Infant* (1985), Daniel Stern draws from his extensive psychiatric practice and research with infants and their families as he emphasizes the importance of the subjective social experiences of the infant during the first 2 years of life. During this time the infant develops four different senses of the self: (1) the emergent self, (2) the core self, (3) the subjective self, and (4) the verbal self. Capturing the dialectic between self and other, Stern suggests that each newly emerging sense of self provides definition for the formation of a new form of relatedness. Stern cites the importance of infants' memories of being with caring others and of their having social dialogues during the first 9 months of life in the formation of healthy life narratives.

USES OF NARRATIVE
IN TEACHING AND COUNSELING

There are two central reasons for the rich use of narrative in teaching and counseling. One has to do with the coherence and the ongoing autobiographical activity of the self, the other with the power of story and metaphor in human action and feeling.

The coherence of the self within its narrative structure is explored by David Carr in *Time, Narrative, and History* (1986) and by Alasdair MacIntyre in *After Virtue* (1981). Carr asks: "Can my life be regarded as an event that I experience, an experience I have . . . or perhaps an action I perform? Is it thus the sort of 'story' in which I am character, story-teller, and audience all at once?" (p. 75). This sense of self is to be taken in the broadest sense, that is, the self that

> is concerned not with the right or wrong of particular actions or even rules for action, but with the question of how to live one's life as a whole, and with questions about the nature of individual human existence, character, and personal identity. (p. 73)

The coherence of the self is grounded in its narrative structure. The narrative of a life is not random; rather, it is given coherence through notions of time, value, and purpose. Carr refers to Dilthey's (1894/1977) notion of reflection on one's life as an ongoing autobiographical activity that acts as a sediment for our actions and decisions. The coherence or structure of the self's narrative is provided through the integration of value, purpose, and meaning, where value represents the valence we attach to the present, purpose entails our sense of future possibility and aspirations, and meaning is our memory and interpretation of the past. Carr acknowledges that our imagination is involved in this activity, but it is an act of practical, rather than literary or aesthetic, imagination. It is "a matter of coping *with* reality, not of providing alternatives to it" (p. 91). It is the narrative structure of one's life that links "the metaphysical, the epistemological, and the moral sense of the notion of personal identity" (p. 73).

This is a notion that is given careful treatment by MacIntyre (1981), who claims that in diminishing the cultural place of narrative (e.g., in sociohistorical, biographical, intellectual, moral, and religious traditions), we have encouraged the disconnection of narrative from life, resulting in an opposition between art and life. MacIntyre further speaks of the moral particularity that is provided to one's life when the nature of one's loyalties, traditions, and inherited roles is acknowledged. These constitute the "given of my life, my moral starting point" (p. 204). We are, at best, MacIntyre asserts, coauthors of our life stories.

The centrality of human narratives in the attainment of moral identity and in the very nature of the moral quest is poignantly illustrated in Elie Wiesel's *Gates of the Forest* (1966). Gavriel discards his Jewish identity as he hides in the forest from the Germans who have robbed him of family, home, community, and traditions. He assumes a non-Jewish name, Gregor. "The future is blank," one of our students wrote. "It is from this vacant cave of meaning that Gregor will venture forth beyond the bounds of his narrative into a world which must be treated and discovered in every moment." The new world is never created, however. Gregor remains a fantasy, a false self, until he reunites with Gavriel, an event that takes place following two experiences. The first is his portrayal of Judas in a dramatization of the passion story, where he purges his anger. The second experience is his participation in the Hasid celebration, where he rediscovers his roots through song and movement, and, thereby, claims the "narrative unity" of his life.[1] It is through drama and dance that he unites many

---

1. MacIntyre (1981) develops the notion of the "narrative unity of a human life" in the context of a narrative quest that is itself situated in "an interlocking set of narratives. . . . I am not only accountable, I am one who can always ask others for an account, who can put others to the question. I am part of their story, as they are part of mine" (p. 203).

narratives — historical, communal, moral, and spiritual; their separateness is no longer a possibility.

The second reason for a prolific use of narrative in teaching and counseling has to do with the power of story and metaphor in offering up possibilities for human action and feeling. Whether inventing, reading, or listening to stories, reading or writing journals and autobiographies, conducting oral history interviews, or engaging in therapeutic dialogue, the teller or receiver of stories can discover connections between self and other, penetrate barriers to understanding, and come to know more deeply the meanings of his or her own historical and cultural narrative. Story and metaphor provide a form of educational encounter that renders us human and frees the moral imagination. They enable us, in Cynthia Ozick's words, to "leap into the other" (1986, p. 65), imagining the experience and the feelings of the other.

Once we envision the activities of teaching and counseling as grounded in the paradoxical relations between self and other, knower and known, subject and object, person and culture, feminine and masculine, thought and feeling, being and doing, and so forth, new possibilities for moral engagement will arise. As we seek to understand these connections in our own lives and in others', we may even learn some things about how to live and invent our lives, lessons that can lead us to a more moral and compassionate life. A new "vision of the Songlines" becomes, then, a vision of connection and relation, and the next stanza of the World Song, "I AM, BECAUSE WE ARE!"

REFERENCES

Allen, Paula Gunn. (1986). *The sacred hoop: Recovering the feminine in American Indian traditions*. Boston: Beacon Press.

Belenky, Mary; Clinchy, Blythe; Goldberger, Nancy; & Tarule, Jill. (1986). *Women's ways of knowing*. New York: Basic Books.

Bruner, Jerome. (1979). *On knowing: Essays for the left hand*. Cambridge, MA: Belknap Press of Harvard University. (Original work published 1962)

Bruner, Jerome. (1983). *In search of mind: Essays in autobiography*. New York: Harper & Row.

Bruner, Jerome. (1986). *Actual minds, possible worlds*. Cambridge, MA: Harvard University Press.

Buber, Martin. (1966). *The knowledge of man* (Maurice Friedman, Ed.). London: George Allen and Unwin.

Carr, David. (1986). *Time, narrative, and history*. Bloomington: Indiana University Press.

Chatwin, Bruce. (1987). *The songlines*. New York: Viking Penguin.

Dilthey, Wilhelm. (1977). *Descriptive psychology and historical understanding* (Richard M. Zaner and Kenneth L. Heiges, Trans.). The Hague: Martinus Nijhoff. (Original work published 1894)

Erikson, Erik. (1964). *Insight and responsibility.* New York: W. W. Norton.

Erikson, Erik. (1975). *Life history and the historical moment.* New York: W. W. Norton.

Field, Joanna. (1981). *A life of one's own.* Los Angeles: J. P. Tarcher.

Gilligan, Carol. (1982). *In a different voice: Psychological theory and women's development.* Cambridge, MA: Harvard University Press.

Hanson, Karen. (1986). *The self imagined: Philosophical reflections on the social character of psyche.* London: Routledge and Kegan Paul.

Jung, Carl G. (1963). *Modern man in search of a soul.* New York: Harcourt Brace & World.

Lifshin, Lyn. (Ed.). (1982). *Ariadne's thread: A collection of contemporary women's journals.* New York: Harper & Row.

MacIntyre, Alasdair. (1981). *After virtue.* Notre Dame, IN: University of Notre Dame Press.

Macmurray, John. (1961). *Persons in relation.* New York: Harper & Row. (Original work published 1954)

Mandler, Jean. (1984). *Stories, scripts, and scenes.* Hillsdale, NJ: Erlbaum.

Manheimer, Ronald. (1977). *Kierkegaard as educator.* Berkeley: University of California Press.

Mead, George Herbert. (1934). *Mind, self, and society: From the standpoint of a social behaviorist* (Charles W. Morris, Ed.). Chicago: University of Chicago Press.

Needleman, Jacob. (1982). *The heart of philosophy.* New York: Harper & Row.

Noddings, Nel. (1984). *Caring: A feminine approach to ethics and moral education.* Berkeley: University of California Press.

Nott, Kathleen. (1971). *Philosophy and human nature.* New York: New York University Press.

Ozick, Cynthia. (1986, May). The moral necessity of metaphor. *Harper's Magazine,* pp. 64–65.

Stern, Daniel. (1985). *The interpersonal world of the infant.* New York: Basic Books.

Stone, Robert. (1988, June). The reason for stories: Toward a moral fiction. *Harper's Magazine,* pp. 71–76.

Sutton-Smith, Brian. (1988). In search of the imagination. In Kieran Egan & Dan Nadaner (Eds.), *Imagination and education* (pp. 3–29). New York: Teachers College Press.

Welty, Eudora. (1984). *One writer's beginnings.* Cambridge, MA: Harvard University Press.

Wiesel, Elie. (1966). *Gates of the forest.* New York: Holt, Rinehart, & Winston.

Wright, J. Eugene, Jr. (1982). *Erikson: Identity and religion.* New York: Seabury Press.

6

Telling Our Own Stories
The Reading and Writing of Journals or Diaries

JOANNE E. COOPER

Joanne Cooper, assistant professor of educational administration at the University of Hawaii, received the Ph.D. degree in educational policy and management from the University of Oregon. She has taught courses in the Graduate Core Program at Lewis & Clark College in Portland, Oregon, and in journal writing at Oregon State University and Western Oregon State College. Her research has focused on journal-writing methods of senior level managers and of contemporary women diarists in education.

> 6:00 am: I go into the kitchen to make coffee. I give the cats water (they have none). I look at the raspberries I bought last week. No one has eaten them and they are moldy. Five bananas rot on top of the cookie jar. I realize I have two choices—make banana bread or write my chapter—and in that realization comes the recognition of the price I pay to be a woman who writes. My body is shot, my children feel neglected, the food in my kitchen is rotting and my partner has moved on to God and a new wife . . . right now I wish my God (or my wife) knew how to make banana bread. No such luck.

I am an addicted diary keeper. I have been keeping a journal or diary (I use the terms synonymously) almost 14 years now. This chapter is about keeping a journal, a notebook, a diary, or a log. It is about writing, writing to tell our own stories, writing to listen to ourselves, and writing to educate ourselves and others about our lives.

This is no easy task. The act of writing requires the neglect of other aspects of one's life. With this huge price to pay, why do I go on writing? Why do any of us write? First of all, we write to tell our stories. As Marilyn Farwell (1988) has stated,

Without a story, we perish. Stories define our lives: they teach us what is possible and good, help set our goals and limits, offer us role models and explain mysteries. Without stories — myths and legends, folktales and sacred texts, romances and comedies and tragedies — our lives would be formless. (p. 29)

Telling our own stories is a way to impose form upon our often chaotic experiences (Grumet, 1988) and, in the process, to develop our own voice. Listening to our own stories is a way for us to nourish, encourage, and sustain ourselves (Howe, 1984), to enter into a caring relationship with all the parts of our self (Noddings, 1984).

Mary Belenky, Blythe Clinchy, Nancy Goldberger, and Jill Tarule (1986) listened carefully to the voices and stories of women. They found that the development of voice was particularly important in the establishment of epistemological perspectives that locate one's self within the context of one's culture. Belenky and her associates concluded that the stories of women they heard during their research "drew us back into a kind of knowing that had too often been silenced by the institutions in which we grew up and of which we were a part. In the end we found that, in our attempt to bring forward the ordinary voice, that voice had educated us" (p. 20).

Just as the voices of ordinary women educated these authors, so the voices of individual diarists are instructive, both in the telling and the listening. Each diarist's voice becomes one of many voices in the culture, voices that articulate individual selves, deepening our understanding of the self, enhancing clear dialogue, and helping us to understand the collective self we call society. Christina Baldwin (1977) states that "introspection takes the human image from the self to the culture instead of imposing a human image from the culture onto the self" (p. 28).

A central task for any diarist, then, may be to ask, "Who am I?" The answer, as Joan Didion (1968) suggests, may be not one self, but many past selves, the people we used to be:

I think we are well advised to keep on nodding terms with the people we used to be, whether we find them attractive company or not. Otherwise they run up unannounced and surprise us, come hammering on the mind's door at 4 a.m. of a bad night and demand to know who deserted them, who betrayed them, who is going to make amends. . . . It is a good idea, then, to keep in touch, and I suppose that keeping in touch is what notebooks are all about. (pp. 142–143)

These past selves have evolved to form a present collective self. This present self can be discerned through a journey back in time, a journey that

threads the past selves, like beads on a string, forming a necklace of existence, a present complex whole. Keeping a notebook is one way to keep in
touch with our past and present selves. A notebook, a diary, or a journal is
a form of narrative as well as a form of research, a way to tell our own
story, a way to learn who we have been, who we are, and who we are
becoming. We literally become teachers and researchers in our own lives,
empowering ourselves in the process.

I was privileged to watch this process in my students when I taught a
class called Shaping Meaning: The Reading and Writing of Diaries and
Journals. One student in my class wrote about the importance of finding
one's own voice through writing, telling, and listening to each other's
stories: "Hearing all of your voices in your journals and speaking in class
gives me confidence. The fact that you sound so good to me helps me
assume that you are hearing me that way too." Students told their own
stories and listened to each other's stories in ways that were honest, caring,
and at times enormously moving. In a farewell letter to the class, one
student wrote:

> The thought of coming to Journal Class on Saturday — even a warm,
> sunny Saturday — left me not with dread but with anticipation. May-
> be it was the comradery with the group, maybe the sanction to write
> freely and fully, maybe the chance to listen and cry and laugh with
> others as they grew through this journey called life. Each of us came
> to the class from our own little crowded world, and many of us won-
> dered and fought this gut-wrenching process called reflection. Yet the
> first day so many weeks ago, we each ventured out a little at a time to
> experiment and trust . . . writing, thinking, writing, sharing, search-
> ing . . . each time we tackled an assignment we felt the challenge —
> spurred on by our honesty — to dig deep and question values . . . it
> has been a wonderful class and has probably been the thread of self
> awareness and willingness to discover — the sanctuary of those pro-
> cesses — that held my life in some sense of perspective this spring.

JOURNAL WRITING AS TELLING

Writing a diary or journal is a powerful form of narrative in which we tell
our own stories, allowing us to rethink our past, our present, and our
future selves. It is a kind of journey, a journey from one moment to the
next, from one entry to the next. We literally write our own stories, simultaneously incorporating our own future, as we reconstruct our past (Culley, 1985). Telling our stories through journal writing becomes a quest for

understanding and integration, a bridging of the inner mindscape and the outer landscape.

Madeleine Grumet suggests that "to tell a story is to impose form on experience" (1988, p. 87). Keeping a journal or diary, even if it is nothing more than the simple recording of events through periodic entries, enables the writer to impose form on the often chaotic experience of life. Journals allow us to examine our own experiences, to gain a fresh perspective, and by that means begin to transform the experiences themselves.

I was startled by the power of this process when our journal writing class met for the second time. When I asked what keeping a journal had felt like for the students, one student announced that she had quit her job as a director of a nursing home. She said writing down what she did every day and how she felt about it drew her to the gradual realization that it was *not* what she wanted to be doing with her life. So she quit! I had hoped the process would prove valuable to my students, but I hadn't expected it to work with such power and immediacy.

As the experience of this student illustrates, it is through telling our own stories that we learn who we are and what we need. Journal writers, through describing the reality of their daily lives, discover their own voices and simultaneously witness to future generations. An example of this "witnessing" can be found in Margo Culley's collection of women's diaries entitled *A Day at a Time* (1985). These diaries, which aided the diarists in finding their own voices when they were being written, today illuminate the details of women's lives from 1600 to 1900. Their words contribute much to what Bell Hooks has called "the struggle of memory against forgetting" (1988). Their diaries become letters to the future, letters which aid both writer and reader.

UNSENT LETTERS

Writing letters one does not intend to send can serve in the telling of our own stories within the context of a particular relationship. Tristine Rainer, in *The New Diary* (1978), addresses four basic principles in writing a diary: writing spontaneously, writing honestly, writing deeply, and writing correctly. Unsent letters are a way to write both honestly and deeply. Because the letters are unsent, diarists are free to write as honestly as possible about all that they feel toward the other. Rainer contends that writing honestly is more than just telling the truth, it "involves an openness about what you really feel, what you really want, what you really believe, what you really decide. Through diary writing this real self can become the vital center of your psychic life" (p. 35). Unsent letters allow diarists the freedom to write deeply, to dig below the surface of a relationship, and thus can become powerful tools in helping to understand one's self in relation to others.

I asked my students to first make a list of people to whom they might want to write an unsent letter, then to pick one person from the list and write a letter to that person in class. One woman wrote a letter to her mother, who was very much on her mind that day. I have preserved the letter's form, including capital letters and line breaks, because I feel what she wrote is more than a letter, it is almost a prose poem. The power, the beauty, and the pain-filled honesty of this letter illustrate how un-sent letters, as a writing form, allow diarists to write spontaneously and deeply:

I am not with you in person today . . . I am with thought . . .
I chose to fulfill an important (to me anyway, needing the credits
to graduate this year) precommitment on this day rather than
Drive to see you today.
I know that your other daughters have all been there . . .
I have talked to them . . . they are in acute distress . . .
And none of them can understand my decision . . .
And I understand the way they feel . . . But I can
Not change what is —
It's unreal to me also — here I sit in a class . . .
While my mother lays in ICU. . . . Another cardiac
arrest . . . And I have not spoken with your doctor
Or the nurses that are caring for you
I'll deal with that tonight
And I did not leave the hall and classroom number that I
would be in just for emergencies . . . Because if you
should die . . .   I'll deal with that tonight
Are three credits more important than rushing to your side?
I know you must be thinking that —
And I guess they are to me . . .
It's not that I dislike you . . . I have always
tried to be very pleasant to you — And I don't
think that I'm angry with you . . . I think I resolved that
long ago
But even a plant needs water
And I have NO recollection of your hand touching me,
A kiss, or a hug — initiated by you . . .
And I still am
And you still are

And we are NOT
I grieved over the loss of a mother,
a relationship that never was . . . many
years ago.

This letter illustrates the relational aspect of Nel Noddings's (1984) feminine ethic of care. Noddings insists that the caring relation is one in which reciprocity must be present. She states, "We are both free—that which I do, *I* do—and bound—I might do far better if you reach out to me and help me and far, far worse if you abuse, taunt or ignore me" (p. 49). My student, within the historical context of her relationship with her mother, has chosen to be in my class on this particular day. Although we do not know the full history of the relationship between this student and her mother, it is clear that she has chosen to turn from the relationship and "properly pay heed to her own condition" (Noddings, 1984, p. 105). The unsent letter becomes a way for this student to care for herself, both clarifying her reasons for such actions and helping her reach resolution. It is within the construct of this writing form that the diarist can be fully honest, addressing that which is most deeply felt, and helping to clarify complex human relations.

Here, too, is an example of a hurtful story that heals, or a healing story that hurts in the telling. Facing the fact that she was not at her mother's deathbed, but instead in a class she took for herself, was not easy, at best, and excruciatingly painful at worst. Examining her past hurtful relationship with her mother and her own longing for love in the face of repeated rejection is even more painful. Yet in examining this relationship, writing about it, the writer reaches some form of resolution: "And I still am/And you still are/And we are NOT." Thus stories that are told deeply and honestly, though painful in their telling, can simultaneously relieve or heal that pain.

METAPHOR AS CONDENSED TELLING

Diarists who generate metaphors for self create new ways of viewing the self within the changing process of one's own life. Aristotle was the first to identify the role of metaphor in the production of knowledge. Gareth Morgan (1986), whose work uses metaphors for organizational diagnosis and analysis, defines metaphor as "the general process of image crossing whereby A is seen as B" (p. 346). Metaphors have greatly influenced language and communication (Lakoff & Johnson, 1980) and have played a role in creative imagination and science (Koestler, 1969; Miller, 1978), in social theory (Brown, 1977), and, as mentioned, in organization theory (Morgan, 1986).

One student, when asked to list possible metaphors for the self and then to pick one and expand upon it, described herself as follows:

> [I am a] diaper pin holding the fabric of our lives together and keep-
> ing the crap cleaned off. My sharp point has been dulled by pulling
> the threads of all of my family together — the point is still there — yet
> one wrong turn without the cushion of the guiding hand — and I in-
> flict pain on the family fabric. I am ready to put the diapers away
> and put the diaper pin to new use — to stretch and pull it out as may-
> be a letter opener. But must I hurt my family, my children, to pull
> out and let the fabric of the diaper find new shape and form — while
> I let the process of reshaping begin?

Through the use of metaphor this student is able to examine both objective and subjective knowledge: the objective knowledge that she is responsible for holding the family together and the subjective knowledge that she is being dulled by that process. She uses the central image of a diaper pin to examine her present sense of self as "holding the fabric of the family together" and the impact of her possible future actions as she re-shapes herself. She is considering returning to school. What will happen if she reshapes herself into a letter opener? Will the fabric of the family hold? The image combines objective and subjective knowledge to assist the diarist in the formulation of a perspective Belenky and her associates (1986) have labeled as constructed knowledge. Through the use of meta-phor this student begins to integrate the voice of societal expectations with the voice from within. She is listening to her inner feelings even as she attends to her world, attempting to balance the voices she hears from each, in order to develop a central integrated voice.

In seeing herself as a diaper pin, the diarist is using a "generative metaphor" (Schön, 1983), a process whereby seeing one thing as something else helps to generate new perceptions, explanations, and inventions. Schön describes the use of metaphor as a three-stage process or life cycle:

1. One notices or feels that A and B are similar, without being able to say similar with respect to what.
2. After some reflection, one presents relations of elements present in both A and B through a restructured perception of both.
3. Later, one develops a general model for which a redescribed A and a redescribed B can be identified as instances.

JOURNAL WRITING AND
WOMEN'S WAYS OF KNOWING

The diarist's choice of a diaper pin as a metaphor is of particular interest because it is distinctly female. Diaper pins are objects central to the everyday experience of mothers. The use of this metaphor serves to bring a fresh viewpoint to life's puzzling situations. It allows women to examine their lives in ways that are unique to their own experience and that validate both their perceptions and their ways of knowing. It is a truncated way of "telling our own story."

Alicia Ostriker, in *Writing like a Woman* (1983), underscores the need for female images and the importance of journal writing as a means of understanding the female experience. She encourages women to write about their own experiences, experiences that are central to their lives:

> If the woman artist has been trained to believe that the activities of motherhood are trivial, tangential to main issues of life, irrelevant to the great themes of literature, she should untrain herself. The training is misogynist, it protects and perpetuates systems of thought and feeling which prefer violence and death to love and birth, and it is a lie. . . . The writer who is a mother should, I think, record everything she can: make notes, keep journals, take photographs, use a tape recorder, and remind herself that there is a subject of incalculably vast significance to humanity, about which virtually nothing is known because writers have not been mothers. (p. 131)

One might easily say, "Well, that was true for Alicia Ostriker in 1965 in England, but not today." Yet the need for these stories, for models, and for ways of knowing that utilize the female experience was recently underscored for me in a conversation with my two teenage daughters. My older daughter, Kim, was listing the authors she had read this year in her honors English class. I realized with a sinking feeling that not a single one was female. Katie, my younger daughter, said scoffingly, "Well, mother, you just overreact. That's probably because none of the stuff written by women is as good as the stuff written by men." The impression our curriculum leaves in the minds of its youth, both male and female, is that women do not write classics. Not only are female students left with little sense of their own history, their own experience, but both male and female students are left with the impression that female experiences (their words, their stories) are not worth recording or, when recorded, are inferior.

Ostriker concludes:

> As our knowledge begins to accumulate, we can imagine what it would signify to all women, and men, to live in a culture where childbirth and

mothering occupied the kind of position that sex and romantic love have occupied in literature and art for the last five hundred years, or the kind of position that warfare has occupied since literature began. (p. 131)

One way for this knowledge to accumulate, for the world to understand the hidden experiences particular to women, is through diary and journal writing. Florence Howe (1984) has asserted that the huge quantity of women's diaries, letters, journals, memoirs, and autobiographies written from the nineteenth century to the present have, perhaps like quilts, both created and recorded history in the manner of art. These art forms record for future generations the real stories of women's lives, loves, and dilemmas, as they simultaneously validate the experiences of the women who are recording them.

JOURNAL WRITING AS LISTENING

Listening to stories is an ancient form of nurturance. Storytelling is a long-standing tribal ritual. In addition, most of us have been read to or told stories since we were very small. Thus listening to our own story through diary or journal writing is a way to nurture ourselves as we simultaneously illuminate our lives and emotions. It is a way to love and replenish ourselves.

Perhaps narrative in any form functions first and foremost to sustain and encourage the writer or storyteller. Even something as simple as a list can uplift both writer and reader, as with this list, entitled "At Least," written by a teacher who had recently been forced into early retirement:

At least I am alive, I have my health.
At least I don't have the gut grinding pain in my stomach anymore.
At least my son can't slip another $50 check by me and overdraw my account because I won't have $50.
At least I wasn't on the Challenger.
At least my children are grown and gone and are financially independent.
At least I'm not in pain and my body isn't twisted like a pretzel like my friend Nan, so what's my excuse for not getting moving?
At least I won't have to go to meaningless meetings without end anymore.
At least I kept my dignity and my freedom of choice. I went out on my convenience.

At least I don't have to prostitute myself by working for a man I don't
trust or respect.

While there are some individuals I will miss, there are others I will
not — this is the asshole capital of the world.

This list goes on for 33 items, which serve to uplift not only the writer but
the reader, as well.

Journal writing places us in relation to ourselves so that we become
both the one who is caring (or one-caring) and the cared-for. Noddings
(1984) defines this caring relation as one in which we are obligated to
care for ourselves even as we care for the other. Through lists such as the
preceding one, writers are able to care for themselves, to "feel with" the
other. In this case the self that is the object of the writer's reflection is
the "other"; the writer "feels with" this other self through a process of
engrossment, a kind of empathy that involves reception rather than projection. Through writing we are able to receive ourselves, our feelings, our
beliefs and to hear our own voices as they tell our stories in ways that help
us grow.

Noddings also suggests that to maintain the ethical ideal, one needs to
build "a reservoir of sustenance from activity in the non-human world" (p.
124). "An ethic of caring strives to maintain the caring attitude. That
means that the one-caring must be maintained, for she is the immediate
source of caring. The one-caring, then, properly pays heed to her own
condition" (p. 105). This remains a central problem in our society today.
Caregivers are often totally depleted before they retreat to the nonhuman
world Noddings mentions above. Yet because society bestows great social
approval on their actions without rewarding them economically and because women often find a sense of self-worth through giving to others,
many caregivers continue to give to the point of depletion.

Writing our own stories works to combat this depletion by reminding
us of who we are, while it focuses on and attends to our needs. Diarists
report that when they sit down and put pen to paper, their most immediate
and pressing concerns emerge before them on the page. There is a feeling
of surprise, "Oh, so that's what's bothering me," that emerges from the
process of engrossment described by Noddings.

Writing in a journal is thus a way to attend to the self, to care for and
to feed oneself. It can be a place to dump anger, guilt, or fear instead of
dumping it on those we love. It can be a place to clarify what it is we feel
angry or guilty about. It can be a place to encourage ourselves, to support
ourselves, in working through that anger or guilt, and it can be a place to
transform silence into language and action.

Journal writing can also help unravel the conflicts women often feel in struggling to meet the needs of others. Noddings suggests that the one-caring may often feel conflict if two of her cared-fors have conflicting needs (a sick child and a husband wanting to go to the theater, for instance), or if the cared-for wants or needs something that the one-caring does not want to provide (Will you help me set this cat on fire? or Even though I'm only 14, will you buy beer for our slumber party?). I would like to suggest a third conflict—one in which the one-caring is torn between the needs of the cared-for, a sick child or an aging mother, and her own needs as she approaches emotional and physical exhaustion. This is the point at which the one-caring needs to withdraw and renew or replenish her own resources.

One way to replenish oneself has been described by Joanna Field (1981) as "discovering joy." Here the diarist uses journal writing to attend to the physical world and to discover joy in the process. This involves an "internal gesture" of expanded awareness, a way to stay in touch with the experience and immediacy of life through active receptivity. Field observed that:

> In certain moods the very simplest things, even the glint of electric light on the water in my bath, gave me the most intense delight, while in others I seemed to be blind, unresponding and shut off, so that music I had loved, a spring day or the company of my friends, gave me no contentment. . . . So now I began to discover that there were a multitude of ways of perceiving, ways that were controllable by what I can only describe as an internal gesture of the mind. (pp. 70–71)

This "internal gesture" can be triggered by describing in detail what you see and hear around you or by making lists of moments in which you felt great joy. Tristine Rainer (1978) states:

> If you were to list in your diary the happiest moments in your life you might be surprised to find that it did not include your graduation or wedding day or the acquisition of things you thought you wanted. Rather it might include the spontaneous wonder and surprise at certain unexpected events in your life, an encounter with a stranger in a strange place, a moment in a play, a feeling of physical exhilaration. . . . One woman's list included:
> Driving through Big Sur with C.
> Kissing W. on the street in Greenwich Village
> Dancing, floating and swimming in my dreams
> Certain lines in Durrell's *Justine*
> When I felt Cathy's new-born cheek with my forefinger and could hardly tell what was her cheek and what was my finger. (pp. 161–162)

These techniques then become ways in which diarists can shed their fears, worries, and physical exhaustion by tuning in to the world around them. This technique for expanded awareness is a way to withdraw and renew or replenish individual resources.

VOICES IN THE CULTURE

My work is to inhabit the silences with which I have lived and fill them with myself until they have the sounds of brightest day and the loudest thunder. (Lorde, 1980, p. 46)

Belenky and her coauthors (1986) have grasped the importance of the development of self and mind as it connects to voice — a voice, as Lorde states, "to inhabit the silences with which I have lived" (1980, p. 46). In their study Belenky and her coauthors found that women inhabiting the epistemological perspective they termed "silence" were often fearful, abused, and buffeted about by the worlds in which they lived. It was only as they began to find their voices and to speak from an intuitive sense, or "from the gut," that they gained some power over their own lives and a growing sense of self. Many reported the use of a diary or journal to facilitate this process. These women grew personally and intellectually as they "found their voices." Lorde (1980) associates silence with oppression. For her the development of voice is a way out of helplessness into a kind of personal power that seeks to transform pain. Struggling with breast cancer, Lorde equates silence with death and her voice with the vitality needed to live in a fully actualized state. She uses her journal to develop that voice and to transform her painful experiences with a mastectomy into a reaffirmation of her right to live. She is determined not to deny the pain and mutilation she experiences, equating cosmetics, such as a prosthesis, with a form of denial that buries fear and shame until they eat away from the inside like a second cancer:

I refuse to have my scars hidden or trivialized behind lambswool or silicone gel. I refuse to be reduced in my own eyes or in the eyes of others from warrior to mere victim, simply because it might render me a fraction more acceptable or less dangerous to the still complacent, those who believe if you cover up a problem it ceases to exist. (p. 60)

If finding a voice is facilitated through the journal process in a way that transforms experience into growth, as Lorde demonstrates, then journal keeping is a powerful tool that combats the oppressions and repressions that prevent us from being fully present to ourselves.

Women have been strongly enculturated by a white male view, by a process of male hegemony that encourages them to be silent, passive, and pretty. Lorde asserts that the encouragement to wear a prosthesis after a mastectomy, and thus to be silent and pretty, denies the real pain and mutilation women feel and leaves them ignorant of their own buried feelings. Adrienne Rich suggests that "ignorance of ourselves has been the key to our powerlessness" (cited in Culley & Portuges, 1985, p. 24). Keeping a diary or journal functions here in what Weiler calls the "building of counter-hegemony" (1988, p. 125), a process that taps into the power of discovering one's own voice, a voice that rises up to support individuals as active agents in their own lives rather than victims. Lorde (1980) seems determined *not* to see herself as victim in her struggle with cancer and her journal is her weapon. She says of her diary:

> I don't want this to be a record of grieving only. I don't want this to be a record only of tears. I want it to be something I can use now or later, something that I can remember, something that I can pass on, something that I can know came out of the kind of strength I have that nothing else can shake for very long or equal. (p. 46)

It is not only important for women to become aware of their own socialization, but as transmitters of the culture through their role, teachers are especially challenged to examine how the culture has impacted on the female self. Grumet (1988) describes how women who gradually entered the workforce as teachers were molded in ways that demanded the transmission of male hegemony to their pupils and thus to future generations. Martha Cox, a young Mormon, describes in her diary the agony she felt in the conflict between her hopes and dreams about what the profession should or could be and the pressure she felt to become an instrument for the continued rigid oppression and harsh discipline of the patriarchal system in which she became enmeshed (pp. 36–37).

Increasingly, society looks to the schools for social change—an instrument to implement integration, sex education, and widespread drug testing, to name a few assignments. Mary Louise Holly (1983), in a research report that describes seven elementary school teachers who kept journals for one year as they reflected upon their lives and roles as classroom teachers, states:

> As teachers we are increasingly becoming aware that we cannot solve many of our children's, or any of society's, problems and that teaching is far more complex than our "methods of teaching" courses lead us to believe. (p. 175)

Teachers must constantly integrate their own needs, values, and desires with the often conflicting expectations of society. Many teachers in this project found writing to be cathartic as well as introspective. During the course of the year, they produced snapshots of their lives that enabled them to view their own role more objectively, embedded as it is in society, and their own actions, embedded in the complex interaction of students, administrators, parents, and community.

Students face similar dilemmas as recipients of society's messages. They struggle with decisions to agree with, acquiesce to, reject, or alter the messages society sends them about how they are to act and think. Students can use journal writing to facilitate finding their voice, a voice needed before any kind of dialogue can ever take place between them and their culture. Without a voice of their own, students are simply dictated to. No real dialogue can take place without the presence of two true voices. One student expressed her confusion about who she was apart from the demands of the culture in a dialogue between herself (her head, her rational self that embodies the culture's expectations of women) and her heart (her feelings and emotional needs):

HEART: I'm lonely. Why can't I have what I want?

ME: You have a husband and four children; you must meet their needs first.

HEART: But don't I count for something too? Can't my needs be an equal part there, too?

ME: Only if you don't ever lose sight of their needs. I became sort of a non-person as a mother and a wife. It is important to give and nurture others without thought to my own need.

HEART: But then what do I do with the rumblings, the rising flood gates, the needs that can no longer be repressed?

ME: You throw crumbs — carrots — little pieces to your needs but remain in the cog of meeting everyone else's needs first.

HEART: Why do I feel like I am dying?

This student is clearly caught between her culture's expectations for women and her own needs. She has embodied the culture's expectations to the point where they are identified in the dialogue as "me." But her heart, her subjective self, answers clearly. Most revealing is the last line. Here we see the uncovering of her own personal truth. Some part of her knows that she will die without the recognition of her heart's needs in the face of the culture's demands. In Noddings's (1984) terms, she is struggling between the needs of those she cares for and her own needs as the one-caring.

She is also searching to find her own voice, the voice of her heart, which can help define the self in the face of the culture's expectations. Her struggle exemplifies both Baldwin's (1977) assertion that one must define the self before that self can be seen in the context of its culture and the perspective Belenky and her coauthors (1986) have defined as constructed knowing. They would describe attending to the voice of "the heart" in the dialogue as "subjective or intuitive knowledge." By contrast, the reception and reproduction of society's expectations would be described as "received knowledge." The application of objective procedures for obtaining and communicating knowledge has been defined as procedural knowledge. At the positions of received and procedural knowledge, other voices and external truths prevail. This student's sense of self, of "me," is embedded in external definitions. She is reaching, however, for the creation of her own frame, a position of constructed knowledge, an attempt to reclaim the self by integrating intuitive knowledge (I feel like I am dying) with received knowledge. Just as Belenky and her associates name the combining of these two voices as constructed knowledge, so Baldwin (1977) names it "finding one's place in society." Voices in the culture are constructed voices that mirror an integration of the individual voice and common cultural voices. Finding a place in the culture is finding one's constructed voice.

Journal writing can serve here as a form of intense self-reflection and self-analysis, a process Belenky and her coauthors (1986) report many of their research participants experienced in reclaiming the self. Like the student just described, these subjects developed a narrative sense of the self, past and future, in an attempt to embrace all the pieces of the self in some ultimate sense of the whole. The use of dialogue, as we have demonstrated, facilitates the integration of these pieces of self and helps the diarist to form a single powerful voice that embraces complexity, paradox, and ambiguity.

DIARISTS AS EDUCATORS AND RESEARCHERS
OF THEIR OWN LIVES

Grumet (1988) argues that women "must construct a special place for ourselves, if our work as teachers is to achieve clarity, communication, and insight of aesthetic practice — if it is in short, to be research and not merely representation" (pp. 88–89). As diarists, we are all researchers of our own lives, researchers who withdraw to a special place, taking our myriad selves with us and writing up our observations. To "do research" on yourself through journal writing seems one way to solve the subject-object split frequently found in traditional research that Susan Florio-Ruane discusses in Chapter 13.

In the field of social work both professionals and their clients benefit from the use of personal logs as a form of research on the self and as a tool for personal growth. Swenson (1988) advocates the use of a personal log "for deepening client self-awareness and therapeutic communication" and for "deepening professional self-awareness" (p. 307), as does Fox (1982). In this context social workers, as researchers, can examine who they are in the context of their own professional lives. Clients are able to examine their lives within their own contexts, to become their own researchers, to move from disempowered and mute to empowered and "voiced."

Audre Lorde's (1980) struggle to be "whole" is both the researcher's struggle and the research subject's struggle to be whole. Each is being silenced in her own way. Lorde is not to speak or display her mutilation. She is to hide it under a prosthesis. Traditionally, researchers are to hide their feelings and their personal observations in a diary, while publishing only the "scholarly accounts" of their work.

Yet, an attempt to publish a narrative account under a false name is a prosthesis for the researcher, a wad of cotton slapped on over the scars of feeling that objective researchers are not supposed to have. Likewise, denial of our own voice and intelligence as women writers attempting to research our own lives is a prosthesis slapped on over the scars created as we are cut off from our own power and intelligence. As diarists, journal keepers, professional log keepers, we seek to reclaim the right to intelligently examine our own lives even as we are deeply and personally embedded in our own context. To be detached from our feelings, our voice, our intelligence, is to be cut off, which in turn leaves scars—scars we have hidden too long and for which we are paying a great price. Telling our own stories, using journal writing to examine our lives, can heal those scars and leave us more whole.

As chroniclers of our own stories, we write to create ourselves, to give voice to our experiences, to learn who we are and who we have been. Our diaries become the stories of our journeys through life, stories that are both instructive and transforming in the telling and the listening. These stories, these myriad voices, then serve to instruct and transform society, to add to the collective voice we call culture. Diarists, then, both as researchers and research subjects, begin to heal themselves and the split society has created between subject and object. Thus diaries, these small, insignificant objects filled with the simple words of our lives, can serve to make us whole.

Acknowledgment. Portions of this paper were made possible through a study funded by the Center for the Study of Women in Society at the University of Oregon.

REFERENCES

Baldwin, Christina. (1977). *One to one: Self-understanding through journal writing*. New York: M. Evans.

Belenky, Mary; Clinchy, Blythe; Goldberger, Nancy; & Tarule, Jill. (1986). *Women's ways of knowing*. New York: Basic Books.

Brown, Richard H. (1977). *A poetic for sociology*. New York: Cambridge University Press.

Culley, Margo. (Ed.). (1985). *A day at a time*. New York: Feminist Press.

Culley, Margo, & Portuges, Catherine. (1985). *Gendered subjects: The dynamics of feminist teaching*. Boston: Routledge and Kegan Paul.

Didion, Joan. (1968). On keeping a notebook. In *Slouching towards Bethlehem* (pp. 135–144). New York: Washington Square Press.

Farwell, Marilyn. (1988, Summer). The female hero. *Old Oregon, 67*(4), 29–31.

Field, Joanna. (1981). *A life of one's own*. Los Angeles: J. P. Tarcher.

Fox, Raymond. (1982, Summer). The personal log: Enriching clinical practice. *Clinical Social Work Journal, 10*, 94–102.

Grumet, Madeleine. (1988). *Bitter milk: Women and teaching*. Amherst: University of Massachusetts Press.

Holly, Mary Louise. (1983, November). *Teacher reflections on classroom life: An empirical base for professional development* (Progress Report No. 3). Kent, OH: Kent State University. (ERIC Document Nos. RIESEP84, ED243865, SPO24308)

Hooks, Bell. (1988, October). *In the presence of my sisters*. Keynote address presented at the NW Women's Studies Conference, Portland, OR.

Howe, Florence. (1984). *Myths of coeducation*. Bloomington: Indiana University Press.

Koestler, Arthur. (1969). *The act of creation*. London: Hutchinson.

Lakoff, George, & Johnson, Mark. (1980). *Metaphors we live by*. Chicago: University of Chicago Press.

Lorde, Audre. (1980). *The cancer journals*. San Francisco: Spinsters/Aunt lute.

Miller, Jonathan. (1978). *The body in question*. New York: Jonathan Cape.

Morgan, Gareth. (1986). *Images of organizations*. Beverly Hills, CA: Sage.

Noddings, Nel. (1984). *Caring: A feminine approach to ethics and moral education*. Berkeley: University of California Press.

Ostriker, Alicia. (1983). *Writing like a woman*. Ann Arbor: University of Michigan Press.

Rainer, Tristine. (1978). *The new diary*. Los Angeles: Jeremy P. Tarcher.

Schön, Donald. (1983). *The reflective practitioner*. New York: Basic Books.

Swenson, Carol R. (1988, May). The professional log: Techniques for self-directed learning. *Social Casework: The Journal of Contemporary Social Work, 69*, 307–311.

Weiler, Kathleen. (1988). *Women teaching for change: Gender, class, and power*. New York: Bergin & Garvey.

7

"According to Their Feelings"
Teaching and Healing with Stories

KIRIN NARAYAN

Kirin Narayan is assistant professor of anthropology and South Asian studies at the University of Wisconsin–Madison. Born in Bombay, she received her B.A. from Sarah Lawrence College in liberal arts and the M.A. and Ph.D. degrees in anthropology at the University of California, Berkeley. She received the Jean P. Steager Memorial Prize in Folklore in 1983 and was first in the Eric Hoffer and Lillian Fabilli Essay Competition in 1985. Dr. Narayan has served on the faculties of Middlebury College and Hampshire College. She is the author of Storytellers, Saints, and Scoundrels: Folk Narrative in Hindu Religious Teaching *and is coeditor of* Creativity: Self and Society.

If game, drama, and text were analogies guiding theory in many disciplines through the 1960s and 1970s (Geertz, 1983), narrative has been central to the 1980s. Whether viewed as a syntagmatic arrangement of concepts or as actual discourse, narrative has colonized territory in a number of fields. Though clearly sweeping in behind the vanguard of the "text" analogy, the use of narrative instead of text emphasizes the subjectivity of active agents and the negotiated unfolding of events. That narrative is a means of making sense of one's own and others' experience has been recurrently argued by theologians (Crites, 1971; Goldberg, 1982; Hoffman, 1986); psychologists (J. Bruner, 1986, 1987; Coles, 1989; Polkinghorne, 1988; Schafer, 1983); philosophers (MacIntyre, 1981; Ricoeur, 1984); historians (Clifford, 1986; Mink, 1978; White, 1973, 1981); and anthropologists (E. Bruner, 1986; R. Rosaldo, 1989) — to cite only a prominent

---

Portions of this chapter are drawn from Chapters 1, 2, and 4 of *Storytellers, Saints, and Scoundrels: Folk Narrative in Hindu Religious Teaching,* by Kirin Narayan, Philadelphia: University of Pennsylvania Press. Copyright © 1989 by University of Pennsylvania Press. Reprinted by permission.

selection of authors and publications. Most generally, these theorists agree that the progression of events in narrative captures the dimension of time in lived experience. By arranging the flux and welter of experience around a narrative line, we make sense of our pasts, plan for our futures, and comprehend the lives of others.

For some years now, I have been interested in folk narrative as a vehicle for religious teaching. My research has attempted to ground theories of narrative and religion in actual interactions by focusing on a Hindu religious teacher in Western India, his stories, and the manifold ways in which these stories are viewed by his disciples (Narayan, 1989). In this essay I explore the therapeutic aspects of storytelling, drawing connections between the ways folk narratives are employed by traditional healers (who are often religious figures) and the ways narratives are elicited, reinterpreted, and retold in contemporary Western schools of psychotherapy. After introducing Swamiji, a Hindu religious teacher, I will reproduce one of his stories and the situation in which it was told, so that the discussion that follows can be rooted in vivid particulars. Following the lead of the Swamiji and his disciples, whose multiple voices I draw into this text, I will argue that the evocation of feeling is central to the choice of a story told and to the impact of a story on the imaginative lives of listeners. Though stories are effective in depicting and evoking powerful feelings, I will argue that antithetically, by providing a perspective outside the tangled flow of experience, stories are also therapeutic in the detachment they evoke.

A HINDU TEACHER AND HIS SETTING

Let us turn then to Nasik, a center of pilgrimage and industry in Western India. On the second floor of an apartment building adjoining a bustling main street, an old holy man (*sādhu*) daily received visitors. I call him Swamiji, a generic name, for as he said, "What need do I have for 'publicity'? Just write that some Swamiji told you all this." Swamiji was a genial round-faced man, whose scalp and cheeks were sometimes smoothly shaved and at other times bore a shaggy white growth of hair. Nearly blind, Swamiji wore enormous black-rimmed spectacles that blurred and magnified his eyes. As a *sannyāsī* "renouncer" he wore ochre robes bound around his waist or tied around the neck. During my first visit to perform research in 1983, Swamiji reclined in an aluminum deck chair as he received visitors; midway through my second visit in 1985 he had moved to a bed. Lying relaxed against cushions with his feet outstretched, he chatted with his visitors and on occasion launched into stories that addressed the concerns of those present.

There are two broad forms of religious authority in Hinduism: the birth-ascribed authority of those born into the castes of Brahman priests and the achieved authority of those who have embarked on a spiritual path. Treading the path toward union with divinity generally involves renouncing the world: an initiation that involves the symbolic death to society, the cutting of caste and kinship ties, and the discarding of possessions in order to lead a celibate and itinerant life. Swamiji himself had been a political activist in the Independence movement that freed India from British colonial rule before he began to wander through the subcontinent in search of a Guru. He was formally initiated into the Dashanami Dandi order of *sannyāsi* renouncers at age 40 in 1956, yet even before he began to wear the ochre robes of this order he was addressed as "Swamiji" since he was single, itinerant, and dedicated to religious concerns. By providing a rare, neutral space in a society traditionally pervaded by ties of caste and kinship, renouncers are often sought out by people who wish to unburden themselves. Renouncers are expected to dispense blessings, heal the sick in body and soul, and guide people in their worldly life and spiritual growth. In any interaction with a renouncer, it is difficult to draw the line between where teaching leaves off and where healing begins.

When a renouncer is regarded by disciples as a teacher, he or she becomes a Guru. Mediating between human and divine worlds, the Guru is viewed as divinity incarnate: in fact, *gurudev*, or "Guru God," is how devotees may address their teachers. Idealized as a center of sacredness, the Guru is often credited with supernatural powers such as the ability to read minds, peer into the past or future, and transform fate. Gurus may preach varying versions of scripture and religious practice. When accepted by disciples, these reformulations of religion by renouncers turned Guru become part of the ongoing dynamic of Hinduism (Dumont, 1970).

Stories are pervasive in Hindu life. Whether animal fables demonstrating morals, legends of saintly Gurus, or myths of the gods' exploits, stories are the chief medium for the transmission of Hindu faith. Folk narratives are told within families, by professional storytellers (*kathākār* or *paurānikā*), by renouncers resting during their travels, by settled Gurus to rapt disciples. The Indian psychoanalyst Sudhir Kakar (1982) has argued that traditional narratives become a Hindu tool for self-understanding:

Incorporating all possible fantasies around core human concerns — birth, love and death, body and bodily functions, relationships with parents, siblings and children — Indian myths, through a process of "creative" listening, reading or watching their enactment in folk plays and dance dramas, are readily available to the person for the lifelong task of strengthening psychic integration and maintaining continuity of the self. (p. 273)

Though stories are present in many spheres of life, their reception is influenced by the sources in which they appear. After all, there is a difference between flipping through a myth in a comic book and hearing it from the lips of a religious teacher perceived as embued with the power to instruct, bless, and heal. The intensity with which many of Swamiji's listeners interacted with his stories, I will show, emerged directly from their perception of him as a Guru.

My account of these folk narratives is in turn shaped by the complex sets of stories that constitute my own life experience. I grew up in India, with a Gujarati Brahman grandmother and American mother who were both inveterate visitors to Gurus. My grandmother conducted her piety within the framework of the Hindu tradition: she was a widow, she had grown children and was aging, and so it was perfectly natural for her to spend greater time with religious concerns (cf. Roy, 1976, pp. 134–147). My mother, on the other hand, was a Westerner who had adopted all the marks of a Hindu wife—a sari, bangles, red bindi on the forehead—and her interest in Gurus was perhaps a personal grappling with the larger historical theme of the West confronting the "mystical East." Observing both relatives in the presence of *sādhus* and Gurus, I took the phenomenon of religious figures for granted while also reflecting on it as an outsider might. The ethnography stemming from my fieldwork, then, was not just a narrative integrating discordant aspects of the self generated by graduate training and fieldwork (Crapanzano, 1977; Kondo, 1986) but also an attempt to bridge portions of myself formed in interaction with two distinct others since childhood.

When I first met Swamiji, I was about 10 years old. He lived near Nasik, the hometown of my father, and also often visited his Guru's ashram near Bombay where my mother also went. Tagging along with my pious relatives, I met him occasionally through the years and was always intrigued and delighted by the stories he told. Though other *sādhus* told stories, he seemed to bear the treasures of a Scheherazade. After attending college in America, I began to write down his stories when I dropped by to visit him: the taken-for-granted flow of events had, for me, become distanced as "culture" worthy of being recorded and studied. As a graduate student in anthropology, I formally returned with a tape recorder, notebook, and research proposal, to Swamiji's indulgent amusement.

Swamiji's repertoire of folk narratives was enormous, and he was a riveting storyteller. He mostly told these stories in what he calls his "topsy-turvy language" (*agaṛam-bagaṛam bhāshā*), which was a mixture of Kannada, his mother tongue; Marathi, the regional language; Sanskrit picked up from the scriptures; and a smattering of English—all set around a framework of colloquial Hindi. This coarse and colorful language bore idiosyncrasies that were clearly Swamiji's, yet it was also comprehensible to his visitors; either they knew one of the languages he was mixing or, better yet, they spoke "Bombay Hindi," which represents the colorful blending of regional languages and practices in this city. Swamiji's language marked him as an earthy, grass-roots *sādhu* who had mingled with people from many different regions and countries. Among his visitors were Maharashtrian peasants in dusty clothes, South Indian blue-collar workers who lived now in Nasik, Hindi-speaking professionals, members of the English-speaking urban elite, and, finally, Westerners from America, Australia, England, and France. (Mixing and matching dialects, Swamiji sometimes drolly enunciated wrong words. For example, in 1985, after a bad bout of arthritis, I heard him informing people that he had developed "arithmetic." "I myself am fine," he said, "but this body (*sharir*), it got 'arithmetic.'") In the story reproduced below, I smooth out the various languages into English, marking only English words with an asterisk: dismiss*, function*, cut* are among the words that appear here.

A STORY

Swamiji's stories were always spontaneously told. During my fieldwork, for example, there would be gaps as long as a week when no stories emerged. Just when I had given up and omitted to bring along extra tapes, Swamiji would switch back into his storytelling mode, narrating as many as five in a day. Each story tended to be closely related to the situation that evoked it. A listener's character or concerns, talk of an absent person, a discussion of related themes, or even the outright request for a story on the part of someone in the room were some of the cues inspiring Swamiji to delve into his rich repertoire of folk narratives.

For example, in September 1985, a group of about 5 or 10 people were sitting around Swamiji, a "focused gathering" (Goffman, 1961, pp. 7–10) with Swamiji as the hub connecting our joint presence and attention. Conversation, as always, was eclectic: we spoke of my brother, who was terminally ill; the shine that comes onto people's faces when they worship; how to rotate a coconut between two coins; the power of the dollar over the rupee; terrorism in the Punjab. All these diverse subjects were discussed in light of a divine presence that pervaded the world with its alternation of opposites, sequences of lives and deaths, cycles of time. Then Swamiji began telling us about a couple, Govindbhai and his wife, who had stopped by the previous night. Govindbhai was an industrialist from Gujarat. Swamiji spoke with affection of the family's lack of pretension despite their wealth. He described Govindbhai's meticulous work, the air-conditioned house, the simple food, the garden lush with fruit trees and full of birds, the warmth and hospitality extended by the family. Some of those present had met these people, but I had not. At the crack of dawn before I had arrived, they had set off for Ellora to visit the Shiva temple there.

Shortly before noon, to everyone's surprise, Govindbhai and his wife were back. They came in through the screen door looking badly shaken. One of the trucks that terrorizes the Indian highways had run right into their Mercedes. The car was smashed. Miraculously, they were alive. "Your blessings protected us," Govindbhai bowed before Swamiji. "Your blessings," his wife agreed, adjusting her sari over her bent head. They were both small people, delicate featured, fair, and wearing simple but obviously expensive clothes.

Swamiji listened to their account of their accident with concern. He asked question after question as though he too wanted to enter the experience: "Did you see the truck coming?" "How did you get back?" "Will you stay over now?" Govindbhai asked Swamiji whether he thought they should make another attempt to get to the temple, procuring a different car or hiring a taxi. Swamiji considered the plan, asked more questions to make sure they were not hurt, then agreed it might be a good thing if they returned.

"Today is Thursday, so there will be a crowd there," said Swamiji. Thursday (*guruvār*) is literally the "Guru's day"; also, we were in the sacred month of Shravan during which pilgrims flock to temples. "If you go in the evening, the crowd will have thinned. You can have audience (*darshan*) in peace."

Govindbhai and his wife nodded: yes, they would set off once again. It was almost noon and the rest of us present had risen. It was time for Swamiji to withdraw inside for lunch and rest. Though the few of us others present had been interjecting comments and exclamations, the conversation was primarily between Swamiji and this couple.

"Maybe God wants to meet you alone," Swamiji continued. His face was serious, his voice low and comforting. "There must be some reason (*kāran*) for this happening. There's always a reason."

Then, without warning, he started in on a story:

> There was a King. He had a Minister. Whatever the King said, the Minister would say, "That's good!" (*acchā huā*). Whatever happened, he would say, "It was good that it occurred."
>
> ["You might have heard this story," Swamiji looks up at Govindbhai standing at the foot of his chair, "to say that whatever happens

is good?" Govindbhai smiles, nodding. In fact, most of the rest of us have heard this story, too, for it is one of Swamiji's favorites.]

One day the King went to hunt somewhere. One of his toes was cut* off. In his assembly, he said, "One of my toes was cut* off."

"That's good," said the Minister.

"What kind of idiot is this? He's my minister and when I tell him my toe was cut off he says that's good! I'll dismiss* him," he said. "You're sacked from your job," he said.

"Very good (*bahut acchā*)," said the Minister.

"Go home!" he said [loud and abrupt].

"That's very good." [Swamiji agreeably rolls his head, voice level and resigned.] He went home.

The King remained silent. He had sent the Minister home. Things continued like this, and then in a few days the King went out hunting. The Minister wasn't around so he took the army (*senā*) with him. Night came. The King went off in one direction and the army went off in the other. The tribal people (*janglī log*) there captured the King. They captured him, and they have a custom for what they catch: the custom of offering sacrifice (*balidān*). "We've found a nice goat," they thought. They were going to offer him to their God. They have a tribal God (*janglī devatā*). They look out for a good day, those people. After finding this day, all the people of the jungle get together for a big function*. They play all kinds of instruments, then they slaughter something. After slaughtering it, everyone takes away a little consecrated food (*prasād*).

They planned this celebration (*utsav*): "Just today we found him." They planned to slaughter him. They decorated him, they played instruments. They said, "You're going to be slaughtered and offered as a sacrifice. We will offer you to our God."

There was nobody to free him. Just as goats are taken, he was being led forward, with a garland around his neck and instruments playing. He was weeping. But who would free him? He was King only in his own house. Now tribals were taking him.

There, from inside the priest (*pūjarī*) was coming forward, dancing like this:

[Swamiji sits upright to wave his right arm above his head, torso swaying. His eyes are widened and fierce, and watching him one's impulse is to shrink away. Yet all of us, knowing we are safe, are grinning instead.]

There was a big sword in his hand. He came and looked at the King. "So this is the animal (*pashu*)!"

["You understand what I mean by 'animal,' don't you?" Swamiji laughs—"Goat!" Govindbhai nods, smiling.]

He walked round* the King three times, holding the sword. The garland had already been put on. He was sprinkling water on the King. He looked at the King from top to bottom. He saw that on his foot, one toe had been cut off.

"Where did you get him from?" he asked [tone indignant].

Those people asked [voice dropping in surprise], "Why? We brought him from just over there."

"This won't do! [loud again]. He has been cut* once before. Something that's already been cut won't do for our God. It can't be offered to God. He's already been cut once. Let him go!" he said.

Once he said the King should be released, he couldn't be offered. So they set him free.

When the King was freed he thought, "My life was saved!"

[Swamiji is laughing, and the rest of us join in at this release of tension.]

He went and sat on his throne. After he sat there, he called for his Minister. He had been saved because his toe was cut off, right? So he remembered the Minister. He called that same Minister who had said that before. He gave the job back to him. "Come brother, what you said was very good. You said it was good that my toe was cut off. This and that happened to me, and it really was good that the toe had been cut off. My life was saved. Yes? This was good. And you said it was good."

[Govindbhai is called next door for a trunk call placed to Bombay. "I'll be right back," he tells Swamiji. Swamiji watches him hurrying out the door. Then after a pause, Swamiji continues for the rest of us present. He fixes his eyes on Govindbhai's wife. She sits on the women's side of the room, nodding her head.]

"You said it was good, and it *was* good. Then when I dismissed you from your job you said it was very good. What was very good for you in that? You were sent home. You said it was good that my toe was cut* off; you said it was very good that you were dismissed* from work. What's very good about losing a job? What was very good about that?"

The Minister said, "Maharaj, what happened is this: I said it was very good because you and I were always together. Your toe was cut* off. We would have wandered there together. Those people let you go because your toe* was cut off. But my toe isn't cut* off. They would have let you go but caught hold of me. I would have been offered as the sacrifice. Because you sent me away my life was saved too. That's why I said it was very good."

[A pleased murmur of laughter rises through the room.]

Both of them were saved! [Swamiji beams.] It's good, it's very good. Whatever God does, there's always some reason or the other.

With the story over, Swamiji returned to his earlier conjecture that the accident would allow the couple to visit the temple in the evening when the crowds had abated. Govindbhai returned from the telephone call and Swamiji quickly summarized the end of the story for him. Swamiji had scooted forward to the foot of his armchair and had lifted a tray of bananas in his lap. Like the tribals anticipating the distribution of consecrated food (*prasād*) in the story, each of us came forward to receive a banana. "It's all the Lord's will," said Govindbhai, accepting the fruit with cupped palms, left hand cradling the right. Then we all trooped out to leave Swamiji alone for his lunch and afternoon rest.

This folktale, which Swamiji referred to as "That's Good, Very Good," is one told in many parts of India.[1] Indian friends from Punjab and Madhya Pradesh said they had encountered it in their childhoods; tracking down the constituent motifs I found a variant of the story in a collection from Tamil Nadu (Natesa Sastri, 1908, pp. 74–76). Swamiji himself retold the story differently on different occasions, collapsing or extending sequences for different audiences. For example, when a man from a royal family was present, Swamiji emphasized the actions of the king. "Now it's the habit of kings to go hunting," he said with a grin. Or when a woman ascetic was present whose Guru was known for stirring up ecstatic experiences, Swamiji elaborated on the theme of the priest's frenzied dancing to the point of parody. The text, then, like all folk narratives, was malleable to the teller's concerns and perceptions of his audience.

As is the case in many of Swamiji's stories (and the wider cycle of stories featuring an exchange between kings and ministers), the minister acts as the wise interpreter of events. Structurally the minister matches the holy man who stands to the side of worldly affairs watching, advising, and never becoming ruffled. In telling the story Swamiji was acting out the part of the minister, assuring the listener—who stood in the position of the king—that whatever had happened undoubtedly carried meaning in the larger scheme of things. Though Swamiji repeated this folk narrative on a number of occasions, the thread connecting all his retellings was that someone present had undergone a loss of some sort: not a serious loss (as in the case of death, when I never heard Swamiji tell this story) but some frustrating or frightening loss that had left the person intact. Although acknowledging that life brought losses, the story also set these losses within a framework of wider meaning, emphasizing that everything occurred under the auspices of a Divine Will. The story forced listeners to reflect on what good might have come out of a mishap; for example, even if the car was smashed, the couple was still alive and could reach the temple at a more peaceful time. Their tale of a terrible accident became transformed into a narrative of God's grace (though, in saying that Swamiji's blessings had saved them, they were already open to a version of their accident that emphasized religious power). Swamiji could, of course, have just assured them that things would have a meaning in the long run, but by couching this assurance in a narrative, he drew listeners into the story line and evoked the emotions of loss, fear, and final resolution. When he so triumphantly finished, "Both of them were saved!" he seemed to be voicing the relief that we all felt on seeing Govindbhai and his wife live to tell their tale. Walking out into the sunlit terrace outside Swamiji's door, I recognized that the telling of this story had been therapeutic not just for the couple but for all the rest of us who had been shaken by their narrow escape.

FEELINGS AND STRATEGIES IN STORYTELLING

Folklorists have recognised that accomplished tellers transform folk narratives into idiosyncratic, artistic creations (e.g., Azadovskii, 1974; Degh, 1969; Ortutay, 1972). Performance theorists have underlined the insight that oral stories emerge in the interaction between teller and audience in particular situations (Bauman, 1977). Yet rarely in the folklore literature have tellers themselves spoken out about their strategies in transforming a story around their apprehension of subjectivities in the audience.

"It's hardly that I make up the stories," Swamiji had said several weeks before I recorded this narrative. I had just complimented him on the beauty of another tale. He ducked my compliment by pointing to tradition. "I only tell what's come to us from the past. This happened, then that happened. I don't make anything up. I just tell what's already there."

"But as you tell a story, don't you change it?" I asked. "Like you —"

"A person tells stories according to the feeling (*bhāvanā*) he has," asserted Swamiji. I murmured assent and the other onlookers who understood Hindi nodded. Swamiji stopped and peered at me through his spectacles, "What were you saying just now? I interrupted you."

"I was just thinking," I said, "it seems to me that every time you tell a story you change it a little so it includes the people sitting there."

"According to their feelings!" said Swamiji, extending a hand to the assembled group: a young celibate ascetic wearing ochre clothes, two slim French women in saris, a male college student in terylene pants, a hotel keeper in a starched white *dhotī*, an American hypnotherapist wearing a T-shirt and lungi with a ponytail at the back of his balding head, a little girl in a frock, and me, the sari-wearing ethnographer.

"When you tell a story," Swamiji said, "You should look at the situation and tell it. Then it turns out well. If you just tell any story any time, it's not really good. You must consider the time and shape the story so it's right. All stories are told for some purpose."

Bhāvanā is a Hindi word, and among its range of meanings are feelings, wish, fantasy, idea, mood. *Bhāvanā* can refer to the overall sense exuded by a person — his or her gestalt — not unlike the ethos of a particular culture that an anthropologist strains to grasp. Rifling through my fieldnotes, I lit upon another conversation in which Swamiji had spoken about feelings. Someone had brought him a magazine with an article about a prominent Hindu Guru and his activities in America. Unable to read because of his near-blindness, Swamiji was examining the photographs through a glass. He paused at a picture that showed the Guru embracing a female disciple. Such activity, he observed, was just fine for America, but in India people would object because a *sādhu* should be both celibate and ascetic. While others looking on clucked with disapproval, I asked whether this might not just be fatherly love. "Just look at the feeling!" Swamiji said, motioning with the magnifying glass. "That's not the feeling between a father and a daughter."

Then he continued, locating the particulars of this picture into a general rule of thumb for life. "When you look at a picture, get a sense of the feeling. When a person comes before you, look at the feeling. The feeling given off by a picture or person is very important in forming an opinion."

Feelings, then, appeared to be Swamiji's measure of other subjectivities. Yet the self that surfaced in feelings was not the Self to which Swamiji most often referred. Hindu theology postulates a pervasive divine Self (*param ātman*) that appears in each person as a life spark (*jīv ātman*) (cf. Bharati, 1985; Paranjpe, 1987). This is the indwelling divine Self that ascetics have renounced the world to realize: indivisible and indestructible, it is a manifestation of the unity underlying the many life forms in the world. As Swamiji explained, drawing on a traditional analogy, a drop of water is part of the ocean, and its difference is only illusory. Rising from the ocean as vapor, it takes many forms (in rain, in sap, in milk, in urine, in a stream, in a river) before it rejoins the sea. Similarly, a soul is reborn through countless incarnations before being reunited with the larger divine Self. The goal of religious practice is to shed desires and burn off the effects of past actions (*karma*) that are blocking the perception of the indwelling divinity. The self that is swayed by feelings, that is transformed through transactions (Marriott, 1977) is, in Swamiji's religious worldview, secondary to the divine Self. As Swamiji said, a Guru helped people in their suffering by reminding them their true identity was divine. The desires and frustrations experienced were part of the illusion (*māyā*) of separateness, they were a "play" (*lila*) that masqueraded as reality but had no enduring substance.

If reality is an illusion, it is on par with a fictional tale. The feelings diagnosed in listeners are of the same powerful yet fleeting substance as the feelings accompanying the adventures of characters within a narrative frame (feelings dramatized in Swamiji's voice, in his actions, on his face). Swamiji's — and other religious teachers' — inveterate telling of stories appears to me to be another means of expressing the message that the phenomenal world experienced by the mutable individual self is unreal. Life unfolds, as stories do, but rather than identifying with its changing movements, it should be witnessed from the perspective of the unchanging divine Self. Yet listeners who scanned these stories for counsel did not appear to start with a distanced philosophical approach: rather, in directly identifying with these stories as commentaries moored in what they had done, would do, or should ideally choose, they were led toward a view of their own lives as composed of stories that could be observed. In constructing an alternative reality that shed light on the here-and-now, each story bequeathed a perspective outside the flow of particulars: a point of view from which to evaluate experience. To illustrate this point, let us turn to the people who were assembled around Swamiji's deck chair as stories were being told.

LISTENERS AND THEIR FEELINGS

Following developments since the close of the last century, Gurus today are best viewed in terms of a world system: many have been abroad gathering disciples, foreign disciples have come to India, and, finally, Indian disciples have emigrated to different parts of the world while maintaining their allegiance to a particular Guru. Around Swamiji the complexity of equating "Hindu" with "Indian" was well illustrated. The people who visited him were not only from different castes, classes, and regions of India; they also came from abroad. Though Guru Purnima — the full moon sacred to the Guru — brought crowds of devotees flooding in to pay their respects and receive blessings, on an average day there were rarely more than 10 or 15 visitors present in Swamiji's narrow room with its bright altar, pale green walls, and green linoleum.

Since Swamiji had no formal ashram to house disciples for extended periods, those who wanted to stay had to arrange their own accommodations in the area, often with other disciples. They would then drop in for chanting at dawn and dusk and for Swamiji's hours of *darshan* (audience) in the morning and afternoon. Stories could emerge at any time when Swamiji was interacting with visitors—for example, just as a chant had ended and people were receiving *prasād*—but they mainly unfolded at a leisurely pace during the hours of *darshan*. When I set out to interview people on what they made of Swamiji's stories, I tried to ambush them by the door after *darshan* or to meet them in their homes. Though these listeners came from a variety of backgrounds, I treat them as a single "interpretive community" (Fish, 1980) because they all saw Swamiji as a Guru with access to higher truths.

The relationship between a Guru and disciple is deeply therapeutic (Carstairs, 1965; Kakar, 1982; Neki, 1973). Since the Guru is viewed as a conduit for divine grace, his or her very presence is comforting. Also, since most Gurus' discourse emphasizes that suffering is inevitable, individuals are assured that they are not alone in their misfortune. Most important, Gurus displace attention from personal suffering by speaking of larger, cosmic realities and reassuring people that their true identity is divine. These teachings, as we have seen, are often phrased in terms of stories.

Because of the idealization of a Guru, his or her very presence is felt to be elevating, whether or not there are words exchanged or instructive stories told. Many of Swamiji's disciples reported that they were deeply moved in his company. Colonel Khanna, a retired officer, said in brisk English, "Although he has not told me in any particular way, 'Do this, do that,' but you *feel*. I go to ask him something, but when I meet him, I forget to ask him that. I mean, that's the least important thing: speaking. I mean his presence itself inspires you for a better living. Isn't it?" "Datta-treya," who is British, wrote in his journal (that he later lent me to read and cite), "When sitting with Swamiji, an invisible current seems to be at work which consoles and pacifies the heart, and eases worries and strain." Or when I asked "Sarasvati," also British, why she sat with Swamiji when conversation rolled on in Hindi, she said, "If I can't understand his words, I can only go on the feelings that I have when I'm with him, right? The peace and tranquility."

Other listeners linked feelings with stories when they described Swamiji's demeanor as a tale was being told. Champa, an enterprising village woman who ran a cold-drink stall, located the effect of Swamiji's stories in the delight he exuded. "He tells the story with happiness on his face," she said in Hindi. "Because he tells it laughing and happy (*hansī khushī se*), because he tells it with affection, the story has an effect on people." Or Isabel, a French nurse, said in her accented English, "Swamiji is so much inside the story. He is *inside* it. His body, his words, everything. He is so happy to tell us a story. . . . Then, he is not one character. He is everyone in the story. When he says a man is sleeping, he becomes that man. Or a bullock. Or a king. He *becomes* each character in the story." In short, a teller's own participation in a story makes the emotions of the characters seem real and draws rapt listeners into the narrative space. As a skillful teller becomes each character through actions and intonation, members of the audience are guided through a sequence of feelings.

As the anthropologist Michelle Rosaldo has observed, "Feelings are not substances to be discovered in our blood but social practices organized by stories that we both enact and tell" (1984, p. 143). Indeed, many of Swamiji's listeners felt that the folk narratives he told spoke directly to the stories and associated feelings they were playing out in their own lives. Sahadeva, a dairy farmer, said, speaking Hindi, "Through stories he tells us about our own feelings. If you've made a mistake on the road, he'll tell a story about it." The road (*rāstā*) could refer to Sahadeva's moral path but also to his perpetual travels between Bombay and central Maharashtra. "If you've done good deeds and said good things, his story will repeat what you did. You feel he was with you. He tells you how to behave and what not to do. His stories are completely advice.*"

Sahadeva's interpretation of the stories told by Swamiji illustrates how a Guru can be seen as either personally omniscient or in touch with an omniscient divinity that inspires his or her words. So even if Swamiji had not been present or had not been told about something that had happened in a disciple's life, he was still invested with the power to comment on it. He was also believed by some to prophesy the future. Manjuben, a woman visiting from Gujarat, said, "His stories are grand and full of morals. . . . It *all* comes to pass." Disciples, in short, seemed to interpret these stories as guidance for living. Gulelal, an American Jew, said, "These are all lesson stories." Lakshmi Amma, a housewife, simply stated (in a Hindi akin to Swamiji's), "He tells us stories so we can change our lives." And Damle Seth, another farmer, said, "He understands what's in someone's mind and tells a story to show them the right path (*mārg*). . . . If you don't listen to what he's saying, you can forget your path. You fall into difficulties. Then if you go back to him and say, 'I had troubles,' he doesn't say, 'I told you so.' Rather, he tells another story."

How is it possible that such a motley array of listeners, male and female, Indian and Western, could all feel that the stories carried personal meanings for them? The answer lies in the ambiguity and multivocal form of the story: by using a story rather than a straightforward assertion, Swamiji allowed different people to read in their own perspectives, to engage with the text in their own way (cf. Jackson, 1982; Bruner & Gorfain, 1984). This interpretive variation was recognized by most listeners and was most eloquently expressed by Nathu Dada, the buck-toothed barber. He explained, "People extract meanings according to their *samskaras*" (*samskara* in this context can variously be translated as inner refinement, rite of passage, or effects of a past life). Nathu Dada went on to draw a poetic analogy: Just as people filled pots of different sizes from the Ganges River, he said, so different people took away meanings according to their own capacity.

This acceptance of interpretive variation in terms of the listeners' inner states is widespread in Hindu thought. A Marathi proverb that Swamiji cited, for example, asserts, "Where the feeling, there the God" (*ticche bhāv, tikre dev*). Or the Tulsi Ramayana bears a much-quoted Hindi line, "According to the feeling within him [or her], each saw the form of the Lord" (*jinhā ke rahi bhāvanā jaisi/ prabhu mūrati tinhā dekhi taisi*) (Hess, 1983, p. 186). Feelings, then, direct the choice of stories told as well as their reception.

THERAPEUTIC STORIES

In cultures of the sort that anthropologists have traditionally studied it is not to psychotherapists that individuals have turned when the coherence of the self is threatened by physical pain and mental distress. Rather, they have approached people like Swamiji: Gurus, shamans, witchdoctors, diviners, singers, and priests. The analogy between the traditional healer and the psychotherapist is by now well illustrated in anthropological literature (e.g., Frank, 1961; Kiev, 1964; Kleinman, 1980), but I will single out Claude Lévi-Strauss' "The Effectiveness of Symbols" (1963) for discussion, as this is the single most influential article on the therapeutic aspects of narrative in the anthropological literature.

Lévi-Strauss starts with a text sung by a Cuna shaman in Panama to a woman undergoing a painful childbirth. The song relates how a midwife summons the shaman and how he marshals tutelary spirits to rescue the soul of the suffering woman from the grips of powerful Muu, who presides over fertility and who has gone awry. The description of the shaman's attack on Muu through white tissue to an arena covered with blood—a "dark whirlpool"—is interpreted by Lévi-Strauss as an entry into the uterus. Through the song, then, the shaman symbolically manipulates the organ and effects a cure. Having convincingly presented the Cuna case, Lévi-Strauss goes on to compare the shaman to a psychoanalyst. He points out that both bring a patient's unconscious conflicts and resistances (that may have bodily corollaries) to the conscious level, allowing for a healing resolution. Through transference, both the psychoanalyst and shaman become protagonists in the narrative that will allow healing to occur, creating a relation in which the patient can restore and clarify an unexpressed or confused initial situation. Yet despite these broad similarities there is an important difference. A psychoanalyst *listens* to a personal "myth" supplied by a patient, whereas a shaman *tells* a collective "myth," speaking for the patient. Lévi-Strauss concludes by arguing that structural parallel between the narrative and the conflict serves to endow inchoate individual experience with form and meaning in both cases. Healing, in short, occurs through an analogy in narrative form.

Yet is the oft-cited distinction between the listening therapist and the orating traditional healer, between individual histories and collective myths, really so clearcut? Mulling over this article in reference to his own psychoanalytic practice and also research among traditional Hindu healers, Sudhir Kakar (1982) has pointed out that psychoanalysis itself operates in terms of the "collective myth" of shared cultural assumptions and that traditional healers do indeed evoke individual histories before dispensing treatment (pp. 114–116). Swamiji, for example, did not tell just *any* story to Govindbhai and his wife; this was chosen specifically in response to their narrative of the accident. Kakar also disagrees with Lévi-Strauss's emphasis on form over content, an objection that would seem to be reinforced by Swamiji and his listeners' articulation of the importance of the feelings evoked by a story.

An excursion into the growing literature on narrative generated by psychoanalysts and psychotherapists of various persuasions also reveals that the supposed rift between Western and traditional healing is not altogether unbridged. Other Freudian analysts now admit that they listen to their patients' free associations in terms of narrative structures of human development and the narrative of analytic process as proposed by Freud. By offering interpretations, they argue, an analyst retells a patient's scattered stories, until there emerges a new, jointly authored story featuring a more coherent and aware self (Sarbin, 1986; Schafer, 1981, 1983). What is at stake is less plodding historical truth than narrative truth that can artfully arrange and encompass the facts of a patient's history (Spence, 1982).

This approach emphasizes the stories told by a patient, even if in dialogue with an analyst. Additionally, discussions of the therapeutic power of storytelling have shifted from a patient's *telling* stories to a patient's *listening* to or reading them, with the therapist taking on the role of teller or bibliographer. So another eminent Freudian, Bruno Bettelheim (1977), writes that fairytales are really about childhood dramas within the family, and that by reading these stories children can project and resolve their conflicts. Joanne Bernstein (1976) has advocated "bibliotherapy" for grieving children; that is, presenting them with books that tell stories of other children encountering death. Richard Gardner (1971) has proposed a "mutual storytelling technique" in which imaginative stories are elicited from children (who pretend they are on a television program for which the therapist serves as host); then, after decoding the metaphorical statement of the child's condition precipitated in the story, the therapist retells the tale with a different resolution. Similarly, the "hypnotherapist" Milton Erickson and his followers tell stories to express metaphorically what they perceive to be a patient's condition. These stories, however, are neither traditional nor recast from a patient's narrative but rather tend to be personal creations drawn from the therapist's imagination or experience (Barker, 1985).

Yet there are also therapists who advocate that patients should be told the folk narratives that have traditionally been the domain of religious teachers in diverse traditions. In *Oriental Stories as Tools in Psychotherapy* (1982), Nossrat Peseschkian, an Iranian emigree to Germany, includes many Islamic, Sufi, and Baha'i teaching tales along with accounts of the therapeutic situations in which he drew upon a particular story and the reflections it provoked in his patient. Similarly, Carl Fellner (1976), a family therapist, employs traditional Hasidic or Sufi teaching stories. The ambiguity of these stories, Fellner argues, allows each member present to orient himself or herself to the story and the problem differently. His account of the ideal storytelling therapist could well be a description of Swamiji!

> He has not expressed an opinion, he has just told a story. However, in so doing, he has commented indirectly on several levels of meaning about an ongoing situation, and he has seeded a number of ideas, set in motion a number of forces. It is now up to the individuals themselves to make their own discoveries, their own interpretation, and thus move towards perceiving relationships in new ways, towards "tasting" new realities. (p. 429)

Many of the people who visit Swamiji straddle two worlds themselves: they are aware of both traditional healing and psychotherapy, and from this vantage they themselves professed a similarity. So "Prabhu," an American hypnotherapist (who aside from listening to Swamiji's stories also used them in his own practice), praised storytelling as persuasive and nonconfrontational, saying, "A *sādhu* is like a therapist, because he doesn't change anything but tells stories so people can recognize their own outlook and make their own choices." Similarly, Dr. Khanna, the colonel's wife, said, speaking convent-accented English, "He really sympathizes. So you unburden yourself. In Western words, it's as though you're talking to a psychiatrist. It's just like that. He acts as your sounding board, then gives you correct advice. He tells you to accept what you get."

This advice, "Accept what you get," echoes the moral of "That's Good, Very Good." The extent to which some of Swamiji's listeners accept the view put forward in "That's Good" is indicated by Nathu Maharaj, the barber who later observed, as we sat in his garret crowded with smoke and grandchildren, "This world is a good place, even when there are difficulties. One should understand that it's a good place. Otherwise you become sad. What's meant to happen will happen." Or as both "Prabhu" and Mr. Karnad, the retired journalist, said, collapsing the story reproduced here into an adage much as a fan is slapped slim, "Everything is for the best." This view could be interpreted as false consciousness, masking imperfections of the present and so defusing the impetus for active change: in this case, the story would be morally debilitating. However, in my understanding of the way this particular story was used and interpreted, it seems that the attitude of acceptance it held was often positive. By straining to comprehend what good could emerge from a mishap, listeners reflected on the past in such a way that numbing bitterness was transformed into positive action for the future.

My mother also spoke of therapeutic aspects of interaction with a *sādhu*. "Everyone comes with their secrets," she said in an accent that blended an American upbringing with years spent in India. "A *sannyāsī* (renouncer) acts also as a psychiatrist. People tell them things they can't tell anyone. And very often, *sannyāsīs* are surrounded by some really weird people. Swamiji has great compassion for them — even a black marketer, a racketeer — because they have told him their innermost fears. Own fears, own innermost reactions; and he has compassion for that person. The person has opened up to him the dark areas of his soul that he will not have opened up to others."

The postmodern world is rapidly shrinking with the cross-cultural flow of communication. Today it is not just Western academics who have the vantage point to comment on the similarities and differences between Western psychotherapy and traditional forms of healing. A holy man like Swamiji, with access to radio, television, and the testimonies of foreign visitors, can himself draw an analogy between the two forms of healing. One September morning in 1985 I was startled to hear Swamiji holding forth on how a *sādhu*, or holy man, could be compared to a "psycho-logishta."

"A person is off-balance," Swamiji said, "and what a psychologist* does is lead them back. The psychologist* sits listening sympathetically, and a person tells the story of his life. Through telling this, people recollect the moment when they went off-balance. They understand the mind and the consequences of their life on the mind. Then they are freed. They are cured.

"A *sādhu* also cures," Swamiji went on, adjusting his glasses, "but not by making people tell of their lives. A *sādhu* cures with love (*prem*), faith in God (*shraddhā*), and trust in people (*vishvās*). People's minds are taken off their troubles and they are freed. All a *sādhu* says is 'worship God.' The worship of God gives you a peace greater than anything else. You eat, but then you have a bad stomach. You give money, but then when you don't, people bear a grudge. Children love you if you speak kindly, but when you get mad, they hate you. The only thing that is constant is the worship of God. It has no ill effects. If you become addicted to worshiping God, all other problems or addictions a therapist cures fall away by themselves."

In other words, whereas a therapist evokes a retelling of personal experience, a *sādhu* ideally extends positive emotions—love, faith, trust—and reminds individuals of a divine self that transcends the vicissitudes of ongoing experience. When Swamiji spoke of worshiping God (*bhagavān*), he did not just mean through ritual. As he explained in other contexts, God was in all people, and so to act with kindness and responsibility in the world was an important form of worship. Though Swamiji did not directly mention stories as a part of a *sādhu's* healing, the feelings evoked and transformed by storytelling, of which he and his disciples spoke earlier, are clearly set within the framework of these positive emotions. Also, like the exhortation to "worship God" amid the ebbs and flows of life, stories point to alternative and psychically liberating realities.

CONCLUSION

This essay has examined a situation in which teaching and healing inter-twine around the use of traditional stories. I have drawn on the testimonies of a religious storyteller and his listeners to demonstrate the importance of feeling in the choice of a story told as well as the imaginative engagement of listeners. The practice of storytelling by traditional healers (who are often teachers) has been compared to the use of narrative in contemporary Western psychotherapy. I would like to finish by reiterating that whether personal or collective, stories construct versions of reality that endow experience with meaning. Stories, I believe, both teach and heal by encouraging individuals to observe and reflect on the personal self rather than to blindly identify with it.

NOTES

Acknowledgments.   Though I have known Swamiji since 1970, the concentrated fieldwork on which this essay is based was conducted between June and September 1983 and July to October 1985. I am grateful for a National Science Foundation Graduate Fellowship, a U.C. Berkeley Graduate Humanities Research Grant, a Robert H. Lowie Fellowship, and a Charlotte W. Newcombe Dissertation Writing Fellowship. I am also grateful to Eytan Bercovich, Maya Brewer, Claudia Henrion, Smadar Lavie, Donald Lopez, and Burke Rochford for their comments on an earlier draft of this essay.

1. This is a well-known folktale with distribution in both North and South India. The following Indic motifs are present: N 25.2 minister always says, "It is for the best when anything happens"; P 12.13 king quick to anger; N 771 king lost on hunt has adventures: V 11.9 sacrifice to deity; V 14 sacrifice found must be without a blemish; P 111 banished minister found indispensable and recalled; J 21,52.8 nothing happens that does not work out for one's good (Thompson & Balys, 1958).

REFERENCES

Azadovskii, Mark. (1974). *A Siberian tale teller* (James Dow, Trans.). Austin: University of Texas Press.

Barker, Philip. (1985). *Using metaphors in psychotherapy.* New York: Brunner/ Magel.

Bauman, Richard. (1977). *Verbal art as performance.* Rowley, MA: Newbury House.

Bernstein, Joanne E. (1975). Helping young children to cope with acute grief: A bibliotherapy approach. In V. R. Pine et al. (Eds.), *Acute grief and the funeral* (pp. 274–280). Springfield, IL: C. C. Thomas.

Bettelheim, Bruno. (1977). *The uses of enchantment: The meaning and importance of fairytales.* New York: Alfred A. Knopf.

Bharati, Agehananda. (1985). The self in Hindu thought and action. In A. J. Marsella, G. De Vos, & F. L. K. Hsu (Eds.), *Culture and self: Asian and Western perspectives* (pp. 185–230). New York and London: Tavistock.

Bruner, Edward M. (1986). Ethnography as narrative. In E. M. Bruner & V.

Turner (Eds.), *The anthropology of experience* (pp. 139–155). Urbana: University of Illinois Press.

Bruner, Edward M., & Gorfain, Phyllis. (1984). Dialogical narration and the paradoxes of Masada. In E. M. Bruner (Ed.), *Text, play and story* (pp. 56–79). Washington, DC: American Ethnological Society.

Bruner, Jerome. (1986). *Actual minds, possible worlds.* Cambridge, MA: Harvard University Press.

Bruner, Jerome. (1987). Life as narrative. *Social Research, 54,* 11–32.

Carstairs, G. Morris. (1965). Cultural elements in response to treatment. In A. V. S. de Reuch & P. Porter (Eds.), *CIBA symposium on transcultural psychiatry* (pp. 169–175). London: J. A. Churchill.

Clifford, James. (1986). On ethnographic allegory. In J. Clifford & G. Marcus (Eds.), *Writing culture* (pp. 98–121). Berkeley: University of California Press.

Coles, Robert. (1989). *The call of stories: Teaching and the moral imagination.* Boston: Houghton Mifflin.

Crapanzano, Vincent. (1977). On the writing of ethnography. *Dialectical Anthropology, 2,* 69–73.

Crites, Stephen D. (1971). The narrative quality of experience. *Journal of the American Academy of Religion, 39,* 291–311.

Degh, Linda. (1969). *Folktales and society: Storytelling in a Hungarian peasant community* (E. M. Schlossberger, Trans.). Bloomington: Indiana University Press.

Dumont, Louis. (1970). World renunciation in Indian religions. In *Religion/politics and history in India* (pp. 33–61). The Hague and Paris: Mouton.

Fellner, Carl. (1976). The use of teaching stories in conjoint family therapy. *Family Process, 15,* 427–431.

Fish, Stanley. (1980). *Is there a text in this class? The authority of interpretive communities.* Cambridge, MA: Harvard University Press.

Frank, Jerome. (1961). *Persuasion and healing: A comparative study of psychotherapy.* Baltimore: Johns Hopkins University Press.

Gardner, Richard. (1971). *Therapeutic communication with children: The mutual storytelling technique.* New York: Jason Aronson.

Geertz, Clifford. (1983). Blurred genres: The refiguration of social thought. In *Local knowledge* (pp. 19–35). New York: Basic Books.

Goffman, Erving. (1961). *Encounters: Two studies in the sociology of interaction.* Indianapolis, IN: Bobbs Merrill.

Goldberg, Michael. (1982). *Theology and narrative: A critical introduction.* Nashville, TN: Abingdon.

Hess, Linda. (1983). Ram lila: The audience experience. In M. Thiel-Horstmann (Ed.), *Bhakti in current research, 1979–1982* (pp. 171–196). Berlin: Dietrich Reimer.

Hoffman, John C. (1986). *Law, freedom and story: The role of narrative in therapy, society and faith.* Waterloo, Ontario, Canada: Wilfred Laurier University Press.

Jackson, Michael. (1982). *Allegories of the wilderness: ethics and ambiguity in Kuranko narrative.* Bloomington: Indiana University Press.

Kakar, Sudhir. (1982). *Shamans, mystics and doctors: A psychological enquiry into India and its healing traditions.* New York: Alfred A. Knopf.

Kiev, Ari (Ed.). (1964). *Magic, faith and healing: Studies in primitive psychiatry today.* New York: Free Press.

Kleinman, Arthur. (1980). *Patients and healers in the context of culture.* Berkeley: University of California Press.

Kondo, Dorinne. (1986). Dissolution and reconstitution of self. *Cultural Anthropology, 2,* 74–88.

Lévi-Strauss, Claude. (1963). The effectiveness of symbols. In *Structural anthropology* (pp. 186–205). New York: Basic Books.

MacIntyre, Alasdair. (1981). *After virtue.* Notre Dame, IN: University of Notre Dame Press.

Marriott, McKim. (1977). Hindu transactions: diversity without dualism. In B. Kapferer (Ed.), *Transaction and meaning* (pp. 109–142). Philadelphia: Institute for the Study of Human Issues.

Mink, Louis. (1978). Narrative form as a cognitive instrument. In R. Canary & H. Kozicki (Eds.), *The writing of history* (pp. 129–149). Madison: University of Wisconsin Press.

Narayan, Kirin. (1989). *Storytellers, saints, and scoundrels: Folk narrative in Hindu religious teaching.* Philadelphia: University of Pennsylvania Press.

Natesa Sastri, S. M. (1908). *Indian folk tales.* Madras: Guardian Press.

Neki, J. S. (1973). Guru-chela relationship: The possibility of a psychotherapeutic paradigm. *American Journal of Orthopsychiatry, 43,* 755–766.

Ortutay, Gyula. (1972). Fedics relates tales. In I. Butyav, (Trans.), *Hungarian folklore: Essays* (pp. 225–285). Budapest: Akademiai Kiada.

Paranjpe, Ananda C. (1987). The self beyond cognition, action, pain and pleasure: An Eastern perspective. In K. Yardley & T. Honess (Eds.), *Self and identity: Psychosocial perspectives* (pp. 27–40). New York: John Wiley.

Peseschkian, Nossrat. (1982). *Oriental stories as tools in psychotherapy: The merchant and the parrot.* Berlin: Springer-Verlag.

Polkinghorne, Donald. (1988). *Narrative knowing and the human sciences.* Albany: State University of New York Press.

Ricoeur, Paul. (1984). *Time and narrative.* Chicago: University of Chicago Press.

Rosaldo, Michelle. (1984). Toward an anthropology of self and feeling. In R. Schweder & R. A. Le Vine (Eds.), *Culture theory* (pp. 137–157). Cambridge: Cambridge University Press.

Rosaldo, Renato. (1989). *Culture and truth.* Boston: Beacon Press.

Roy, Manisha. (1976). *Bengali women.* Chicago and London: University of Chicago Press.

Sarbin, Theodore. (Ed.). (1986). *Narrative psychology: The storied nature of human conduct.* New York: Praeger.

Schafer, Roy. (1981). *Narrative actions in psychoanalysis.* Worcester, MA: Clark University Press.

Schafer, Roy. (1983). *The analytic attitude.* New York: Basic Books.

Spence, Donald P. (1982). *Narrative truth and historical truth: Meaning and interpretation in psychoanalysis.* New York: W. W. Norton.

Thompson, Stith, & Balys, Jonas. (1958). *The oral tales of India.* Bloomington: Indiana University Press.

White, Hayden V. (1973). *Metahistory: The historical imagination in nineteenth century Europe.* Baltimore: Johns Hopkins University Press.

White, Hayden V. (1981). *The content of the form: Narrative discourse and historical representation.* Baltimore: Johns Hopkins University Press.

8

The Stranger's Story
Who Calls and Who Answers?

VIRGINIA SHABATAY

Virginia Shabatay, Ph.D., lives with her husband in San Diego, California, and teaches in the English Department at Grossmount College. Dr. Shabatay has taught at several colleges around the country, and for one year at Universiti Kebangsaan in Kuala Lumpur, Malaysia. For the past several years she has incorporated the thought of Martin Buber into her work. At present, Dr. Shabatay is writing a book on "The Stranger's Story."

The experience of being a stranger is a primary concern of many educators, writers, and social scientists. We all experience being strangers at different times, and we become aware that strangerhood has many nuances. We can be strangers by being in a new land; we can be strangers by virtue of any difference: physical, psychological, social, cultural, religious, political, racial, personal. One can be a stranger by remaining within oneself or by being at odds with the world.

Whatever the situation, the stranger is one who lives on the edge between her unique world and the world of others that she has just entered. The stranger, by her presence, asks something of us: she asks that her heritage or her condition be respected. This requires that those with whom she comes in contact enter into a dialogical relationship with her. Real dialogue allows for the uniqueness of the other to be brought forth. Such openness to differences is an essential component of caring relationships like that of teacher and student or counselor and client.

We may first ask ourselves the following: what is a stranger? And when? What makes strangers and how do we treat strangers? With what conflicts must they deal? What problems are exposed by the stranger? Why are strangers a problem for our world? The stranger has often been the character in literature who is the prophet in disguise or the wise person who has something to reveal to us if we pay attention. In many fables and stories, when the stranger is ignored, destruction or failure ensues.

The community can be redeemed by the stranger who presents himself in all his otherness and who asks by his presence to be met. Because the stranger is often at the heart of conflict, he can reveal to us a way through that conflict. The stranger lives with a feeling of not belonging, of being different, of having lost a sense of self, of being alienated from God. How the community responds to the stranger will either alienate one from the other or will serve in the work toward peace.

How do those of us in the helping professions discover the strangers among us? How can we develop sensitive, caring relationships with those who feel set apart? Whether working in classroom settings, in group therapy sessions, at organizational meetings, or with families, we meet as persons with varying backgrounds and with perhaps little information about the history and culture from which the others in the group come. We bring certain attitudes to those whom we don't know: suspicion, mistrust, caution, and bias, or trust, openness, and welcome. Stories allow us to break through barriers and to share in another's experience; they warm us. Like a rap on the window, they call us to attention. Through literature and people's stories we discover a variety of situations that make people feel like strangers. We discover what strangers have to teach us.

It has been said that literature is psychology done gracefully. That is true as long as we don't impose psychological theory upon the literature. What shines through the stories we read and the stories we tell reveals, in Maurice Friedman's terms, "an image of the human" (1974, p. 4). This image is that wholeness of the human that is manifested in the story. Literature retains a quality of the concrete and the unique, and thus reveals what it means to be human. Stories abound with dilemmas faced by strangers and conflicts created for others by them. We have only to look at selected works by Albert Camus, Richard Rodriguez, Elie Wiesel, and Richard Wright, to name but a few, to discover who the stranger is.

Finally, why is it important not to deny a stranger? If we want to live in a world that will not destroy itself, the stranger has to be drawn in. We see where xenophobia takes us: it belongs with those failures of the human spirit that lead us into wars. Perhaps Elie Wiesel, recipient of the 1986 Nobel Peace Prize, more than any other writer, brings together the connection between the way we perceive and treat strangers and the violence we unleash on one another. When we read about the threat of a nuclear war, we might not connect the relationship between war and our attitude toward strangers, but as soon as the two are juxtaposed, we do. In the preface to Camus's *Neither Victims nor Executioners* (1972), Robert Pickus writes that "we can count on injustice in human affairs; on privilege, exploitation, and violence. Violence, which in its ability to turn a living man into a thing, inflicts the final unalterable injustice" (p. 7). One of the many aspects of being a stranger is that we turn or are turned into someone who does not count, someone who can be destroyed directly or indirectly.

The way we treat strangers reveals as much about us as it does about them. Meeting the stranger requires of us that we respond in one way or another: with indifference, disdain, and suspicion, or with interest, friendship, and openness. Further, the stranger may represent that which is very different, and how we respond to his or her distinctiveness affects not only the personal realm but the social and political as well. How we respond is a reflection, also, of our ethical and religious views and commitments.

Strangers may ask of us to honor their history and their customs. They may ask us for justice when they have been denied their rights. Communities that fear strangers tend to become communities of affinity. Such communities are "based on what people feel they have in common — race, sex, religion, nationality, politics, a common formula, a common creed" (Friedman, 1983, p. 135). Such a group suppresses difference, dialogue, personhood. These are sacrificed in order to gain the security of allegiance, a "likemindedness." Strangers could be guests of such a community, but if they wished to become members, they would have to mimic the ways of the others.

Friedman defines real communities as communities of otherness that allow divergent points of view:

> What makes community real is people finding themselves in a common situation — a situation which they approach in different ways yet which calls each of them out. The very existence in genuine community is already a common concern, a caring for one another. The caring begins with understanding from within the actual people present. Only then does it extend to gather other people in and then to a dialogue with other communities. (p. 135)

The Jewish philosophical anthropologist Martin Buber devoted much of his work to relationships. For Buber, each person has a voice that must be heard. Only by individuals' working together in free exchange can we hope to work toward some measure of justice for all. "Buber," writes Eugene Borowitz, "gave us the ideal of community, of a society in which people could be persons" (1978, p. 322). What Buber is interested in is an arena where claims from each group can be heard, where conflict and resolution can be met through renewed meeting. Buber stands in opposition to reductionism that turns the other into the stranger whom we cannot understand and that allows us to identify ever more strongly with our own group. The sociologist Alfred Schutz (1975) speaks of groups treating each other as strangers, where each looks at the other and sees only itself. This is similar to Buber's noting the self-absorbed person who is unable to perceive the unique individual who stands opposite. In contrast to this way of responding to one's fellows is the life of dialogue, humankind's contribution to the work of redemption. Such work demands "responsible engagement with the social problematics of this unredeemed world" (Woocher, 1978, p. 242).

It is consistent with this thinking that Buber believed indefensible the use of drugs to alter one's state of consciousness. Drugs place the user in a state of "situationlessness," and no true dialogue can take place when either one or many people are removed from the common order. In "What Is Common to All," Buber writes that

> The fugitive flight out of the claim of the situation into situationlessness is no legitimate affair of man. And the true name of all the paradises which man creates for himself by chemical or other means is situationlessness. They are situationless like the dream state and like schizophrenia because they are in their essence uncommunal, while every situation, even the situation of those who enter into solitude, is enclosed in the community of logos and cosmos. (1965b, p. 100)

Whatever draws us away from the common order of existence contributes to our isolation and to our sense of separation.

THE STRANGER DEFINED

Anthropologist Paul Bohannan writes in his article on "The Stranger" that

> Traditionally, before urban society existed, there were two ways to deal with strangers: Either lump them with your enemies and kill them before they killed you, or turn them into "guests" who deserved elaborate courtesy and the best available lodging, food, and drink. In return, as guests, they were bound to protect and to dwell with the host in honesty and peace. In such societies for either the host or the guest to infringe upon the code of hospitality was a heinous offense against God.
>
> For urban dwellers, however, hospitality won't work. There are just too many strangers. Most of them are not enemies, and most of them are too busy to be guests. Yet dealing with the strangers who populate urban space is the task of those of us who live urban lives. (1981, p. 18)

Being a stranger means that we have entered the interpersonal realm and that we experience ourselves as being apart from others. Strangerhood occurs when a person enters another's world in which that person does not inherently belong. The stranger is not fully a part of, and that not fully being a part of means that he or she is coming up against something that is very different — very Other. The experience of being a stranger is thus twofold: I here and someone else there.

But that twofoldness in itself does not make a person uncomfortable. In fact, out of the exchange and the relationship between two very different persons can come, as we know, increased appreciation and a broadened, fuller life. The type and degree of strangerhood depend on whether inclusion takes place and to what degree it exists. Inclusion, to use Martin Buber's term, can occur when an event is shared by two persons and at least one of the two "without forfeiting anything of the felt reality of his activity, at the same time lives through the common event from the standpoint of the other" (1947/1965a, p. 97). One person is able to know enough of her partner that she can understand how that partner is experiencing the shared event. It requires that each person be open and receptive; such exchange breaks down the barrier of strangerhood.

A member of a group lives at ease with his habits, with the ways of his group. But the stranger must be always on the alert; he must struggle to learn the different ways: the idioms of language, the idioms of emotion, the meaning of unspoken glances. He has to learn the history, possibly the language, certainly the customs and traditions of his adopted community. His antennae are always out: Who may expel me? Who may be threatened by me? Who may be suspicious of my loyalty? Did I commit a faux pas? Whom did I insult? The stranger must learn how to blend, to belong, to be beyond mistrust. He must live through the uncomfortableness of awkwardness, of ignorance, of his "greenhornness." He must gain acceptance, and then he must live with the tension of his two cultures: new and old. Schutz points out that "the stranger becomes essentially the man who has to place in question nearly everything that seems to be unquestionable to the members of the approached group" (1975, p. 87). When we look at the stranger from his point of view as opposed to that of the group, we see that he stands in precarious relation to the new society he has entered.

If the stranger does not threaten me and is only passing through my land, I can be a gracious hostess. If she and I meet on a chance encounter, she can use me as a confidante. But if the stranger comes closer for a longer period of time, then the pressure of a demand, the emergence of a fear may appear. I may become xenophobic. The stranger behaves in ways that I do not understand. A Hasidic story illustrates one judgment made about the stranger:

> Rabbi Moshe Hayyim Efraim, the Baal Shem's grandson told: "I heard this from my grandfather: Once a fiddler played so sweetly that all who heard

him began to dance, and whoever came near enough to hear, joined in the dance. Then a deaf man who knew nothing of music happened along, and to him all he saw seemed the action of madmen — senseless and in bad taste." (Buber, 1970, p. 53)

This tale reveals more about the observer than the observed. The fiddler, the dancers, and the deaf man are bound together; the deaf man first responds with a judgment and puts the others and not himself in the position of strangers. That may force a reaction in the others, who now have been viewed as "mad." The group could, particularly because there is strength in numbers, begin to ridicule and ostracize the deaf man for his ignorance and deafness. The key that may unlock the mystery of the stranger lies in the words "whoever came near enough to hear." We seldom consider what our reaction does to the stranger. The tendency when we don't understand something is to claim it inferior or threatening. When we learn to value otherness or when we understand from within the ways of others, we can be accepting and appreciative.

The great paradox of strangers is that we neither want to redeem strangers out of existence nor abandon them. If we were to decide that in an ideal world there would be no strangers, we would be left with monotony. Thus, although the condition of being a stranger poses problems both for the stranger and the others with whom she lives, that condition is inevitable if we value differences; it is also inevitable given the complex nature of human beings. What we can do is hear the stranger's story and discern what it reveals and what it possibly asks of us. Thus, we may accept the gift of the stranger as it is offered.

STORIES OF STRANGERS

A Story About an Immigrant as Stranger

In *Hunger of Memory*, Richard Rodriguez, who grew up in a Mexican-American home where no English was spoken, tells of his discovery that the price of success in America meant his letting go of the ways of his family (1982). Rodriguez, in fact, is outspoken against the sort of bilingual education that allows students from immigrant families to study in their native language rather than be placed in classes where the language of the land is used. Anything that allows for distance from the culture at large will only keep the immigrants in ghettos. Much of Rodriguez's youth was spent in pain and loneliness, fear and depression because he was caught between two worlds. Though Rodriguez's parents encouraged him to learn English, they did not suspect the disunity and confusion that learning would bring into all their lives. Rodriguez tells of his experience of being thrust far from the world of his parents:

> For my part, I felt that I somehow committed a sin of betrayal by learning English. . . . I *knew* that my parents had encouraged me to learn English. I *knew* that I had turned to English only with angry reluctance. But once I spoke English with ease, I came to *feel* guilty. . . . I felt that I had shattered the intimate bond that had once held the family close. This original sin against my family told whenever anyone addressed me in Spanish and I responded, confounded. (p. 3)

In a monograph entitled *Culture Change, Symbolic Object Loss, and Restitutional Process*, psychiatrist Howard Stein introduces an interesting premise: the stranger struggles with his new situation because he has not yet given up the old (1985). Whether the stranger has left a country, a tribe, a family, or the past, he will need to "mourn the loss of [his] past" before he can "embark upon a future based upon something other than a panic-ridden flight into the romantically edited past or by reviving it in the present" (p. 323). For Stein, a stranger will never resolve his dilemma until he has grieved over what was and over what he thought was, so that he will not be projecting his idealized past onto his present reality. Such grieving even means letting go of the mother, or of the fear of separation anxiety that holds one captive to a group unity, a unity that continually changes. In his new situation, the stranger needs to reaffirm the foundation of his past. He must decide what he needs to relinquish and what price he has to pay for subsequent adaptation.

Rodriguez had to grieve and let go. He discovered that he lived in two cultures, neither of which provided him with a secure place. As he became adept in American culture, he felt more estranged from his family and friends. But the name on his passport he proudly retains; his heritage he does not deny. His book he dedicates to his parents.

A Story About Catharsis

Paul Bohannan tells of a time when he was sitting in the window seat of an airplane and was confided in by a fellow passenger who sat next to him (1981). Bohannan found himself listening to the most intimate details of his neighbor's failing marriage, of his difficult mother-in-law, of his pain. "We did not exchange names, let alone telephone numbers. I doubt that I would recognize him on second meeting. I do not know where he lives or anything else about him except the intimacies of his collapsed marriage" (p. 18).

Yet this sharing of the most intimate details of one's life is really a pseudo-intimacy. No mutual exchange had taken place gradually over an extended period of time. In a position consonant with that of Martin Buber, Bohannan recognizes that "the innermost self becomes clear only in the reciprocity" (p. 20). However, such an exchange between two strangers can be important, he believes, because it enables the revealer to "learn something about himself. A stranger is sometimes the best person for that purpose, for he is neither guest nor enemy. More significantly, a stranger doesn't strike back" (p. 20). In such a situation, familiar to all of us, the benign stranger becomes one to whom another confesses. This encounter may lead to a developing relationship, but more often it remains a passing meeting, a chance to reveal oneself without fear of a judgment or of harm.

What is the significance of the stranger's revealing such intimate details to Bohannan? Certainly we tell our stories over and over again. The man may have had others with whom he could speak thus. But we can raise the question of whether the isolation imposed on us by contemporary society has resulted in the weakening of long-lived, close friendships, so that the absence of proven loyalty and trust often means that we have no one to talk to. When we share openly with a friend with whom there exists mutual caring, the give and take is a part of a fuller, shared life. Our friend may confront us with issues that the stranger on the plane never would. We respond to our friend's story more deeply than we do to the stranger's. When there is no reciprocity, there is limited awareness of the other. We may feel safe confiding to a stranger precisely because she will hear only one side. But we may also find value in speaking to someone who knows so little; and finally it may be as Bohannan suggests, that when we confide to strangers we are really speaking more to ourselves (particularly because we are not in relationship with the stranger).

A Story About "Intimate Strangers"

Our experience as strangers, we discover, moves along a continuum. At one end there is no knowledge or recognition; at the other, there is the greatest familiarity. In Albert Camus's story "The Adulterous Woman" (1957), Janine realizes that she has never lived her own life; rather she has lived the life directed for her by her husband. Not having been her own person, and therefore not having been able to be in a real relationship, she was a stranger to her husband and to herself.

Janine comes to recognize that she had a great need for security, both emotional and financial. Driven by fear, she married Marcel and maintained the marriage for 25 years. She remembers feeling the fear of growing old alone as she struggled with the decision between independent life and marriage. She had been obsessed with being provided for. Yet she knows that at various times in her life she had wondered about that part of life that remained beyond the essentials of survival. How to provide for them? This question she has repressed.

She dreams of the tall and sturdy girl she had once been. The ensuing years have passed in "semi-darkness," without children, without much life. Her husband Marcel has been driven by money, enjoying his piece-goods business. It is clear that he loves Janine, and he has, she admits, always been generous and considerate of her. But his generosity, although it does include love, is limited; he too is closed off to a fuller life, to an inner life brought forth into the world. Janine recognizes that she has been waiting for something, though for what she does not know.

The setting of the story is appropriate. It takes place in winter and opens with a bus ride in the desert where all is stone and blowing sand: one sees nothing growing "among the stones except dry grasses" (p. 10). Thus Janine's life does not open until after her travels through the desert and she comes to an oasis where she and Marcel stay while he conducts business.

Although we are called into existence by relationship, we have to be a self to be a part of that relation. Janine experiences herself as not being *alone* because she exists for her husband. She knows that "by so often making her aware that she existed for him, he made her exist in reality" (p. 6). Yet that is not a full relationship. Janine is a stranger to her husband, living a shadowlike existence. She is something of a stranger to herself too: she has not allowed herself to come into her own. She cut off uniqueness for security's sake. As long as she is not fully a person, she cannot really be known to Marcel. For her, existence has been more important than essence. Such denial of self and lack of participation in life lies at the heart of strangerhood.

One evening Janine is moved by the sight of the nomads; she is struck by their ability to value freedom and to choose poverty rather than slavery. She knows that she has lacked the courage to make such a choice, and she recognizes the price she has paid for security. Before her is the image of what freedom could be like; it is her self that weeps within her heart for the loss. Janine begins to see her exile as she experiences the kingdom before her. She sees Marcel's reliance on her as an avoidance of aging and death and her need of that reliance. If only she could overcome her fear, Janine reasons, then she would be happy. At that moment she does not want to die without having been liberated.

> Fully awake, she sat up in bed and listened to a call that seemed very close. But from the edges of night the exhausted and yet indefatigable voices of the dogs of the oasis were all that reached her ears. A slight wind had risen and she heard its light waters flow in the palm grove. (p. 29)

Out of this moment she hears a call that promises meaning if she would but answer it. She slips away from Marcel in the middle of the night, goes to the parapet, and looks out at the vast desert and the star-filled sky where she had been earlier in the day.

Janine gives herself to the freedom of the open space; she lets go of her fear of death and solitude. When she returns home, she sobs deeply and is only able to tell her husband that "it's nothing."

Her venture in the night, like an adulterous affair, was a giving of herself for a moment. She brought herself to that freedom, knew intimacy with it, knew what she had lost and would probably not be able to claim for herself. Janine faces a kind of suicide of the soul, a remaining within self and subordinating her being to her fear via Marcel.

To be outwardly intimate with another but to remain inwardly unknown by one's "intimate" is the core of strangerhood. When a person remains locked within herself, any I-Thou relation is impossible.

Intimacy can be affected not only by the involvement of the persons; it can be affected by change as well. Thus, we can become strangers to people who previously have been close friends. Elie Wiesel writes:

> To reject a friend—or to be rejected by him—is painful. Here I am, there he is; and I thought we belonged to the same intimate circle; that we were allies, bound by the same utopian dreams, projects and discoveries—and suddenly I discover: a stranger. I thought I could count on him—or her; I thought I counted for him—or her. Wrong. And when I see the stranger in him, it means also that I am a stranger to him. Worse: the stranger in him may very likely be me. (1980, p. 42)

In essence, the person facing such a change asks: If the stranger in him is me, am I not a stranger to myself as well? What changes have taken place that I have been unaware of? When we become strangers to ourselves, we know changes have occurred. What has been lost? What gained?

A Story About Group Loyalty

Daru, a schoolteacher in Algeria and the central figure in Camus's "The Guest" (1957), is caught in the age-old battle between peoples, a bitter conflict between claims of loyalty. The Arabs and the French are pitted one against the other, and Daru, whose heritage is French, is expected to be loyal to the French. But Daru has been teacher to the Arab children. In this story the guest is an Arab who has been taken prisoner because of a family squabble that left one man dead. He is delivered by Balducci, a gendarme, to Daru, a schoolteacher, both of whom are *pieds-noir*, Algerians of European descent. Balducci says that there are orders for Daru to deliver the Arab to the police headquarters in Tinguit. Daru protests: he is a schoolmaster and not subject to orders; but the gendarme says that things are brewing, that there are not enough police to patrol the territory, and that he must return at once to El Ameur. Daru asks, "Is he against us?" The gendarme doesn't think so, though he adds, "One can never be sure."

Balducci will not denounce Daru if the latter does not turn in the Arab; but Balducci accuses Daru of being disloyal and of having insulted him because Daru will not be judge. Daru treats the suspect with kindness by giving him food and supplies and allows him to take a path either to prison or to freedom with the nomads. The Arab, who has his own code of honor, heads off toward the jail. But the Arabs are angry that their brother is not returned to them. When Daru returns to his schoolroom, he finds scrawled on the blackboard, "You will pay for this." English Showalter, Jr., points out that:

> Daru is a humanist in an inhuman or dehumanized world. He genuinely sees a brother in the Arab, but Balducci and the Arab's brothers can see only a criminal or a victim, a pretext for vengeance or a problem, an object within a system of objectified relationships. Daru is furthermore a respecter of ambiguity. . . . But his world is growing increasingly polarized; one must be for or "against us," as Daru puts it, an act must be right or wrong, a person must be guilty or innocent. (1984, p. 82)

Cultural pluralism is written about but not yet lived. Communities of affinity rather than communities of otherness remain too often the pattern among groups vying for position and for all the benefits that go with it.

From the perspective of the individual, how does the approached group appear? What is the reaction of the individual to that group? Howard Stein (1985) points out that not only do we fear separation anxiety as children, we are often affected by an "unconscious family injunction against emotional (even physical) separation" (p. 323). Writes Stein:

> "Group" is repository, container, and target alike for all unfinished developmental business. Little wonder, then, that when one feels that one's group-identity is under assault, one not only "cures" the resulting depression through a cult of the group (or by joining yet another group and becoming its cultist) but also by a fierce and unrelenting assault against the perceived assailant. (p. 319)

Our need for belonging both to people and place is so strong that we will fight those who threaten in any way. The group gives us an identity; we respond with loyalty. We don't have to look far to see the quick escalation of animosity between groups. What Stein implies is not that group identity per se is bad; rather the individual has to become conscious of his own identity and become free of blind allegiance, particularly at the expense of others — because perceived threats from other groups usually lead to counterattack rather than to dialogue.

Stein further suggests that wars have been used to solve depressions and that combined with the drive to belong to a group, group identities are used to project inner aggressions onto another group.

> This certainly obtains for the "extended family," so to speak, of contemporary complementary, syncretizing, and competing social experiments whose focus of attention is upon the family, whether rescuing or vying with it (e.g., the family therapy movement; the family medicine movement; the Unification Church, which calls itself "the one true family," the Family Temple cult, which culminated in the mass "family" suicide at Jonestown, Guyana, in November 1978). These together are to be understood as symptoms of the more widespread societal escape from differentiation . . . through togetherness and oneness, if not through the choice of death itself. One shudders at the prospect that we may indeed unconsciously opt for "the nuclear alternative" in international affairs as a collective final solution to the problem of separation. (p. 325)

Some situations of strangerhood, Stein says, stir up unresolved issues, such as attachments, separations, and losses. Adhering to a group postpones or "aborts the grief work necessary for resolution." Stein also implies that grasping onto group identity can reinforce the pattern of We vs. Them and can hinder an appreciation for uniqueness. Adhering to groups seems to be a way of avoiding differences.

It is not to be understood, however, that belonging to a group is undesirable. Our identity is bound to family, race, religion, culture; but such identity, we may be learning, need not preclude respecting the very other person who comes from elsewhere.

In spite of a fascination with and enrichment from other cultures, individual societies have great difficulty in not seeing others as inferior or as a threat. Our identity is so wrapped up in our history that we have not yet learned that we can hold onto our own ways while respecting and even enjoying the ways of others. John Cruickshank (1960) reprints a section of a letter written by Camus to *Le Monde* in which he was much opposed to the shooting of North Africans by the French in Paris in July of 1953. The great concern of Camus for the rights of all peoples is again made clear:

> There is no question here of pleading on behalf of a ridiculous sentimentalism which seeks to mix up all races in one tender-hearted confusion. It is true that

all men are not alike; I am well aware of the deep differences in tradition between myself and an African or a Mohammedan. But I am also well aware of what binds me to them — something in each of them which I cannot despise without degrading myself. (p. 138)

A Story About Prejudice

Richard Wright, author of *Black Boy*, tells how as a child he remembers seeing white people.

> To me they were merely people like other people, yet somehow strangely different because I had never come in close touch with any of them. For the most part I never thought of them; they simply existed somewhere in the background of the city as a whole. (1966, pp. 30–31)

Before long Wright learns of the lynchings, the always-suspected rape of a white woman by a black man, and of eternal hunger and poverty. No matter how he tried, he would never experience a sense of confirmation from the world at large, for such confirmation was denied him as a black. What alienated Wright from life was white people. Life, he writes, trapped him "in a realm of emotional rejection. I had not embraced insurgency through open choice" (p. 282). The southern culture placed him in a ghetto, kept him apart, refused to grant him anything other than an inferior status, an exile in his own land. He tells us what this kind of living did to him:

> In the main, my hope was merely a kind of self-defence, a conviction that if I did not leave I would perish either because of possible violence against me, or because of my possible violence against them. The substance of my hope was formless and devoid of any real sense of direction, for in my southern living I had seen no looming landmark by which I could, in a positive sense, guide my daily actions. The shocks of southern living had rendered my personality tender and swollen, tense and volatile, and my flight was more a shunning of external and internal dangers than an attempt to embrace what I felt I wanted. (pp. 282–283)

The force of prejudice kept him from discovering who he was and what he was capable of. He conformed as little as possible — just enough to stay alive, meeting the dictates of the whites, being what the whites said he must be. He came to understand that "the South could recognize but a part of a man, could accept but a fragment of his personality, and all the rest — the best and deepest things of heart and mind — were tossed away in blind ignorance and hate" (p. 284).

Denied access to a full life, African-Americans (and other minorities) have too often been kept strangers to themselves and to the culture of the whites with whom they are citizens of the same country. Keeping one people apart from the society at large serves many purposes, all of which have been discussed by social scientists and mental health professionals. In addition to the economic advantages and the sense of power, there are opportunities to use the stranger as an outcast. The stranger is a ready scapegoat for another's aggressions. Psychologist Gordon Allport (1954) cites Herman Bahr, a German Social Democrat, as claiming that "the rich take to opium and hashish. Those who cannot afford them become anti-Semites. Anti-Semitism is the morphine of the small people" (p. 343). Bahr observes that if Jews did not exist, they would have to be invented. The same is true for the stranger. We keep looking for the stranger because it may be to our advantage to do so. The stranger is a weapon we store away until we want to use him. If all is well, we can be a cordial host; if we feel threatened or frustrated, we can dredge up the stranger as scapegoat and whipping boy. Natan Sharansky (Anatoly Shcharansky), the former Russian political prisoner who was finally given permission to leave for Israel in the late 1980s, says that the Jew has been the litmus test for all societies. Where the Jew is allowed to live and be free, that society is free; where the Jew is imprisoned, that society is imprisoned.

The stranger lives with a sense of insecurity, with a sense of never quite knowing the rules. He learns that there is one set of rules for society at large and another for him; the rules can be turned against him at a whim.

ANSWERING THE STRANGER'S CALL

We learn something of the other person through genuine meeting with her. Martin Buber (1965b), whose philosophy of I and Thou rests on dialogue, tells us that the life of dialogue reaches its height when we are able to "make present" the other as just that other that he is. We are able to think, imagine, and feel how the other is thinking, imagining, and feeling. We do this neither by projecting our own feelings onto the other nor by remaining detached but by being open to that which is taking place in the person before us. This we can do to some extent before we know a person well. But a full "making present" occurs in closer relationships where we are able to experience what the other is experiencing. Buber refers to this as "imagining the real," or "experiencing the other side" or "inclusion."

We know a stranger in a limited way—that is, something remains unfamiliar or undisclosed to us. All we can do is respond to what the stranger shares with us. But that response can be a caring response.

Strangers in literature offer us images of individuals who live in some way separate from the community. When we share stories from our lives, we begin to open ourselves to others, and perhaps nowhere are others more willing to come close enough to hear than when they are being told a story. Faithful listening means that we turn our attention to the words of another. We begin to imagine an event from the side of another person, to grasp his or her uniqueness.

Sometimes it matters whether strangers become part of us; more often, it is important that strangers become others whom we learn to value. The term *stranger* has built in it the absence of intimacy. We have seen that issues of trust and loyalty surround our caution with strangers. But, like Daru in "The Guest," we can treat strangers with respect. When we don't, we may become prey to passions of greed, suspicion, power. And we know where these lead us.

Sister Mary Jegen writes in her profound article "Seeing Through Peaceful Eyes" of the relation between peace and the stranger:

> Peacemaking and contemplating are so intimately related that one can hardly exist without the other. This truth can be appreciated by recognizing that violence depends on distorting the object of the victim of violence, turning the victim into an impersonal object which can then be injured or even killed. An army officer told me that killing in war is easier today because soldiers do not have to look enemies in the eye as they are coming over the hill. Psychologically, it would be impossible to kill anyone on whom one had just been casting a loving glance. Modern technology enables the killer to maintain a distance from the victim. In war simulation exercises, when a target is bombed, the people in the vicinity are considered collateral damage — that is, burned, bleeding, and dead children, women and men. It is impossible to cast a benevolent glance on "collateral damage." The day we teach people to look at the persons behind the abstraction, to glance benevolently at them, the military-industrial complex will have a very serious problem. (1987, p. 7)

There is no more urgent case for addressing the issue of strangers than the one that faces us today: we must counter the technology that has created the possibility of our taking one last photo of the earth as it goes up in flames.

Wiesel asks why Abraham did not protest God's terms: "Know Abraham, that your descendants will be treated as strangers in foreign lands; they will be sold into slavery; they will be persecuted, tormented. But it will not last forever. For their oppressors will be punished" (1980, p. 22).

> He understood that the covenant contained a blueprint for life in society. To live without strangers could result in an impoverished system; to live only

amongst ourselves, constantly in-breeding, never facing an outsider to make us question again and again our certainties and rules, would inevitably lead to atrophy. The experience of encountering a stranger—like that of suffering—is important and creative, provided we know how to distinguish between them and when to stop. (p. 47)

If we live monologically, if we treat others as objects to be exploited, if we remain hidden, if we close ourselves to others, then we live like strangers.

The community that allows for diversity is, as we have seen, a strong, vital organization. Perhaps it is the stranger who teaches us how to treat strangers. The ability to appreciate otherness in individuals and communities is a way of redeeming the stranger and of redeeming the world. It is not up to humankind alone to bring redemption, but redemption will not come until we make way for it through doing our share in perfecting the world. Is it not perhaps the stranger who calls us to account and who shows us the way?

REFERENCES

Allport, Gordon. (1954). *The nature of prejudice*. Reading, MA: Addison-Wesley.

Bohannan, Paul. (1981, April). The stranger. *Science, 81*, 18–20.

Borowitz, Eugene. (1978). Humanism and religious belief in Martin Buber. *Thought: A Review of Culture and Idea, 53*, 320–328.

Buber, Martin. (1965a). *Between man and man* (Ronald Gregor Smith, Trans.). Intro. by Maurice Friedman. New York: Macmillan. (Originally published 1947).

Buber, Martin. (1965b). *The knowledge of man*. New York: Harper & Row.

Buber, Martin. (1970). *Tales of the Hasidim: The early masters* (Olga Marx, Trans.). New York: Schocken.

Camus, Albert. (1957). *Exile and the Kingdom* (Justin O'Brien, Trans.). New York: Random House.

Camus, Albert. (1972). *Neither victims nor executioners* (Dwight McDonald, Trans.). Chicago: World Without War Publications.

Cruickshank, John. (1960). *Albert Camus and the literature of revolt*. New York: Oxford University Press.

Friedman, Maurice. (1974). *The hidden human image*. New York: Delacorte.

Friedman, Maurice. (1983). *The confirmation of otherness in family, community, and society*. New York: Pilgrim Press.

Jegen, Mary Evelyn. (1987, July/August). Seeing through peaceful eyes. *Fellowship, 53*, 6–8.

Rodriguez, Richard. (1982). *Hunger of memory: The education of Richard Rodriguez*. Toronto, Ontario, Canada: Bantam.

Schutz, Alfred. (1975). *On phenomenology and social relations*. Chicago: University of Chicago Press.

Showalter, English, Jr. (1984). *Exiles and strangers: A reading of Camus' Exile and the Kingdom*. Columbus: Ohio State University Press.

Stein, Howard. (1985). Culture change, symbolic object loss, and restitutional process. *Psychoanalysis and Contemporary Thought, 8*, 301–332.

Wiesel, Elie. (1980). *Inside a library and The stranger in the Bible*. New York: Hebrew Union College-Jewish Institute of Religion.

Woocher, Jonathan. (1978). Martin Buber's politics of dialogue. *Thought: A Review of Culture and Idea, 53*, 241–257.

Wright, Richard. (1966). *Black boy*. New York: Harper & Row.

PART III

Narrative and Dialogue as a Paradigm for Teaching and Learning

Stories, Paul Ricoeur tells us, offer us models for the "redescription of the world." In the previous parts of this book we have explored narrative and ways of knowing and caring, and the power of narrative as a tool for grasping the self in relation to the other. The authors in this final part provide descriptions of uses of story and dialogue in classrooms and in research efforts. The samplings presented here build a case for narrative and dialogue as a paradigm for teaching and learning in any subject, setting, or level of understanding. These authors grasp that we are all teachers and learners, in nearly every human encounter.

In Chapter 9, "Stories in Dialogue: Caring and Interpersonal Reasoning," Nel Noddings discusses interpersonal reasoning and how schools might encourage its development. She asks us to consider that the capacity of moral agents to talk appreciatively with each other regardless of fundamental differences is crucial in friendship, marriage, politics, business, and world peace. Pointing to a long-standing neglect of this capacity in education, she explores three basic questions: "What *is* interpersonal reasoning? What are its components? How does it develop?"

Mark Tappan and Lyn Mikel Brown, in Chapter 10, "Stories Told and Lessons Learned: Toward a Narrative Approach to Moral Development and Moral Education," invite us to listen to the stories of children and adolescents struggling with moral conflicts as illustrations of their emerging authorship and authority in the moral realm. We have selected this chapter, originally published in the *Harvard Educational Review*, because it conveys lively firsthand narratives of young people exploring moral conflicts in their lives in ways that should prove highly useful to those who wish to understand something of the moral fabric of childhood within contemporary society.

In Chapter 11, "Moral Fictions: The Dilemma of Theory and Practice," Jo Anne Pagano offers accounts of student teachers' experiences interpreted against a background of theory. Through examining the different interpretations of classroom events held by the student teacher, her students, and the college faculty supervisor, the author explores ways that practice can defy (or appear to defy) theory. Through acknowledging the importance of interpretive communities in the process of becoming a teacher, Pagano suggests ways that the negotiation of meaning within these communities has enabled her to identify and reformulate her own theories of teaching and learning.

> There is more than one way to tell a story and more than one story. Teaching is, among other things, a discursive and interpretive practice, just as the writing of autobiography is. Teaching is textual. When we teach, we tell stories about the world. Some stories are scientific, some historical, some philosophical, some literary, and so on. Educational theories are stories about how teaching and learning work, about who does what to whom and for what purposes; and, most particularly, educational theories are stories about the kind of world we want to live in and about what we should do to make that world. Stories obey a narrative logic and, like mythologies, help us to find our place in the world.

In Chapter 12, "Teacher Lore: A Basis for Understanding Praxis," William Schubert introduces *teacher lore* as a necessary and neglected construct in educational literature, exploring its relevance to the theory and practice of curriculum, teaching, supervision, and school improvement. Schubert characterizes teacher lore as the knowledge, ideas, perspectives, and understandings of teachers. When teachers are invited to share in the creation of knowledge about education, they often communicate their knowledge best through stories about their practical experiences. The chapter describes the results of this approach within the Teacher Lore Project, a research venture at the University of Illinois at Chicago.

Susan Florio-Ruane, in Chapter 13, "Conversation and Narrative in Collaborative Research: An Ethnography of the Written Literacy Forum," describes the workings of a group of teachers and the researchers who had carried out ethnographic research in their classrooms. The participants met regularly over a period of a year to hold conversations about how research on writing instruction can be made more meaningful to educators. The author describes the Forum's deliberations about educational research as a means for its members to articulate and examine their assumptions about what researchers and teachers claim to know, how they express that knowledge, and the views they hold of themselves and each other as professionals. The author further relates how incorporating the teachers' voices and stories into texts written for diverse audiences taught the researchers that not all knowledge can be represented by structural models.

> Sometimes a story or a conversation is the best way to represent or share some important kinds of knowledge. We . . . grew to appreciate that such forms of language are not extraneous to inquiry but central to a valid portrayal of teachers' work. . . . Once we [teachers and researchers] began conversations with one another, we learned a great deal more about the processes of teaching and learning writing in school than any of us could have learned in isolation.

This project stands out as an exemplary approach to the use of narrative and dialogue in educational research. The author conveys the importance of the development of caring, respectful relations among participating teachers and researchers, relations that proved fundamental to the success of the project.

In Chapter 14, "Story and Voice in the Education of Professionals," Celeste Brody and Carol Witherell draw on excerpts of autobiographical writing from their students Ken Donald and Ruth Lundblad to describe the use of narrative and dialogue within their course Individual and Societal Perspectives on Adulthood, offered at the Graduate School of Professional Studies of Lewis & Clark College. The course was designed to explore themes of culture, race, ethnicity, age, and gender as they shape identity throughout the life span and as they present both challenges and opportunities to the professional. Several activities of the course, including an outdoor "Challenge Course," and a sampling of several of their students' writings are presented in rich detail. The descriptions reveal the power of experiential learning and of narrative and dialogue as tools for addressing human and ethical dilemmas in the professions.

9

Stories in Dialogue
Caring and Interpersonal Reasoning

NEL NODDINGS

Nel Noddings is professor of education at Stanford University, where she teaches courses in philosophy of education, ethics, and feminist studies. Her areas of special interest are feminist ethics, moral education, and mathematical problem solving. In addition to three books, Caring: A Feminine Approach to Ethics and Moral Education, Women and Evil, *and* Awakening the Inner Eye: Intuition in Education *(with Paul Shore), she is author of more than 60 articles and chapters on various topics ranging from the ethics of caring to mathematical problem solving. Dr. Noddings recently served as a Phi Beta Kappa Visiting Scholar, lecturing at 10 colleges throughout the country.*

There is a great deal of concern today about critical thinking and reasoning skills. The latest results from the National Assessment of Educational Progress (NAEP) indicate that American schoolchildren have improved some on routine measures of learning, but many still do not understand what they read nor can they apply their mathematical knowledge to any but the simplest kind of word problem. So there's reason for concern, and one can understand why current educational publishing is adrift in critical thinking books.

I want to suggest, however, that we face an even more important challenge in the area of *interpersonal* reasoning. The capacity of moral agents to talk appreciatively with each other regardless of fundamental differences is crucial in friendship, marriage, politics, business, and world peace. We see evidence everywhere that the capacity is sorely underdeveloped, and yet we have so far given the task little attention in educational circles.

What I plan to do in this brief discussion is to explore three questions: What *is* interpersonal reasoning? What are its components? How does it develop?

WHAT IS INTERPERSONAL REASONING?

Let me start out with an imaginary dialogue between two high school girls, Mary Jane (M.J.) and Carolyn (C.). Carolyn has confided to Mary Jane that she plans to cut school for the afternoon to counsel her boyfriend, Robbie, who is depressed and threatening to run away.

M.J.: I don't think that's a good idea. You can't just cut classes when you're doing so well and your academic status really matters to you. Robbie never did care about school, but he ought to realize that you *do*.

C.: He isn't thinking about school at all. I'm worried that he'll do something crazy. I'm not asking you to cover for me or anything.

M.J.: Can't it wait until tonight or the weekend?

C.: I don't think so.

M.J.: Well, . . . Carolyn, don't get mad. I've just got to say this. Robbie isn't worth the risks you take.

C.: You may be right. As a matter of fact, we're breaking up. But I can't just ignore how miserable he is right now.

M.J.: Your sense of responsibility! Tell you what. Go now. I can cover for you with the old "She just went to the nurse" line as long as you get back in time for math. Old Lady Biggs will never buy it, and you've got a shot at the math prize. Don't blow it! Okay?

C.: Thanks, Mary Jane. I'll be back for math.

Now, however much we may have wished for a different outcome — no cut classes, no small lies to teachers, a bit more respect for "Old Lady Biggs" — we can appreciate the skill of Carolyn and Mary Jane as interpersonal reasoners. As Norma Haan (1978) describes it, interpersonal reasoning involves "moral dialogue between agents who strive to achieve balanced agreement, based on compromise they reach or on their joint discovery of interests they hold in common" (p. 303). In contrast to logico-mathematical reasoning that proceeds step by step according to a priori rules, interpersonal reasoning is open, flexible, and responsive. It is guided by an attitude that values the relationship of the reasoners over any particular outcome, and it is marked by attachment and connection rather than separation and abstraction.

The short dialogue between Carolyn and Mary Jane reveals two people who care for each other. They differ on the best course of action, but they listen to each other. Just as Carolyn takes responsibility for her relationship with Robbie, Mary Jane accepts the responsibility of supporting and protecting Carolyn. Both girls seem tacitly to have established two goals: to maintain their own relation of trust and affection and to seek a resolution of the problem that will be satisfactory to Carolyn. Mary Jane recognizes her friend's need.

Social scientists—in contrast to novelists, biographers, poets, and dramatists—are only just beginning to look at interpersonal reasoning as Haan describes it. Developmentalists such as Robert Selman (1980) have studied "interpersonal understanding," but their approach has been typically individualistic; that is, they have assumed the usual Western view of moral agents wrestling in lonely isolation with great moral principles. For an individual to score well in Selman's developmentalist version of interpersonal understanding, he or she must demonstrate a capacity to take the perspectives of several parties in a social/moral dilemma. Obviously, people may be able to do this—just as they may become adept at interpreting literature—without actually being able or disposed to engage in genuine interpersonal reasoning. Interesting and useful as this work is, some theorists—feminists among them—have raised serious objections to it because it overemphasizes the intellectual aspect of interpersonal understanding and largely ignores what people actually do in real social situations. It doesn't help us much in listening to the stories that develop in dialogue.

Following Carol Gilligan's (1982) challenge to Kohlberg's description of moral development, Nona Lyons (1983) initiated a similar challenge in the area of interpersonal reasoning. She emphasized the centrality of listening, connecting, and taking responsibility for the relationship itself. Similarly, Mary Belenky, Blythe Clinchy, Nancy Goldberger, and Jill Tarule (1986) have revealed the power and reality of connected ways of knowing and relating in women's lives. The practicality of the new approach has been recognized by feminist theorists in the professions as well. In both law and nursing, for example, theorists and educators are drawing directly on the experience-centered research just cited to fashion a new pedagogy as well as a fresh approach to ethics. (See, for example, "Women in Legal Education," 1988; on nursing, see Watson, 1985.)

We are, then, at a point where we are beginning to appreciate a capacity historically associated with women. We still have a great deal to learn.

WHAT ARE THE COMPONENTS OF INTERPERSONAL REASONING?

In traditional philosophy we find little analysis of interpersonal reasoning. Indeed, ancient efforts to describe or teach skills in this area often deteriorated to rhetoric and, even when they did not, they were highly criticized by philosophers who sought absolute truth. Moral philosophy in the last two centuries has moved even further from analysis of actual situations and interrelatedness. Following Descartes and Kant, it has tried to develop a method (universalizability) that should enable any person — reasoning well and in solitude — to arrive at a conclusion that should be binding on any other agent using the same method. From this perspective, who we are, to whom we are connected, what our projects are, what our situation is — all are irrelevant.

Philosophers are beginning to reject the loss of person and community implied in the highly individualistic quest for a method (MacIntyre, 1981). The great recent interest in ethics of care (Gilligan, 1982; Noddings, 1984), for example, shows that people are concerned about the whole of moral life in real situations and not just abstract decision making in dramatic moments of moral conflict. Guided by an ethic of care, we cannot decide a priori, on the basis of principles alone, what to do or how to respond to the needs of others. We must enter dialogue to find out. The following analysis is speculative and tentative — a first cut at a phenomenology of interpersonal reasoning.

The first thing we notice when we listen to a bit of interpersonal reasoning is an attitude. The attitude is one of care and solicitude. It can be mistaken for timidness and lack of self-confidence. A speaker may, for example, seem fearful of offending another, may give way on points she might have pressed, or may offer what seem to be unwarranted compliments. The way of speaking that accompanies an ethic of care has often been scorned by masculinists like Nietzsche, for example, as an indication of slave mentality. So the first task — one that has been ably undertaken by the black feminist theologian Toinette Eugene (1989) — is to see an ethic of care and its style of engagement as *liberational*. The attitude of care liberates us from the fear that parties in the conversation will use gross power to seize what they want. It also requires *all* people to care — to respond to expressed needs — and therefore should lighten the traditional burden on women.

It may well be true that this unobtrusive, often tentative, way of reasoning and conversing developed in women because of centuries of powerlessness. This, as Eugene explains, cannot be the whole reason, however; powerlessness can as easily induce rage and violence. The mode we are discussing has been chosen under stress, and it has been employed with great courage in behalf of others — not merely in self-protection. For many black women, it has been a free choice to follow the example of Jesus. Further, regardless of its origins, the attitude is one that can be taken freely by one who rejects the use of coercive power even when power is available as an option.

The attitude of care is characterized by attention (or engrossment, as I referred to it in *Caring*, 1984). This concept has a history; it has been treated by Iris Murdoch (1970), for example, who traces it to Simone Weil (1951). Weil's development of the concept is especially useful for our purposes. She situates her discussion in the story of the Holy Grail:

> In the first legend of the Grail, it is said that the Grail . . . belongs to the first comer who asks the guardian of the vessel, a king three quarters paralyzed by the most painful wound, "What are you going through?"
>   The love of our neighbor in all its fullness simply means being able to say to him: "What are you going through?" It is a recognition that the sufferer exists, not only as a unit in a collection, or a specimen from the social category labeled "unfortunate," but as a man, exactly like us. (p. 115)

Weil goes on to say:

> This way of looking is first of all attentive. The soul empties itself of all its own contents in order to receive into itself the being it is looking at, just as he is, in all his truth. Only he who is capable of attention can do this. (p. 115)

These passages appear in an essay entitled "Reflections on the Right Use of School Studies with a View to the Love of God." Weil contends that the capacity for attention can be developed intellectually—through, for example, the study of geometry—and that the capacity so developed can be used to enhance one's concentration in prayer. Thence, we may conclude, would come a still greater patience and compassion for our fellow beings.

I accept Weil's description of attention and the fundamental role it plays in the love of our neighbors, but I think she was wrong in supposing that the capacity for intellectual attention can "make us better able to give someone in affliction exactly the help required to save him." Here I think Weil confused her own devotion to other people, to ideas, and to God with a general correlation among the three devotions. So far as can be judged by available evidence, people quite capable of intellectual concentration are neither more nor less likely to attend compassionately to the afflictions of others. Further, sadly, there seems to be little reason to believe that attention in prayer produces the humane result Weil sought. Indeed, Weil seems to have made an error similar to the one made by developmentalists; she overintellectualized and overindividualized the capacity for attention and response.

Another feature of competent interpersonal reasoning seems to be flexibility. In contrast to analytical reasoning where the end remains fixed and only the means are adjusted, interpersonal reasoning involves shifting ends as well. Carolyn and Mary Jane, for example, explored several possibilities before Mary Jane accepted an end desired by Carolyn. Both parties may revise the goals they seek as the dialogue unfolds. Often a decision must be made on how much to talk and how much to listen, and typically much more is thought than said. Sometimes empathic silence and body language dominate the conversation.

Much of what goes on in interpersonal reasoning is aimed at cultivating the relation. One cannot proceed by working backwards from the desired goal, as in geometry — by, for example, establishing a set of intermediate or subgoals to be accomplished in order. Rather, one must use clues from the other's words to decide when to divert the conversation. When guilt threatens to overwhelm one party, for example, the other can remind her or him of good and wise decisions made in the past. The attribution of best possible motive is fundamental and of great importance in this kind of reasoning. Mary Jane, for example, recognized and complimented Carolyn's sense of responsibility, even though she thought it was somewhat misdirected. Interpersonal reasoners build each other's confidence and self-esteem, and they direct their efforts toward strengthening the relation.

A major aim of interpersonal reasoning is to identify a range of possible responses and to find a satisfactory mode of delivery for the response. In one sense, of course, the whole dialogue can be characterized as "address and response," but, in another sense, at least one party is often wrestling with the problem of how to respond. There is usually a range of responses that will be acceptable to the one who needs help. Not all of these will necessarily be acceptable to the one who must respond. It is a delicate matter to avoid rejecting or being rejected. Hence much of what is said takes the form of suggestion or possibility. One does not want to push the other into a hardened position that must be defended.

All of this stands in sharp contrast to the kind of reasoning that is so highly prized in academic life. At meetings of philosophical societies, for example, speakers and "respondents" use each other's words to build separate and potentially winning arguments. There are notorious examples on record. The Hutchins-Dewey (Dewey, 1937a, 1937b; Hutchins, 1937) debates come readily to mind. Here we have an example of two highly intelligent men who accused each other perennially of misunderstanding and misinterpretation. Hutchins even made jokes about Dewey's inability to understand his positions, but he never really made an effort to get Dewey to understand nor did Dewey try very hard to clarify his ideas for Hutchins. Both men cared more about winning points in the debate than about building a constructive relation. And the public absorbed little more than a caricature of either man's position. Even today, in studying the Hutchins-Dewey arguments, a reader can feel the two men growing farther and farther apart.

Not too many years ago it was common for male mentors to advise young women entering philosophy to be more aggressive, to push their arguments harder. Fortunately, many women resisted that advice, and a new tone is heard at philosophical meetings—one that, happily, seems congenial to many men as well. None of this should be taken to mean that the argumentative style has no place in debate. It does, of course. But it is by no means necessary for this style to pervade all of public academic discussion. There may be optimally effective combinations of interpersonal and analytic reasoning for public debate. It may be worth mentioning here that we really are at a research frontier in this work. We have not yet, for example, studied examples of public debate and dialogue from this perspective. We know that some people have reputations as "gracious respondents"—and we certainly have an intuitive understanding of what this means—but we have not studied their dialogue in any technical way to identify "moves" that are typical of interpersonal (rather than analytical) reasoning.

In this brief attempt to analyze interpersonal reasoning, I have identified several important features:

An attitude of solicitude or care
Attention
Flexibility
Effort aimed at cultivating the relation
A search for an appropriate response

There are no doubt other features that will emerge as further analyses are conducted.

Before undertaking the question of how interpersonal reasoning develops, I should say that there is also a form of executive monitoring or metacognition that accompanies interpersonal reasoning. We monitor our own contributions to the dialogue. Typical internal talk might include comments such as the following:

I didn't know he was in such pain!
Will she reject this suggestion?
Will this make him so mad he'll withdraw?
How can I possibly meet a need of this magnitude?

As in analytical reasoning, internal talk can be facilitative or debilitating. If internal talk takes over, we drift away from the other, our attention is diverted to ourselves, and we cease telling and hearing stories. Clearly, this is another potentially fruitful area of study.

Before turning to questions concerning the learning and teaching of interpersonal reasoning, I should make clear that interpersonal reasoning does not guarantee an ethical result. Two people who care deeply for each other may make a decision that is morally deplorable when the interests of others are considered, or without caring for each other at all, people may communicate effectively and cooperatively for evil ends. Interpersonal reasoning is necessary for ethical decision making, but it is not sufficient. So far I have concentrated on interpersonal reasoning, not the status of its results.

HOW DOES INTERPERSONAL REASONING DEVELOP?

How can we help children to develop a capacity for interpersonal reasoning? Many of us believe that it develops in the actual activities of care, and if it develops there, our worries about the moral status of its outcomes are considerably reduced. People develop a moral orientation of caring, we suggest, through direct contact with those who need to be cared for. In contrast to what Weil believed, this is *not* a capacity that develops in isolated study. It requires sustained interpersonal contact.

There is both anecdotal and inferential evidence for this claim. An example of the first appears dramatically in the dissertation of a nurse-theorist. Carole Anderson (1977) describes the change in a minister's moral orientation when he gave up his authority as a minister and became an orderly in a nursing home. He confesses:

> "I learned my perception as a minister in a nursing home and as an orderly in a nursing home were two different games. I saw things differently. And one of the things I became involved in was patients' rights. They had none." (p. 116)

Here we see that—just as argumentative language in debate need not be entirely eliminated—the language of rights and justice need not be entirely abandoned in a caring orientation toward ethical life. This minister had been aware before of rights—their exercise, their denial, their suspension. But now he saw these rights in the light of concrete experience; he felt the need to respond to suffering that came to him directly. Experiences of this sort have led nurse-theorists to suggest that physicians in training might profit greatly from a period of service as nurses. One has to engage in the activities of care in order to develop the capacity for attentive love, and central to these activities are dialogue and interpersonal reasoning.

As inferential evidence, we might offer the fact that more than 75% of the caregivers in this nation are women. These women do not develop their skills as caregivers in intellectual settings. They learn what to do by engaging in the activities of care. Indeed, it is assumed that they can be and should be caregivers simply because they are women. I am not arguing that there is no need for training in the skills of caregiving; not all private caregiving is good, and sometimes it is not even loving. To the contrary, I am arguing that we should study the best performance of these women and try humbly to find out how they developed the attitudes, dispositions, and skills to care effectively. We need to know in order to provide all our children with experience likely to develop this capacity.

We can see that attention is central in the caring orientation to moral life. To do the work of attentive love requires practice. One must engage in the activities of care, preferably under the loving supervision of an experienced caregiver. In the past, most females have undergone apprenticeship in caring under their own mothers. Males have only rarely received such preparation. Now, as mothers and daughters spend less time together in caring activities, there is a real risk that few people will grow up with the attitudes, dispositions, and skills to care.

I have suggested that interpersonal reasoning is part of the rationality of caring. James Comer (1988) says that the single greatest complaint directed at teachers is, "They don't care!" (p. 35). Uncaring homes and uncaring schools are likely to produce uncaring students. Further, at a time when it is difficult to maintain an optimal level of caring even in loving homes, schools simply must help young people to learn how to contribute to caring relations. The crisis of caring that I will discuss now is directly related to the neglect of interpersonal reasoning that I alluded to at the beginning of this discussion.

Young human beings enter their first caring relations as receivers of care. Normal babies who are wanted and loved contribute generously and naturally to their relation with a caregiver. They wriggle, and coo, and smile, and engage in delightful, prolonged eye contact. When infants are incapable of this sort of response, the burden on caregivers is enormous. I mention this for two reasons: first, to underscore that caring relations require a contribution from both carer and cared for; second, to remind us that being cared for may be a necessary prerequisite to learning to care. More and more children are being born with drug damage and other handicaps that limit their capacity to respond; further, the lives of more severely handicapped children are being preserved. The caregivers for

these children suffer greatly. They need the support of other caring relations in order to continue their difficult work. When we consider the
growing need for care among the elderly, the handicapped, the emotionally ill, and the young, there is little doubt that a crisis exists. Schools by
themselves cannot do much to remove the crisis, but educators can begin to
address the fundamental problem instead of aggravating it by promoting
technical and mechanistic solutions. It may be impossible for regular
schools to provide the sort of care required by children who have never
experienced caring relations, but schools can help most children to learn
more about how to care and be cared for, and our society ought to make
education for caring a top priority.

To participate genuinely as cared-for in a relation requires discernment and receptivity. This is another area of skill to be explored. It is
delightful to do things for people who notice that we care, and it is very
difficult to go on trying to care when the cared-for does not respond. The
response does not need to be one of gratitude and need not always be
directed at the carer. A spouse who exclaims, "I just love meat loaf!" cheers
the cook and supports continued caring. A student who dives into a science
project—even if she doesn't say a word of appreciation to her science
teacher—supports her teacher's effort. These are responses that indicate a
form of receptivity; the efforts at caring have been received.

Discernment is often necessary. Sometimes caring is not completed in
a natural and easy receptivity. Carers differ widely in their expressions of
caring. A gruff old algebra teacher may care deeply about his students. (So
may "Old Lady Biggs"!) He may believe that making them toe the mark is
in their best interests. On the other end of the spectrum, a long-haired,
bearded young teacher who lets students call him "Bill" may also care
deeply and believe that students fully respected will make wise choices.
Students are not always capable of assessing their teachers' attempts to
care, and we have done little to prepare them for the task of evaluating
others for their capacity to do the work of attentive love. Indeed, we
usually make the task of discernment more difficult for students by establishing a rigid description of what constitutes good—or caring—teaching.
In one decade, the gruff old algebra teacher is out—"caring" teachers
don't behave this way. In another decade, he is "in" and bearded Bill is out.
Further, when kids can't get along with teachers and request a change, we
rarely credit them with discernment or help them to develop it; we usually
say they have to stick it out—"You have to get along with all kinds of
people," we say. We fail to hear the stories they try so hard to tell.

I suspect we cannot teach the skill of discernment directly. It develops
in close relationships over time, and even then children and teenagers often
make mistakes. Teenagers, for example, often fail to receive their own

parents' attempts at caring, especially if there is little family time for conversation. This observation suggests that teachers and students need more time together. If trust is to develop, people need to know something about each other, to talk to each other. It seems reasonable, then, to recommend that teachers stay with a group of students for, say, 3 years rather than 1. In elementary school, this seems fairly easy to do. At the high school level, a mathematics teacher, for example, might take on a group of students when they enter and guide them through their entire high school mathematics curriculum. Such an arrangement must, of course, be by mutual consent. The object of such extended contact is at least threefold:

1. It provides time for a caring relation to develop; in this relation of trust, interpersonal skills can be nourished. Students, in the care of good teachers, learn that they are indeed the recipients of care, and they have an opportunity to learn more about appropriate forms of response.
2. The cognitive capacity for discernment and thus for more fruitful dialogue may be better developed as students study for an extended period of time with teachers who regard this capacity as a legitimate target of development.
3. Students can begin the sensitive work of learning to be carers as they see caregiving modeled.

No doubt there are other ways of extending teacher-student contact. Ted Sizer's (1984) recommendation that high school teachers teach two subjects to 30 students rather than one subject to 60 is worth considering. Reinstatement of homeroom periods could be useful, if the time is used for genuine dialogue. Integrating lunchtime into the education program could be wonderful. Just as families do much of the loving work of moral education at mealtime, so might teachers. Eating together can provide a powerful opportunity for caring relations to develop, and, in such settings, teachers have a chance to guide the growth of peer relations as well. Creating examples of extended contact is illustrative of a general change in thinking that is long overdue in education. Instead of depending entirely on programmatic changes in curriculum, renewed emphasis on critical thinking, or new systems of discipline, educators must begin to face the social changes that have occurred in the last 40 years and to think in terms of providing care and educating for interpersonal reasoning.

It could be argued, and I anticipate that it will be argued, that staying together for 3 years will not do much good if the teacher is not a good one. Someone is sure to suggest that teachers will need considerable training if they are to work this way, and so forth. I am certainly not going to argue that teacher training is irrelevant. There are things teacher educators can do to facilitate the program I am trying to describe. But I put a good deal of faith in the activities of care and in legitimating what nurse-theoretician Jean Watson (1985) calls "occasions of caring." These are the moments when nurse and patient or teacher and student meet and must decide what to do with the moment—what attitude to take, what needs are present, what to share, whether to remain silent. This way of meeting the living other in caring situations needs legitimation. It needs to be the guiding spirit of what we do in education. It cannot be accomplished through an extra course or specified form of training. Rather it requires that we look at education from a different perspective.

When we take this other perspective, one that brings us to a consideration of the school as a familylike setting in which interpersonal reasoning is to be developed, we see that there are essential tasks with which teachers may need help. They must learn how to engage in genuine dialogue, for example, and they need to develop teaching strategies that provide students with opportunities to care for each other. Among the latter, small-group work appears to be a promising possibility. It can be an excellent way to get students working together, helping each other. But teachers have to think about this purpose and use it to guide group formation and activity (Noddings, 1989). Children can behave dreadfully toward each other, and verbal abuse by peers is not an unusual event. Because small-group learning is now all the rage, teachers are likely to employ such arrangements either mechanically or arbitrarily. Used mindlessly, small groups may not only fail to accomplish important cognitive goals; they may actually do damage to some group members. From the perspective I've taken here, teachers would have to make clear to their students that the object of small-group work is to help each other—and this means in interpersonal as well as intellectual tasks. One cannot judge whether this is happening simply by looking at final products. The process has to be monitored. Here, extra adults could very useful, and, with a minimum of preparation, parents might participate in such sessions regularly. Their task would be to remind group members how they are to treat each other.

A focus on helping children learn how to be cared for and how to become carers changes the way we look at everything. Some years ago educators came up with the idea that middle schools should be created to attend to the special developmental needs of preadolescents. (Junior highs were obviously a disaster, and this bit of renaming gave us a chance to rethink what should be provided for this feisty age group.) What still has not occurred to most school people is that isolating a particular group may not be the best way to provide for its developmental needs. Suppose one of the great developmental tasks is a moral one — to develop the skills needed to care effectively for others. Middle school children, most of us would agree, have exactly this need. They should be in schools where there are younger children to be helped, and it should be part of their education — an important part — to learn how to do so.

Schools, I have suggested, should function more like families. They should also try to promote sound family relations. It is desirable to involve parents in the school activities of their children, but not all parents are free at the appropriate times to be part of actual school events. Sometimes parents have to take their children out of school in order to spend time with them. Schools, generally, take a dim view of this sort of thing, but this is another area where we have been affected by tunnel vision — where, indeed, we fail to employ the best interpersonal reasoning. Teachers should be delighted when children have opportunities to travel with their parents or just to be with them — even if it's a day at the beach or an afternoon in the city. They come back with grand stories to tell! But it makes more work for teachers, we protest. It doesn't have to. If we focus our attention on caring and interpersonal reasoning, every student can belong to a support group that will tell him or her what has been missed, what assignments are due, when makeup tests are scheduled, and the like. *One teacher* does not have to do all the teaching, managing, caring. We just have not thought things through carefully. We have not learned to listen well, and we do not put high enough value on the skills discussed here.

In summary, I've suggested that schools should become places in which teachers and students live together, talk to each other, reason together, take delight in each other's company. Like good parents, teachers should be concerned first and foremost with the kind of people their charges are becoming. My guess is that when schools focus on what really matters in life, the cognitive ends we are now striving toward in such painful and artificial ways will be met as natural culminations of the means we have wisely chosen.

REFERENCES

Anderson, Carole. (1977). *All the troubles and all that they're worth: Accounts of physically disabled persons attempting ordinary life*. Unpublished doctoral dissertation, University of Colorado, Boulder.

Belenky, Mary; Clinchy, Blythe; Goldberger, Nancy; & Tarule, Jill. (1986). *Women's ways of knowing*. New York: Basic Books.

Comer, James P. (1988). Is "parenting" essential to good teaching? *NEA Today, 6*, 34–40.

Dewey, John. (1937a). President Hutchins' proposals to remake higher education. *The Social Frontier, 3,* 103–104.

Dewey, John. (1937b). The higher learning in America. *The Social Frontier, 3,* 167–169.

Eugene, Toinette. (1989). Sometimes I feel like a motherless child: The call and response for a liberational ethic of care by black feminists. In Mary M. Brabeck (Ed.), *Who cares? Theory, research and educational implications of the ethic of care* (pp. 45–62). Westport, CT: Praeger.

Gilligan, Carol. (1982). *In a different voice.* Cambridge, MA: Harvard University Press.

Haan, Norma. (1978). Two moralities in action contexts: Relationship to thought, ego regulation, and development. *Journal of Personality and Social Psychology, 36,* 286–305.

Hutchins, Robert Maynard. (1937). Grammar, rhetoric, and Mr. Dewey. *The Social Frontier, 3,* 137–139.

Lyons, Nona Plesser. (1983). Two perspectives: On self, relationships, and morality. *Harvard Educational Review, 53*(2), 125–145.

MacIntyre, Alasdair. (1981). *After virtue.* Notre Dame, IN: University of Notre Dame Press.

Murdoch, Iris. (1970). *The sovereignty of good.* London: Routledge and Kegan Paul.

Noddings, Nel. (1984). *Caring: A feminine approach to ethics and moral education.* Berkeley: University of California Press.

Noddings, Nel. (1989). Theoretical and practical concerns about small group mathematics. *Elementary School Journal, 89*(5), 607–624.

Selman, Robert L. (1980). *The growth of interpersonal understanding: Development and clinical analyses.* New York: Academic Press.

Sizer, Theodore R. (1984). *Horace's compromise: The dilemma of the American high school.* Boston: Houghton Mifflin.

Watson, Jean. (1985). *Nursing: The philosophy and science of caring.* Boulder: Colorado Associated University Press.

Weil, Simone. (1951). *Waiting for God.* New York: G. P. Putnam's Sons.

Women in legal education: Pedagogy, law, theory, and practice [Special issue]. (1988, May/June). *Journal of Legal Education.*

10

Stories Told and Lessons Learned
Toward a Narrative Approach
to Moral Development and Moral Education

MARK B. TAPPAN and LYN MIKEL BROWN

Mark Tappan and Lyn Mikel Brown are research associates in education, human development, and psychology at the Harvard Graduate School of Education. They are currently working with Carol Gilligan on the Project on the Psychology of Women and the Development of Girls. Dr. Tappan's research interests are in late adolescent moral development and in narrative and interpretive approaches to the study of human development. Dr. Brown's interests are in female social and personality development and in feminist methodology. The authors are married to each other and live in Cambridge, Massachusetts.

Asked whether she has ever been in a situation where she experienced a conflict and had to make a difficult choice or decision, 11-year-old Rachel, a white fifth-grader, tells the following story[1]:

> Like telling the truth or not telling the truth? Okay, this spring, my dad and I went to this paint gallery — it was where you buy stuff — and there was dirt on my coat, from a pigeon, some dirt. So I went upstairs to the bathroom and when I was washing it off I dropped a piece of tissue down into the toilet and it got clogged, and I didn't know what to do because I was afraid that if I left it there it would

This chapter is a revised and condensed version of an article that first appeared as Tappan, Mark B., and Brown, Lyn Mikel, "Stories Told and Lessons Learned: Toward a Narrative Approach to Moral Development and Moral Education," *Harvard Educational Review*, 59:2, pp. 182–205. Copyright © 1989 by the President and Fellows of Harvard College. All rights reserved. Used by permission.

flood the thing and all these paintings would be ruined. I didn't know what to do.

Okay, so what did you end up doing?

Well, okay, at first I was really nervous because I wasn't going to tell them and then right before I left I said, "I got this thing caught," and he goes, "Thank you for telling me," and it got unclogged by itself, so I didn't need to tell, but it was okay.

So what was the conflict for you?

Well, I didn't know whether . . . because if it was clogged, then I would probably get in big trouble and my dad would yell at me. But if I didn't tell, then the paintings could be ruined and it would be really expensive, because I would have to pay for all of them.

Okay, do you think that what you did was the right thing to do?

Yes.

Why?

Because I made my family trust me more because I told the truth, and it didn't have any chance to get caught, it went by itself, so then it made my family trust me more, because they knew I told the truth.

We begin with this story of moral conflict and choice because it highlights three issues we want to explore in this chapter:

1. Rachel recounts this particular experience in her life by telling a story about it — that is, she constructs a narrative to represent it.
2. Rachel's narrative account of her real-life conflict is especially engaging because it is a story about a moral conflict — that is, about whether or not to tell the truth.
3. Rachel's story is also about an important lesson she learned as a result of her experience — hence we would argue that a crucial aspect of her own moral development is, in fact, expressed in the story she tells.

Thus, when asked about a difficult decision, Rachel not only tells a story, she tells a *moral story* — a moral story about what she learned regarding the importance of telling the truth.

Our aim in this chapter is to reflect on this complex relationship between narrative, morality, and moral development. Our goal is to sketch the broad outlines of a narrative approach to moral development and moral education — an approach that offers an alternative to the models and methods currently in use (see Chazan, 1985; Hersh, Miller, & Fielding, 1980). As such, our goal is also to argue for the recovery and reappreciation of the role story telling and narrative—particularly oral narrative—can play in moral education. There is a long, diverse, and well-respected history of story telling across a wide variety of cultures, but by and large, given social, cultural, and technological changes, the power of these oral narrative traditions has been lost to the modern Western world (see Ong, 1982; Scholes & Kellogg, 1966). Thus, given that much public and political attention has recently focused on the importance of moral education in the schools, and given that there is widespread dissatisfaction with the available approaches (see Damon, 1988), the time is ripe, it seems, to rethink some of the central issues involved in designing educational programs to facilitate moral development in children and adolescents.

We begin with a brief discussion of narrative, in general, focusing on how individuals give meaning to their life experiences by representing them in narrative form. We then turn to a consideration of the psychological dimensions of moral experience, suggesting, in particular, that individuals represent their lived experience of moral decision making and moral action primarily through narrative. We argue, therefore, in the third section, that individuals develop morally by "authoring" their own moral stories and by learning the moral lessons in the stories they tell about their own experiences. This sets the stage for our description, in the fourth and final section, of the basic principles of a narrative approach to moral education designed to facilitate moral development by providing students with the opportunity to "author" their own moral stories. Throughout this chapter we illustrate the relationship between narrative, moral development, and moral education through excerpts from interviews with children and adolescents who, like Rachel, have been invited to tell their own moral stories. In addition, we also highlight the role hermeneutics (that is, the art and practice of interpretation) necessarily plays in a narrative approach to moral development and moral education.

NARRATIVE

Robert, a 16-year-old Puerto Rican sophomore, tells the following story about a recent moral conflict in his life:

> Well, last week, my friends, they wanted to rob somebody, and then I was going to go down with them, be with them, but then when I saw they were going to do it, I just said, "naw," so I just turned back. It was hard, though, 'cause for a couple of weeks they called me all these names. I told them that it's wrong. They felt the same way I did—some of them felt the same way I did.

Did they?

Yeah. Now I don't hang with some of the persons. It's wrong. I got arrested once. That was a couple of years ago. I don't do that no more.

Can you tell me what the problem was for you in that situation?

It went through my mind real fast, it's, you know, my conscience got the best of me. Told me to turn back, something told me to turn back. They went on through it, they went, I left, they went, and a couple of them got arrested.

Can you tell me what went through your mind in deciding what to do?

If I get arrested, a lot of things . . . if I get arrested, what if my mother finds out, my father finds out? What a reputation I have.

How would your reputation come into it?

I have a nice reputation now. I don't do nothing, smoke or anything. Like some of my friends, they might not think I would hang with them.

How come?

'Cause some of my friends, they ain't like that. They think, "that cat's straight," and it's true, he's straight, he ain't uptight.

What about your parents — what went through your mind about them?

I don't know, I just said, "naw," and turned around. I said, "these are suckers," that's what I said, and I just changed my mind.

How come you think they're suckers?

It's wrong, it's just wrong.

Narrative is a fundamental human activity — "international, transhistorical, transcultural: it is simply there, like life itself" (Barthes, 1977, p. 79). Whenever it is necessary to report "the way it really happened," the natural impulse is to compose a narrative, to tell a story that recounts the actions and events of interest in some kind of temporal sequence. Such a story, however, does more than simply outline a series of incidents: It places those incidents in a particular narrative context, thereby giving them a particular meaning. That is, "narrative might well be considered a solution to a problem of general human concern, namely, the problem of how to translate *knowing* into *telling*, the problem of fashioning human experience into a form assimilable to structures of meaning that are generally human" (White, 1981, p. 1).

Thus, in order to understand the actions of others we tend to place those actions in a narrative context — as do historians (see Danto, 1985; White, 1973) or psychoanalysts (see Schafer, 1981; Spence, 1982). Similarly, in order to give meaning to our *own* actions, we tend to tell stories about those actions (as Rachel and Robert do) and hence to place them in the context of the ongoing narratives of our lives.

NARRATIVE AND MORAL EXPERIENCE

Carmen, a young Hispanic woman (age 16) who is a classmate of Robert's, tells the following story about a recent moral conflict in her life:

> I had a lot of family problems at my home, especially with my father. Once came a time when I had to decide whether he should go out or I should go out, and I didn't know what to do, because we were arguing, and it was real hard for me. I told him, "I can't argue with you and have all these problems, and I can't concentrate on my work, going to school." "I don't have any time for myself," I said to him, "either it's you going out or me going out."
>
> *What do you mean by going out?*
>
> Move out of the house. Because it's just going to be war all the time, and my mother she's real nerve-sick, and I can't just have her listen to us arguing all the time. It was real hard for me, even though it's like, God, if I should go, I could spend time with my aunt, or he should just move out and go to [another city]. And I didn't really know what to do.
>
> *What was the most difficult thing about deciding what to do?*
>
> It was difficult, I thought, if he leaves, then the kids are going to blame it on me. "And he left because of your fault," this and that, and that's going to be on my conscience and I'm going to feel real bad about it. And then if I leave, they're going to go, "my father made her leave and I missed her" . . . it's going to be the kids that are going to start talking.
>
> *Your brothers and sisters?*
>
> Right. At the end, I made a decision and he left the house for about a year, then he came back, and talked to me, and he promised me that things would be different. Since then it has been different.

In moving from a general discussion of narrative to a more focused discussion of the role narrative can play in moral development and moral education, we want to offer a brief analysis of the psychological dimensions of moral experience. We use the term "moral experience" to capture the "lived experience" of an individual faced with a situation, conflict, or dilemma that requires a moral decision and a moral action — that is, an individual faced with the question, What is the "right" or the "moral" thing to do in this situation? Thus, for example, we would argue that Rachel, Robert, and Carmen, in the interview excerpts quoted above, all represent their own moral experience as they describe their respective responses to situations in which they had to decide what was the "right" thing to do, and do it.

The key to understanding the psychological complexity of moral experience, however, is to sustain as a fundamental unity its cognitive, affective, and conative dimensions. To this end we have extended Wilhelm Dilthey's (1894/1977) conception of the tripartite structure of "psychic life" to focus specifically on the three-dimensional nature of moral experience (see Tappan, 1987, in press). Such an analysis does not divorce cognition, emotion, and action, as has traditionally been done in the study of moral development (see, for example, Hoffman, 1976, 1982; Kohlberg, 1981, 1984), but instead highlights three interrelated and fundamentally indissociable dimensions of moral experience.

Thus, we would claim that Rachel's narrative representation of her moral experience implies a complicated and complex interaction of cognitive (what she thought), affective (how she felt), and conative (what she did) dimensions: She thought "the paintings could be ruined" and that she "would probably get in big trouble," she felt "afraid" and "really nervous," but yet she finally decided to act by telling the gallery owner "I got this thing caught." As such, while what she thought and felt both influenced what she did, ultimately her act of telling the truth also influenced how she thought and felt about herself—"I made my family trust me more because I told the truth."

Similarly, Robert represents what he thought ("I saw they were going to do it"), what he felt ("it was hard"), and what he did ("I just turned back") in his narrative. Yet in Robert's moral story we can also see how fundamentally indissociable these three dimensions really are. In particular, Robert's representation of how he thought about the problem—"It went through my mind real fast . . . my conscience got the best of me . . . told me to turn back, something told me to turn back"—clearly involves cognitive, affective, and conative elements. Yet it is virtually impossible to distinguish between the thoughts and feelings that "went through his mind real fast" and the thoughts, feelings, and actions that came together in his "conscience," ultimately "telling" him "to turn back."

Without such a focus on the cognitive, affective, and conative dimensions of Rachel's and Robert's representations of their respective moral experiences, and on the circular interactions among them (how, for example, what Robert thinks influences how he feels; or how what Rachel does influences both what she thinks and how she feels), a listener (or reader) runs a very substantial risk of misunderstanding their stories. Our purpose here, however, is not to spell out all the implications of this view of moral experience and its representation (see, instead, Tappan, in press). Rather, we want to return to the issue of narrative and argue, based on three related assumptions, that when we make moral choices and decisions in our lives, we represent those choices and decisions, and give them meaning, primarily by telling stories about them. Narrative thus becomes a very important means for understanding both moral experience and moral development.

Although the term *moral experience* is used to capture the complex nature of an individual's response—in real life and in real time—to moral conflicts and dilemmas, the only way to gain access to and study the dimensions of that experience is through retrospective accounts of specific choices and decisions. We cannot tag along with an individual until she is faced with a moral conflict and then ask her, in the moment, what she is thinking, how she is feeling, and what she is going to do. Rather, we must be content to hear about her decision after the fact—and as she chooses to report it—in its *narrative* form (see MacIntyre, 1981). Despite obvious questions about the veracity of retrospective accounts and the relationship between "historical truth" and "narrative truth" (see Spence, 1982; also Walsh, 1958), we have no other choice. For it is through narrative that we represent and give meaning to our life experiences, whether as mundane as going to the grocery store or as momentous as a moral crisis that changes our lives forever.

Jerome Bruner's (1986, 1987) recent work is particularly helpful in describing the relationship between narrative and the cognitive, affective, conative unity, primarily because of his focus on what he calls the "narrative mode" of psychological functioning. Bruner (1986) argues both that cognition, affect, and action cannot be easily separated—that a "real poverty is bred" (p. 69) by making too sharp a distinction among these three dimensions—and that one of the functions of narrative in culture is to hold these three dimensions together:

> We *can* abstract each of these [dimensions] from the unified whole, but if we do so too rigidly we lose sight of the fact that it is one of the functions of a culture to keep them related and together in those images, stories, and the like by which our experience is given cultural relevance. (p. 69)

In other words, if one of the functions of narrative is to hold cognition, emotion, and action together, and thereby to give meaning to human experience through the representation of such a unity, then we should also expect that narratives of moral decision making would provide a valuable

window through which to view the interrelationship between the cognitive, affective, and conative dimensions of moral experience.

This connection between narrative and the representation of specifically moral choices and values constitutes our third line of argument. This
argument assumes that another function of narrative in culture is to endow
a certain sequence of events with moral meaning; it is based on Hayden
White's (1981) analysis of the role that what he calls "narrativity" plays in
historiography. White argues that what distinguishes a historical narrative
of certain events from a simple listing of those events in a temporal sequence is that such a narrative, by definition, stands in relation to a particular moral perspective, on behalf of which that narrative attempts to assert
authority. A historical narrative, therefore, attempts to endow a sequence
of events with the kind of legitimacy and meaning that would justify and
sustain the moral perspective on behalf of which it is written:

> If every fully realized story . . . is a kind of allegory, points to a moral, or
> endows events, whether real or imaginary, with a significance that they do
> not possess as a mere sequence, then it seems possible to conclude that every
> historical narrative has as its latent or manifest purpose the desire to moralize
> the events of which it treats. (pp. 13–14)

Thus, according to White, the author of a historical narrative asserts
his authority by giving meaning to a particular series of events by telling a
story: "The plot of a narrative imposes a meaning on the events that
comprise its story . . . by revealing at the end a structure that was imma-
nent in the events *all along*" (p. 19; see also Kermode, 1967). The author,
by imposing a narrative form and plot on a sequence of "real events," gives
to those events the meaning, value, and formal coherence that only stories
possess: "The demand for closure in the historical story is a demand, [there-
fore], for moral meaning, a demand that sequences of events be assessed as
to their significance as elements of a *moral* drama" (p. 20). "Could we ever
narrativize *without* moralizing?" (p. 23) is White's rhetorical final question. His answer, clearly, is no.

This connection between telling stories and moralizing is as clear in
the individual stories we tell about our lives and our real-life experiences as
it is in the writing of historical narratives about, for example, wars or
social movements. Thus Rachel, when asked about a situation in which she
faced a difficult choice, does not simply list a series of events that occurred
on the day she and her father visited the art gallery. Rather, she tells a story
about her experience that day — a moral story about "telling the truth" and
the trust she gained from her decision and her actions. Similarly, Robert
tells a moral story about why he did the right thing in deciding not to join

his friends in a robbery, and Carmen tells a moral story about her decision to ask her father to move out of the house, and why that turned out to be the right thing to do, both for her and for her family. These are moral stories, furthermore, that represent the complex and complicated interrelationship between the cognitive, affective, and conative dimensions of lived moral experience. As such, they again illustrate the ways in which narrative serves to give meaning to lived experiences of moral conflict and choice.

NARRATIVE AND MORAL DEVELOPMENT

Malcolm, a young African-American classmate of Robert's and Carmen's (age 15), tells the following story about a recent moral conflict in his life:

I've been in a lot of situations where usually I didn't make the decision, usually it was my mother that made the decision, and she usually made the right decision. But I did have a situation when my father, he doesn't live here any more, he lives [in another state], he wanted me to come live with him and go to school. My mother wanted me to go to school up here, so I didn't know what to decide. I thought if I would decide to go live with my father, it would be wrong to my mother, and I thought if I decided to live with my mother, it would be wrong to my father. But then I started thinking about what was best for me, because I'm adjusted to my area, I know everybody around here, and I just didn't want to up and move just to please one of them, or whatever. I wanted to make sure I was happy, so I stayed where I was at and just decided to stay here.

Was it a hard decision?

Yeah, it was, because I thought if I decided, I would be wrong to one of them, but I just started thinking what would be right for me, so I just stayed.

What sort of things did you think about?

I think I remember . . . I was thinking about going to a strange school in a state I know nothing about . . . strange. And I'm already adjusted up here.

How did your parents feel?

They felt my decision was good, all right, well, so they didn't argue with me.

How did that make you feel?

Better.

We now turn to a discussion of the relationship between narrative and moral development. If individuals tend to represent and give meaning to their real-life moral experiences through narrative, then it makes sense to assume that a central aspect of the process of moral development is both expressed and enhanced through the moral stories they tell about their lives. Thus our aim in this section is to sketch the outlines of the following argument: Individuals develop morally by "authoring" their own moral stories and by learning the lessons in the stories they tell about the moral experiences in their lives. This argument will set the stage and provide the rationale for our description, in the next section, of the basic principles of a narrative approach to moral education.

One of the key features of any developmental theory is the stipulation of the valued goal, or *telos*, toward which developmental progress is assumed to proceed (Kaplan, 1983). In traditional cognitive-developmental stage theories such a telos has taken the form of Formal Operations (Inhelder & Piaget, 1958) or Universal Ethical Principles (Kohlberg, 1981, 1984). Although our conception of moral development as expressed through narrative is not a traditional developmental stage theory, it nevertheless does have a telos toward which, we would argue, moral development proceeds: Authorship.

An individual achieves authorship by authoring his or her own moral story. Authoring, in this view, entails more than simply recounting a series of events in a temporal sequence; it involves telling a *story*; constructing a *narrative*; "narrativizing," in White's (1981) terms. As such, it also entails *moralizing*: imbuing a story or narrative with moral value, thereby asserting or claiming moral *authority* on behalf of an individual's own moral perspective.[2] The attainment of authorship, as expressed in the moral story (or stories) an individual tells, indicates, therefore, that she has claimed authority for the moral thoughts, feelings, and actions that comprise the psychological dimensions of her moral experience (see also Brown, 1989).

What does it mean to claim authority for one's moral thoughts, feelings, and actions in the context of a moral story that one tells, and why is such authority valuable? It means, for one thing, clearly expressing and acknowledging one's own moral perspective, as does Robert when he says "it's wrong" to rob somebody, and as does Rachel when she says her story is about "telling the truth." It also means honoring (or "authorizing") what one thinks, feels, and does with respect to what is right and what is wrong—even in the face of potential conflict and disagreement—as does Malcolm, when he says, "I just started thinking what would be right for me, so I just stayed." And, finally, it means assuming *responsibility* for one's moral actions, and for acting on behalf of one's moral perspective, as does Carmen when she says "at the end I made a decision and he [her father] left the house." For, as Augusto Blasi (1984, 1985) argues, moral responsibility (when an action, evaluated as moral, is also judged to be strictly necessary) is tied directly to an individual's sense of his or her moral *identity* and *authenticity*.

Consequently, authoring contrasts with a simple listing of the events in a situation of moral conflict in which the individual assumes virtually no responsibility, and hence claims virtually no moral authority or authorization, with respect to his thoughts, feelings, and actions. Furthermore, although the analogies are not direct, evidence from social psychological research on bystander intervention (Darley & Latane, 1968) and obedience to authority (Milgram, 1974) suggests that individuals who experience little or no responsibility or authority in crisis situations are much more likely to act in ways that are harmful to their fellow human beings than are individuals who assume responsibility or claim authority for their actions.

To help us further make the link between a conception of authorship as the telos of moral development, narrative, and the psychological dimensions of moral experience, we turn to the work of Mikhail Bakhtin (1986). For Bakhtin, a Russian literary critic and philosopher, the activity of authoring is a central component of his analysis of human experience (Clark & Holquist, 1984). Meaning, in general, and values, in particular, are expressed in dynamic form through the activity of authoring. All of us who make utterances, therefore, whether they are spoken or written, are authors: "We operate out of a point of view and shape values into forms" (Clark & Holquist, 1984, p. 10). How we "author" our lives through articulating who we are influences what we think, how we feel, and what we do. In addition, because Bakhtin treats morality and values not in the context of an abstract philosophical system, but rather as the "practical work of building," he helps us to see that "by shaping answers in the constant activity of our dialogue with the world, we enact the architectonics of our own responsibility" (Clark & Holquist, 1984, p. 10).

This notion of dialogue with others in the world is key to understanding the relationship Bakhtin sees between authorship and responsibility for moral action. Bakhtin emphasizes action, movement, energy, and, ultimately, performance:

> Life as event presumes selves that are performers. To be successful, the relation between me and the other must be shaped into a coherent performance, and thus the architectonic activity of authorship, which is the building of a text, parallels the activity of human existence, which is the building of a self. (Clark & Holquist, 1984, p. 64)

For Bakhtin, then, what differentiates humans from other living creatures is, indeed, the potential for authorship:

> The means by which a specific ratio of self-to-other responsibility is achieved in any given action — a deed being understood as an answer — comes about as the result of efforts by the self to shape meaning out of the encounter between them. What self is answerable to is the social environment; what self is answerable for is the authorship of its responses. (pp. 67–68)

We argue, following Bakhtin, that such authorship is most clearly expressed in the stories the self tells about its own moral experience. For Bakhtin, the analogy between literary authorship and his view of "life as authoring" (see Kozulin, 1988) represents a deliberate attempt to use the paradigmatic case of the creation of literary texts to explore how the relations between self and other are crafted, both in art and in life. We argue, literally, that just as an author of a novel (or a historical narrative) expresses her authorship — thereby asserting her moral authority — in the process of creating and writing her book (see White, 1981), so do we, as individual moral agents, express our authorship — thereby asserting our own authority and responsibility — through the moral stories we tell about our lives.

Returning now to the question of development, we suggest that authorship not only expresses itself through narrative, it also develops through narrative. This is because when an individual tells a moral story about an experience in his life, he must necessarily *reflect* on that experience: "To narrate a story is already to reflect upon the event narrated" (Ricoeur, 1986, p. 61). Consequently, such reflection also entails *learning* from the event narrated, in the sense that the individual has the opportunity to consider what happened, what he thought, felt, and did, and how things turned out. Authoring, furthermore, is enabled and encouraged by just such a reflective consideration of one's experience in the process of narrating a story of moral conflict, because to claim authority and assume responsibility one must be fully aware of the consequences of one's thoughts, feelings, and actions. This is what we have called "learning the lessons" in the stories individuals tell about the moral experiences in their lives.

We would argue, finally, that Rachel's, Robert's, Carmen's, and Malcolm's narratives all illustrate this conception of moral development. That is, although the development of authorship is a gradual, long-term process, these short excerpts nevertheless all show evidence of authorship, in the sense that each of these authors claims authority for his or her particular moral perspective, and each assumes responsibility to act on behalf of his or her perspective.

These preliminary and provisional ideas about the relationship between narrative and moral development can be summarized as follows:
When an individual is invited and encouraged to tell a story about her own
real-life moral experience, two related things happen: First, because constructing a narrative necessarily entails moralizing, based on a particular
moral perspective, telling a moral story requires that she authorize that
perspective — hence telling a moral story also provides an opportunity for
her authorship (and authority) to be expressed. Second, telling a moral
story also necessarily entails reflecting on the experience narrated, thereby
encouraging her to learn more from her experience — by claiming more
authority and assuming more responsibility for her thoughts, feelings, and
actions — than would be possible if she were simply to list or describe the
events in question. Consequently, authorship (and authority) is both expressed and developed through opportunities to tell one's own moral stories.

NARRATIVE AND MORAL EDUCATION

Jennifer, a white seventh grader (age 13), tells the following story about an
important moral conflict in her life:

> In fourth grade I was in a big jam, okay. I was with these group of
> friends who weren't really my friends, but I didn't realize it then.
> And, I tried to fit in, but I just couldn't, you know. And then finally
> the time came when I had to make a choice of either staying with
> them and being miserable or finding a new set of friends, and, you
> know, starting over with friends. And, I wasn't sure what to do. And
> . . . but I did . . . but then I realized that good things weren't hap-
> pening, let's put it that way. Because I wasn't happy, and I wasn't
> sure of myself, so I decided to find a new set of friends, and it
> worked.
>   *In thinking about what to do, what did you consider?*
>   I considered where I was at the moment, you know, which
> wasn't a great position, because I wasn't being honest with myself
> and I wasn't thinking about myself, I just wanted to have these group
> of friends.
>   *So what did you finally decide to do?*
>   Find a new set of friends.
>   *Do you think what you did was the right thing to do?*
>   Yeah, definitely.
>   *Why?*

My grades were dropping, and so I was always a straight A student, and then my grades started dropping, and I went down to Cs and Ds and stuff, and the teacher was really worried about me, and I think it was best for my education.

Now how can that kind of thing affect your education?

Because I was having trouble with my friends, and it seemed like they'd like me one day and they didn't the next, and I used to come home and I'd be like, "Oh mom, what am I going to do, they don't like me?" Then, "Oh ma, they like me!" And my mom thought I was really confused, you know. I didn't know what was going on around me. So, she sort of pointed me in the right direction, and I started to take one step, you know, and then I took another, and they were bad for my education because I was losing confidence in myself. I was losing myself, really, and losing the kind of person I was. So, I just got back on track.

What might be the central features of a narrative approach to moral education, based on the conception of the relationship between narrative and moral development outlined earlier? In particular, what new insight does this view of narrative offer teachers as they evoke and respond to students' stories? Although these ideas are again preliminary and provisional, we offer the following brief outline of the major components of a moral education program based on narrative as a starting point for further discussion, debate, elaboration, and clarification.

Most important, a narrative approach to moral education provides students with the opportunity to tell their own moral stories and thus to express and enhance their own authority and responsibility through the process of authoring. By representing the cognitive, affective, and conative dimensions of their own moral experience through narrative, students will therefore be encouraged to reflect on their own experience from the standpoint of their own moral perspective. This will lead to not only an increased sense of authority and authorization on behalf of that perspective but also an increased sense of responsibility for action.

Consequently, the narrative approach to moral education we propose here is concerned solely with inviting and encouraging students to tell their own moral stories. As such, it differs from other narrative approaches to moral education that highlight the ways stories, novels, and other works of literature that students read and discuss can also be powerfully educative (see, for example, Coles, 1989). We would certainly agree that providing students with the opportunity to engage the moral stories in great works of literature is a very important component of any overall moral education program. Our focus here, however, is on another aspect of a narrative approach to moral education that has not been widely practiced to date: having students author their own moral stories.

This opportunity for students to author their own moral stories can, and should, take several forms. One is to provide the opportunity for students to be formally interviewed, by teachers, fellow students, or, perhaps, even outside interviewers, so they can tell their stories of real-life conflict and choice in great detail. An in-depth interview designed to evoke stories of moral experience is a powerful means of enhancing authorship because it provides a live *audience*, in the form of a sympathetic and engaged listener, to whom the student can tell his story.[3] The presence of a real audience serves to encourage authoring, as the author/interviewee seeks to arouse and fulfill desires and expectations in the mind of his audience/interviewer (Burke, 1931). This is because, unlike someone who simply lists a sequence of events, the author of a story has a particular moral perspective on behalf of which he wants to claim authority and, therefore, on behalf of which he wants to argue. Consequently, his role as an author is to convince his audience of both the legitimacy of his moral perspective and the righteousness of his actions in the story he tells. Thus the author must engage the "psychology of the audience" (Burke, 1931) in ways that enable him to make his case most convincingly and authoritatively. This, again, is what we have called *authoring*.

Students can also be given the opportunity to author their own moral stories in written form, by keeping a journal or through essay assignments that focus on the moral decisions they have made in their own lives. Here, again, the teacher is the audience for these stories; hence she must be not only sensitive and sympathetic, but she must also provide students with the kind of response to their stories that indicates she has heard and understood them. Although this response can be either oral or written, it must acknowledge the author's own moral perspective and encourage the continued authorization of that perspective — that is, it must support the gradual emergence of authorship.

Finally, students may even be given the opportunity to dramatize their own moral stories, through skits and plays or through video productions. Such an option would necessarily involve sharing a story with a peer audience in a way not required by the first two approaches. Although this may be uncomfortable for some, it may also provide the opportunity for students to learn important lessons from the stories of their peers — lessons that may not be learned in any other way.

Needless to say, in order for any of these options to succeed they must occur in the context of a relationship with a sensitive and caring teacher. The power of this approach comes from the authority students can gain by authoring their moral stories and sharing them with an audience; the danger of this approach is the vulnerability that goes along with sharing difficult, painful, and perhaps even tragic stories. Teachers, therefore, must recognize both the opportunities and the risks inherent in such an approach and be prepared to respond accordingly.

One of the central issues that teachers must confront directly with respect to this approach is the problem of interpretation. Stories are often ambiguous and, even, opaque; thus any approach that focuses on the detailed stories people tell about the moral conflicts and decisions they have faced in their lives must deal with how to interpret and understand those "texts" (see Brown, 1988; Brown, Tappan, Gilligan, Miller, & Argyris, 1989; Dilthey, 1900/1976; Mishler, 1986). What is demanded, therefore, is a hermeneutic or interpretive methodology sensitive to the subtle nuance of voice, language, and perspective and open to the possibility that the same text can be read in a number of different ways—a story, in other words, may not be read in the same way by all readers. In particular, gender, cultural, and social-class differences may profoundly affect how a particular story is read and understood (see Flynn & Schweickart, 1986; Schweickart, 1986; Showalter, 1985).

Thus, in practice, teachers can exhibit their concern for and involvement with their students by taking great care in how they interpret and understand the stories they are told. This means that teachers must neither assume automatically they know what a student's story means nor be too quick to judge a particular story as "inappropriate," "immoral," or, simply, "wrong." Rather, teachers must cultivate an openness to and a tolerance of the stories they hear, and they must be willing to work with their students so that both come to understand and appreciate the lessons inherent in these stories. Then, and only then, will students' authorship of their own stories—hence their authorization of their own moral perspective—be encouraged and enabled.

How, specifically, might teachers work with students' stories in this way? Jennifer's narrative, above, provides another example of a "text" that can be interpreted and understood from the standpoint of this approach. Jennifer (like Rachel, Robert, Carmen, and Malcolm) tells a story that clearly represents the psychological complexity of her own lived moral experience. The dynamic interplay of thoughts, feelings, and actions is evident in her discussion of how her thinking about this problem with her friends influenced how she felt about herself ("I wasn't being honest with myself and I wasn't thinking about myself"), how her feelings influenced her thinking ("I wasn't happy and I wasn't sure of myself"), and, perhaps most important, how her thoughts and feelings both influenced, and were influenced by, her actions ("I was losing myself, really, and losing the kind of person I was. So, I just got back on track"). In addition, Jennifer's story also expresses the gradual development of her own authorship. She describes a problem in which her own voice was silenced and her authority limited. The lesson she learns, however, has to do with the importance of asserting her own authority and taking responsibility for solving her problem by finding a new set of friends ("I started to take one step, you know, and then I took another"). Her story has a happy ending because she ultimately makes a choice that honors her own perspective, thereby authorizing her own voice ("I wasn't happy, and I wasn't sure of myself, so I decided to find a new set of friends, and it worked") (see also Brown, 1989).

In sum, then, we argue that the narrative approach to moral education we have outlined above is unique in its emphasis on having students tell their own moral stories and in its focus on authorship and self-authorization as the goals of moral development. As such, it offers a perspective on moral education not often found in other contemporary approaches (see Chazan, 1985). We do not want to claim, however, that this approach should be used alone, as the sole means to facilitate moral development — the process of moral development is too varied and complex and the moral world we live in too complicated to justify such hubris. Rather, we suggest that this approach be used in conjunction with other approaches with which it is cor ,atible, in order to provide students with a full range of experiences and ipportunities designed to facilitate moral development. In that way studen\s not only can be encouraged to claim authority and assume responsibility for their own moral perspectives, but they can also be encouraged to explore — in all of its irreducible richness and complexity — what it means to live a moral life (see Nussbaum, 1986).

CONCLUSION

In this chapter we have tried to sketch the broad outlines of a narrative approach to moral development and moral education, an approach that takes seriously the moral stories individuals — especially children and adolescents — tell about their lives. We have based this approach on a three-dimensional view of the psychology of "moral experience," and we have argued that the stories children and adolescents tell about their own real-life moral decisions not only represent the cognitive, affective, and conative dimensions of this experience but also express the gradual emergence of authorship and authority that are key to moral development. We have also discussed several possible components of a moral education program based on narrative, focusing specifically on providing students with the opportunity to author their own moral stories. And, throughout this chapter, we have provided examples of stories told and lessons learned by children and adolescents from different school contexts to illustrate the ways in which teachers and researchers can listen to and understand the stories they are told.

As we reflect, finally, on the larger intellectual and cultural climate from which this approach has emerged, it is important to acknowledge that this is what might be called a "poststructuralist" or "postmodern" approach to moral development and moral education. It is, therefore, influenced by recent trends in literary theory (see Culler, 1982), by recent hermeneutic approaches to social science theory and research (Packer, 1985; Packer & Addison, 1989), and, specifically, by Gilligan's (1982, 1983, 1986; Gilligan, Brown, & Rogers, 1990; Gilligan & Wiggins, 1987) critique of traditional approaches to developmental psychology. As such this approach attempts to move beyond the genetic structuralism of the cognitive developmental paradigm — the dominant paradigm in moral development and education over the past 20 years (see Kohlberg, 1981, 1984; Mosher, 1980) — toward a new vision of the relationship between developmental psychology and education. This vision, still in its nascent form, seeks to use education less to facilitate development along a hierarchical progression of structurally defined stages and more to enable each student to resist and overcome social and cultural repression, and hence to authorize his or her own moral voice. Consequently, this vision does not see "education as a function of society," where the function of education is to prepare the minds of the young to maintain and uphold the basic principles of society, but rather sees "society as a function of education," where the function of education is to remake or reform society, because the principles and directives of society are by and large unreasonable (Lentricchia, 1985, pp. 1–2; also Burke, 1961; Giroux, 1988).

Clearly there is an inherent danger in any narrative approach to moral development and moral education — a danger that educators and/or researchers using such an approach will assume the right to choose, unilaterally, which stories children and adolescents can tell (as well as which stories they are told), even when those stories continue to foster psychological or social oppression or fail to represent the students' own cultural traditions. Stories can be instruments of indoctrination and hence can be used to perpetuate the status quo; that is, the view that "education should be a function of society." It is our hope, however, that by listening to the voices of children and adolescents as they tell their own stories, educators and/or researchers will come to appreciate how powerfully educative and truly liberating such an experience can be. The narrative approach to moral development and moral education as we have envisioned it and outlined it above, therefore, promises a measure of freedom from the arbitrary imposition of culturally bound values and conventional stereotypes, as it seeks to encourage students to authorize their own voices and moral perspectives. For, as Bakhtin (1986) argues, "The search for one's own (authorial) voice [means] to be embodied, to become more clearly defined . . . to cast off reservations . . . not to remain tangential [but] to burst into the circle of life [and] become one among other people" (p. 147).

NOTES

Acknowledgments. The completion of this chapter was supported by the Lilly Endowment and by a grant from the Cleveland Foundation to Laurel School. The inner-city interviews were collected under a grant from the Mailman Family Foundation. We would like to thank Annie Rogers, Carol Gilligan, Elizabeth Debold, and Carol Witherell for their very helpful comments on earlier versions of the manuscript.

1. The narratives of Rachel and Jennifer come from interviews conducted as part of a 4-year research project at a private all-girls school in the suburbs of a large midwestern city (see Brown, 1989; Brown & Gilligan, 1989). The narratives of Robert, Carmen, and Malcolm come from interviews conducted as part of a research project designed to listen specifically to the voices of adolescents attending a large urban high school in the Northeast and to explore issues of violence and oppression in their lives (see Ward, 1986, 1989). All names are fictitious.

2. One key to our argument here is to note that the words *author* and *authority* are etymologically similar — they both come from the Latin *auctor*, meaning "promoter," "originator," or "author."

3. It is important to note, however, that stories elicited in a formal interview differ in fundamental ways from stories told spontaneously, in either oral or written form. The interviewer asks questions of the storyteller, thereby both interrupting his narrative and perhaps even directing it in ways the narrator might not have otherwise chosen to go. Thus it is important to acknowledge that stories told in such interviews are clearly *co-constructed*, in the context of the *dialogue* that necessarily occurs between interviewer and interviewee. For "the word," argues Bakhtin, "is a two-sided act. It is determined equally by whose word it is and for whom it is meant. . . . A word is territory *shared* by both addresser and addressee, by the speaker *and* [the] interlocutor" (Volosinov & Bakhtin, 1986, p. 86; italics in original).

REFERENCES

Bakhtin, M. (1986). *Speech genres and other late essays* (V. McGee, Trans.). Austin: University of Texas Press.

Barthes, R. (1977). Introduction to the structural analysis of narratives. In R. Barthes, *Image, music, text* (S. Heath, Trans.). London: Fontana/Collins.

Blasi, A. (1984). Moral identity: Its role in moral functioning. In W. Kurtines & J. Gewirtz (Eds.), *Morality, moral behavior, and moral development.* New York: Wiley & Sons.

Blasi, A. (1985). The moral personality: Reflections for social science and education. In M. Berkowitz & F. Oser (Eds.), *Moral education: Theory and application.* Hillsdale, NJ: Erlbaum.

Brown, L. (Ed.). (1988). *A guide to reading narratives of conflict and choice for self and moral voice* (Monograph No. 1). Cambridge, MA: Harvard Graduate School of Education, Center for the Study of Gender, Education, and Human Development.

Brown, L. (1989). *Narratives of relationship: The development of a care voice in girls ages 7 to 16.* Unpublished doctoral dissertation, Harvard University.

Brown, L., & Gilligan, C. (Eds.). (1989). *Relational voice, ways of knowing, and female development: Implications for education.* Cambridge, MA: Harvard Graduate School of Education, Center for the Study of Gender, Education, and Human Development.

Brown, L., Tappan, M., Gilligan, C., Miller, B., & Argyris, D. (1989). Reading for self and moral voice: A method for interpreting narratives of real-life moral conflict and choice. In M. Packer & R. Addison (Eds.), *Entering the circle: Hermeneutic investigation in psychology.* Albany: State University of New York Press.

Bruner, J. (1986). *Actual minds, possible worlds.* Cambridge, MA: Harvard University Press.

Bruner, J. (1987). Life as narrative. *Social Research, 54,* 11–32.

Burke, K. (1931). *Counter-statement.* Berkeley: University of California Press.

Burke, K. (1961). *Attitudes toward history.* Boston: Beacon Press.

Chazan, B. (1985). *Contemporary approaches to moral education.* New York: Teachers College Press.

Clark, K., & Holquist, M. (1984). *Mikhail Bakhtin.* Cambridge, MA: Harvard University Press.

Coles, R. (1989). *The call of stories: Teaching and the moral imagination.* Boston: Houghton-Mifflin.

Culler, J. (1982). *On deconstruction: Theory and criticism after structuralism.* Ithaca, NY: Cornell University Press.

Damon, W. (1988). *The moral child: Nurturing children's natural moral growth.* New York: Free Press.

Danto, A. (1985). *Narration and knowledge.* New York: Columbia University Press.

Darley, J., & Latane, B. (1968). Bystander intervention in emergencies: Diffusion of responsibility. *Journal of Personality and Social Psychology, 10,* 202–214.

Dilthey, W. (1976). The development of hermeneutics. In H. Rickman (Ed. & Trans.), *Dilthey: Selected writings.* Cambridge: Cambridge University Press. (Original work published 1900)

Dilthey, W. (1977). Ideas concerning a descriptive and analytic psychology. In W. Dilthey, *Descriptive psychology and historical understanding* (R. Zaner & K.

Heiges, Trans.). The Hague: Martinus Nijhoff. (Original work published 1894)

Flynn, E., & Schweickart, P. (Eds.). (1986). *Gender and reading: Essays on readers, texts, and contexts*. Baltimore: Johns Hopkins University Press.

Gilligan, C. (1982). *In a different voice: Psychological theory and women's development*. Cambridge, MA: Harvard University Press.

Gilligan, C. (1983). Do the social sciences have an adequate theory of moral development? In N. Haan, R. Bellah, P. Rabinow, & W. Sullivan (Eds.), *Social science as moral inquiry*. New York: Columbia University Press.

Gilligan, C. (1986). Remapping the moral domain: New images of self in relationship. In T. Heller, M. Sosna, & D. Wellbery (Eds.), *Reconstructing individualism: Autonomy, individuality, and the self in Western thought*. Stanford, CA: Stanford University Press.

Gilligan, C., Brown, L., & Rogers, A. (1990). Psyche embedded: A place for body, relationships, and culture in personality theory. In A. Rabin (Ed.), *Studying persons and lives*. New York: Springer-Verlag.

Gilligan, C., & Wiggins, G. (1987). The origins of morality in early childhood relationships. In J. Kagan & S. Lamb (Eds.), *The emergence of morality in young children*. Chicago: University of Chicago Press.

Giroux, H. (1988). *Schooling and the struggle for public life*. Minneapolis: University of Minnesota Press.

Hersh, R., Miller, J., & Fielding, G. (1980). *Models of moral education: An appraisal*. New York: Longman.

Hoffman, M. (1976). Empathy, role-taking, guilt, and development of altruistic motives. In T. Lickona (Ed.), *Moral development and behavior*. New York: Holt, Rinehart, & Winston.

Hoffman, M. (1982). Affect and moral development. In D. Cicchetti & P. Hesse (Eds.), *New directions for child development: Emotional development*. San Francisco: Jossey-Bass.

Inhelder, B., & Piaget, J. (1958). *The growth of logical thinking from childhood to adolescence*. New York: Basic Books.

Kaplan, B. (1983). A trio of trials. In R. Lerner (Ed.), *Developmental psychology: Historical and philosophical perspectives*. Hillsdale, NJ: Erlbaum.

Kermode, F. (1967). *The sense of an ending*. Oxford: Oxford University Press.

Kohlberg, L. (1981). *Essays on moral development: Vol. 1. The philosophy of moral development*. San Francisco: Harper & Row.

Kohlberg, L. (1984). *Essays on moral development: Vol. 2. The psychology of moral development*. San Francisco: Harper & Row.

Kozulin, A. (1988). *Life as authoring: The humanistic tradition in Russian psychology*. Unpublished manuscript, Boston University.

Lentricchia, F. (1985). *Criticism and social change*. Chicago: University of Chicago Press.

MacIntyre, A. (1981). *After virtue: A study in moral theory*. Notre Dame, IN: University of Notre Dame Press.

Milgram, S. (1974). *Obedience to authority*. New York: Harper & Row.

Mishler, E. (1986). *Research interviewing: Context and narrative.* Cambridge, MA: Harvard University Press.

Mosher, R. (Ed.). (1980). *Moral education: A first generation of research and development.* New York: Praeger.

Nussbaum, M. (1986). *The fragility of goodness.* New York: Cambridge University Press.

Ong, W. (1982). *Orality and literacy: The technologizing of the word.* London: Methuen.

Packer, M. (1985). Hermeneutic inquiry in the study of human conduct. *American Psychologist, 40,* 1081–1093.

Packer, M., & Addison, R. (Eds.). (1989). *Entering the circle: Hermeneutic investigation in psychology.* Albany: State University of New York Press.

Ricoeur, P. (1986). *Time and narrative* (Vol. 2). Chicago: University of Chicago Press.

Schafer, R. (1981). Narration in the psychoanalytic dialogue. In W. Mitchell (Ed.), *On narrative.* Chicago: University of Chicago Press.

Scholes, R., & Kellogg, R. (1966). *The nature of narrative.* New York: Oxford University Press.

Schweickart, P. (1986). Reading ourselves: Toward a feminist theory of reading. In E. Flynn & P. Schweickart (Eds.), *Gender and reading: Essays on readers, texts, and contexts.* Baltimore: Johns Hopkins University Press.

Showalter, E. (Ed.). (1985). *The new feminist criticism: Essays on women, literature, and theory.* New York: Pantheon Books.

Spence, D. (1982). *Narrative truth and historical truth: Meaning and interpretation in psychoanalysis.* New York: W. W. Norton.

Tappan, M. (1987). *Hermeneutics and moral development: A developmental analysis of short-term change in moral functioning during late adolescence.* Unpublished doctoral dissertation, Harvard University.

Tappan, M. (in press). Hermeneutics and moral development: Interpreting narrative representations of moral experience. *Developmental Review.*

Volosinov, V., & Bakhtin, M. (1986). *Marxism and the philosophy of language* (L. Matejka & I. Titunik, Trans.). Cambridge, MA: Harvard University Press.

Walsh, W. (1958). "Plain" and "significant" narrative in history. *Journal of Philosophy, 55,* 479–484.

Ward, J. (1986). *A study of urban adolescents' thinking about violence following a course on the Holocaust.* Unpublished doctoral dissertation, Harvard University.

Ward, J. (1989). Urban adolescents' conceptions of violence. In C. Gilligan, J. Ward, & J. Taylor (Eds.), *Mapping the moral domain: A contribution of women's thinking to psychological theory and education.* Cambridge, MA: Harvard University Press.

White, H. (1973). *Metahistory: The historical imagination in nineteenth-century Europe.* Baltimore: Johns Hopkins University Press.

White, H. (1981). The value of narrativity in the representation of reality. In W. Mitchell (Ed.), *On narrative.* Chicago: University of Chicago Press.

11

Moral Fictions
The Dilemma of Theory and Practice

JO ANNE PAGANO

Jo Anne Pagano is associate professor at Colgate University, Hamilton, New York, where she teaches courses in philosophy of education, women's studies, and curriculum and teaching in English and social studies. She has published in JCT: An Interdisciplinary Journal of Curriculum Studies; Educational Theory; Curriculum Inquiry; *and* Journal of Curriculum Studies. *Dr. Pagano is coauthor with Landon Beyer, Walter Feinberg, and Anthony Whitson of* Preparing Teachers as Professionals. *She is the author of* Exiles and Communities: Teaching in the Patriarchal Wilderness.

Many of us have used students' autobiographical writings in a variety of situations and for a variety of purposes. When I began to use autobiographical writing in my senior seminar on curriculum and teaching in the humanities, it was for the purpose of encouraging students to bring curriculum theory to their lives and to theorize their lives in schools. Autobiography promised to be a passage between theory and practice and to make it possible for students to develop the habit of critical self-reflection. This project seemed necessary to me in view of what was revealed over and over again in my observations of student teachers.

The students I teach are by and large well prepared for college. They are also socially and economically privileged; they have lived sheltered lives, and most of them can, if they choose, look forward to sheltered and protected futures. Those who choose teaching as their profession are unusual in this population, many of whom will have no trouble walking into high-paying, high-visibility jobs immediately after graduation. Their political and social commitments tend to be to the left of most of their classmates'. They care intensely about questions of social justice, about freedom, equality, and peace. Many of them have connections to our women's studies and peace studies programs. They want to teach for the same reason that they fast for Oxfam, demonstrate against apartheid, join Amnesty International, and participate in a variety of volunteer activities. They teach because they think they can help make the world a better place and all of us better people by doing so. I think that they can.

Nearly all of the courses offered in the education department at the university are highly theoretical, including the curriculum and teaching seminar. All of my colleagues teach courses that ask students to explore the political, social, and ethical dimensions of schooling from multiple perspectives. By the time they have begun their student teaching, which they undertake at the same time that they are enrolled in the curriculum seminar, students have a fairly sophisticated understanding of political and theoretical questions in education. But neither that education nor any previous experience of their own is sufficient preparation for the actual experience of student teaching, for the actual alienness of students who fall asleep in class, for the actual prejudices often found in rural communities, for the actual problems of poverty and disease and the actual psychological problems that attend these.

We are all aware of the often uneasy relationship between teaching and theory. We know how often teachers' practices appear to be at odds with the theory they profess. For example, teachers who know that a behavior problem is in the eye of the beholder, teachers who know that what appears to an adult as misbehavior is to the child a reasonable solution to a problem, succumb readily to the seductions of assertive discipline. Ditto worksheets are dealt efficiently from the hands of teachers who know that students learn best when they have some control and some choice. I have always suspected that this happens for two reasons. One reason is that we are not accustomed to theorizing daily life. Theory exists on some metalevel, in some domain where thought and logic rule. But daily life is often so noisy that we can't even hear ourselves think. The other reason is that the language of theory is rarely the language of things. The world of theory is too often a sensible emptiness. I've used autobiographical writing then as the source of the language of things and as a way of picking the meaning from the noise.

To act is to theorize. That is one of the things that I try to teach my students as I teach them to evaluate both theory and action in terms of each other. Raw experience is inscrutable; therefore it is an insufficient motive to action. If I try to describe my day, if I try to describe a moment in the classroom, I find that I cannot do so without recourse to intentions, my own and others'; I cannot do so without assuming that certain things constitute certain explanations of other things. We act in the ways that we act because we believe certain things about the way the world works. We judge others' actions in the ways that we do because we believe certain things about persons and the freedoms and constraints on their actions. To write autobiographically is, among other things, to theorize as well.

Surely it is commonplace by now to note that gestures, utterances, situations, and so on, do not contain meaning; they are produced as the gestures, utterances, and situations they are taken to signify as part of the process of making meaning. We are accustomed to think that all experience is theory laden and that all theory is value laden. And we are accustomed to think that personal history influences one's reading of history, or of science, or of anything else. It seems to me that our contemporary ways of thinking can cause big problems for teachers. It also seems that we have no alternative and that our contemporary understanding makes very clear to us the moral imperatives of teaching.

I wrote an early draft of this essay in 1983. I had just then begun experimenting with fiction writing in my seminar as a way of accomplishing what I had hoped to accomplish in using autobiography. I was becoming distrustful of autobiography, suspecting my students of either an unwillingness or an inability to achieve the distance required for self-criticism and of an inability to theorize the everyday. I began it then and ended it in the same way—with a question. The question, as it always was and continues to be, is one of practice. Specifically, as I became more and more engrossed in the dailiness of my own life, the question became increasingly one to be answered in my own practice. Working from the hypothesis that curriculum and teaching practices make a story and can be read as texts that interpret the world or some part of it, I began an investigation of the moral dimensions of interpretation.

My investigations led me to suspect that autobiography was inadequate to the purposes for which I intended it. I think we all have a tendency to fictionalize ourselves when we write about ourselves. Force is added to the impulse when autobiographical work will function in some judgmental scheme. The threat is not diminished if the work is not graded. The complications are even greater if those who are asked to write autobiographically are at the point of simultaneously imagining and fearing entry into the "adult world." A self constructed as an ego ideal is the likely subject of such an autobiography. This is understandable. I do not believe that the vulnerability of teachers, particularly beginning teachers, can be underestimated. I do not mean to imply that the fictionalized self of an autobiography is a lie or a masquerade. It is a theoretical construct.

I recently reread an autobiographical essay that I submitted as part of my tenure dossier. My assignment was to talk about the way I think about teaching, to develop a "philosophy" of teaching, and to evaluate my performance as teacher, scholar, and citizen of the university community. I was terrified. Nothing I've ever written, including my Ph.D. dissertation, was ever as difficult for me as that autobiographical essay. Never had I felt more vulnerable.

On the surface, my essay reads as a fairly straightforward representation of a career beginning with my first teaching at the secondary level. The narrator is myself. The events I describe occurred, the attitudes I claimed are mine. No one will be surprised to learn that I represented the author of my autobiography as a very good teacher indeed. She is committed to student empowerment, she is sensitive to student needs, she knows about the importance of listening, is self-reflective and critical, and so on. And I hope she is. But when I read this essay now, certain apparently marginal, or at least inessential, moments strike me. To begin with I inform my readers that I never meant to be a teacher and certainly never considered the study of education. I say I meant to be a philosopher. Of what am I assuring my colleagues when I include this information in the story of my professional development? I teach at a liberal arts college. The partnership between education and other departments at such places can be an uneasy one. When I tell my colleagues that I never meant to teach, I assure them that I am one of them. I say (between the lines) that I am smart enough and talented enough to have shared once their prejudices against teacher education. In this essay, I also assert my working-class origins. The context in which I do so is one that permits me to claim (again between the lines) a privileged knowledge. I am the one who knows.

My essay also conceals certain repudiations. The language in which I claim my social-class origins is the language that has enabled me to distance myself from them. I interpret a particular student's claim about freedom and education to mean escape from working-class life. In this context, claiming my working-class childhood can be read as charged with the worst sort of sentimentalism. Perhaps it is not merely sentimental, but the possibility must be considered. Reading my essay as a feminist, I am forced to remind myself that teaching is a profession associated with women. How should I read my rejection of women's work? I am forced, as a feminist, to interrogate my decision to align myself with philosophy — with the rational, the logical, and the abstract.

I can read my essay as flawed by the kind of arrogance that comforts the fear of inferiority. I am defending myself against the possibility that my colleagues will suspect that I am not as smart as they are. The essay reveals the possibility that I retain some conflict myself about my career choice. When I read my essay, I can interpret much of what I say as undercutting the pluralistic and nonauthoritarian positions I claim to be committed to. I can read my essay as thoroughly saturated with the monist and monolithic values of patriarchy despite my avowed rejection of those values. I can interpret my essay as wholly embedded in the binary oppositions of logocentric and, from my own theoretical position, oppressive thinking.

This distance from an autobiographical piece of my own writing enables a critical perspective, and a departure for interpretation that is important to me in dealing with my students and with colleagues who are now in as vulnerable a position with respect to me as I once was with respect to the tenured faculty. I did not read my essay in those terms when I wrote it 2 years ago. Nor could anyone have taught me to do so. Does that mean I lied? Does it mean I willfully dissembled? Does it mean that I failed to know myself? I don't believe that it means any of those things. It means that there's more than one way to tell a story and more than one story to be told.

In May Sarton's novel, *The Small Room* (1961), one professor remarks to another that it is a pity that we expect people to be students at the time in their lives when they are least suited for it. Learning, she suggests, demands humility, and the young do not have humility. I think they do not, because they cannot afford it. Humility requires the solidness of a life behind one to secure the unknown future.

It should be obvious that questions of interpretation, even the interpretation of one's own life, are enormously complicated by questions of power. Autobiographical work produced in the context of unequal power relations for some supervisory or other pedagogical purpose puts the teacher/reader in a tricky spot. The author of an autobiography is the one who knows. Here the epistemological problems of interpretation join with the ethical questions of pedagogy. Knowledge and authority are all mixed up with trust. Judgment of another's autobiographical work in the classroom may produce results that counter our intentions to foster critical self-reflexivity. And judgment may be impossible anyway if the author is presumed to know.

There is more than one way to tell a story and more than one story. Teaching is, among other things, a discursive and interpretive practice, just as the writing of autobiography is. Teaching is textual. When we teach, we tell stories about the world. Some stories are scientific, some historical, some philosophical, some literary, and so on. Educational theories are stories about how teaching and learning work, about who does what to whom and for what purposes, and, most particularly, educational theories are stories about the kind of world we want to live in and about what we should do to make that world. Stories obey a narrative logic and, like mythologies, help us to find our place in the world. The stories we tell in our disciplines are faithful to certain narrative conventions that define those disciplines. What separates philosophy from literature is narrative convention and presumed epistemological status.

One of our most cherished prejudices is the belief that there is a clearcut distinction between imaginative and other kinds of writing. But Raymond Williams (1977), for example, argues persuasively that the distinction between literature and other kinds of writing is a modern one and must be understood as part of the Enlightenment project of securing to certain kinds of discourse incontestable authority grounded not in the supernatural but in the imperatives of human possibility.

In an essay entitled "How Ordinary is Ordinary Language?" Stanley Fish (1980) argues that there is no such thing as ordinary language. The argument is a response to the apparent dilemma posed by J. L. Austin's (1962) theory of performatives. Austin had claimed that to speak is to perform an act. To say "I promise to marry you" is to engage in the act of promising. This claim gets fiction into some trouble. What is the "illocutionary" force of a fictional utterance? Is a fictional utterance a lie? What is its epistemological status? Fish says the dilemma seems forced on us only because we assume that literature, or imaginative writing, is somehow a special case, or an aberration of ordinary language use. Jonathan Culler (1982) makes a similar claim in his reading of Derrida's reading of Austin and Searle. According to Fish (1980),

> Literature is language around which we draw a frame, a frame that indicates a decision to regard with a particular self-consciousness the resources that language has always possessed. . . . What characterizes literature is not formal properties, but an attitude . . . always within our power to assume toward properties that belong by constitutive right to language. (This raises the intriguing possibility that literary language may be the norm, and message-bearing language a device we carve out to perform the special, but certainly not normative, task of imparting information.) (pp. 108, 109)

If we take a literary attitude to our stories about teaching, we direct our attention to narrative and actual effects and away from the troublesome, and possibly repressive, questions of truth and falsity. The effects we shall be concerned with have to do with the ways that we produce meaning, with notions of persons' varied relationships to the intersubjectively available meanings that make up our repertoires, and with the sense of power or limit available in the range of human meanings produced in the act of narration.

A story about educational experience has, as does the experience it represents and constitutes and hence the experience it *intends*, the same dual nature that Dewey associated with experience in general. The story is at once a doing and undergoing even in the act of "writing about." When we follow a narrative, we must be able to follow its construction as well as its content, for content is produced through narrative strategy. The distinction between factual and fictional tales distinguished among the attitudes of readers and writers to the tales at hand.

Teaching is textual. We make sense of our own and others' teaching by interpreting acts and utterances according to certain narrative conventions. These conventions serve to mobilize in us, as readers of the teaching text, certain structures of expectation and constraint. The activity of interpretation is an activity in which we form expectations about what will be said or what will happen next. Our anticipations regarding the future figure prominently in the sense we make of the present moment. We bring to this activity a set of personal and institutional assumptions and interests regarding the teaching of texts. The content of teaching narratives may be characterized as some knowledge domain taken with its associated skills. In the narrative enactment participated in by both teachers and students, knowledge and skill are produced. Content is produced through deploying the strategies of the narrative codes of our disciplines and of our profession.

Narrative codes also specify relationships. In the codes of teaching three sets of relationships are specified during the enactment: the relationship between teachers and knowledge or skill (author and subject), the relationship between students and that same knowledge or skill (reader and subject), and the relationship between teachers and students (author and reader). Obviously these are neither stable nor exhaustive identifications. In the relationship to subject, teacher/authors are at some point readers as they are with respect to their students. As characters in the classroom drama, all of us read each other.

Through knowledge and through our stories about our knowledge, we bring a sense of our own identity into focus as much as we do in our autobiographical writings. My stories about the natural world, about literature, about philosophy, about history, all reveal my values and attitudes, my sense of my own cares and responsibilities. My stories about my work as a teacher and a student disclose those same aspects of my life. The same is true of my stories of teachers and students in general, whether I tell these stories within the codes of theory or the codes of gossip. Through these stories we consolidate our connections to each other as well. Some have claimed that narration is a displacement of an inner reality onto an outer reality. To know himself or herself becomes, then, a teacher's primary obligation. We can come to know ourselves as well through the fictions we concoct, and through the interpretations of those read, as through the truths that we assert, and perhaps we can come to know ourselves more easily in fictive discourse.

Fish (1980) argues that interpreting a text is never, in any case, a matter of being faithful to the facts. Interpretation, he says, is an activity in which we specify what it means to be faithful to the facts. The obvious question leaps unbidden. What, then, makes discourse possible? Suppose each of us employs different narrative codes, mobilizes different strategies of expectation? Fish solves this problem by introducing the notion of shared pretense in our conversation. Discourse is made possible by "shared pretense." We agree on the parameters of the narrative codes in which we should be operating. (Fish uses the term *universe of discourse*, but I find that language too elaborate for my purposes.) What exonerates us from the charge of relativism is the fact that narrative codes are public. There is no such thing as a private language. Even autobiography in this view is a narrative enactment producing certain conventional effects through the deployment of certain strategies. Even autobiography ceases to enjoy the privilege of certain knowledge.

Fish argues that the charge of relativism already presumes a particular way of cutting up the world in language. Reader-response theory holds that our commonsense distinctions between subjective and objective, internal and external, private and public, the individual and the collective are specious distinctions. Objectivity is simply intersubjectivity, the individual exists only as communicant in a form of life, all that we know of the world emerges through our speaking it, and all language is public. Cognizing and judging are strategies in particular narrative codes.

The distinction between fiction and, say, ethnography or even laboratory report is a distinction among narrative codes. It is not a distinction between fact and fantasy or between real and not real. What then enables us to make judgments? It seems now as if I have just saddled all narration with the epistemological and ethical problems of autobiography. Far from improving the situation, my investigation seems to have introduced endless complications.

Fish's solution is not really much help to teachers. Perhaps it is a prejudice, but I cannot help thinking that considerably more is at stake in the business of education than is at stake in literary criticism. In *A World of Difference*, a sustained meditation on the political consequences of deconstruction, Barbara Johnson (1987) argues that the very possibility of leveling the charge of relativism against deconstructive readings of texts depends on a binary logic of antagonism. In this logic, if a claim is not absolute, then it is necessarily relative. This she argues is the logic that entitles us to read difference as deficit. This is a logic embedded in a psychology of intolerance for difference.

Deconstructionists introduce us to a logic of difference/differance. For the deconstructionist, as Derrida said in *Dissemination* (1981), there is nothing that is not a text. Traditionalist theorists reject deconstruction because it seems to them that they would have to relinquish judgment. If there is nothing that is not a text, then all readings must be equally plausible. This conclusion betrays a hunger for something outside, something beyond judgment according to which we might be absolutely certain — according to which any one of us might be the one presumed to know. This is, of course, the logic of domination. We cannot be vindicated of the charge of relativism within the binary logic of domination. Nor can anyone, as any number of writers have pointed out, actually *be* a relativist. In order to act we must act as if we believe in something like truth and knowledge. The logic of difference presumes that every text is different from itself, that meaning is always nonimmediate, that there is no identity between the act of meaning and what is meant. So how does anyone presume to know anything?

Johnson (1987) recommends that we talk about teaching and interpretation in terms that acknowledge that any reading is "motivated and undercut by its own interests, blindnesses, desires, and fatigue, and that the *role* of truth cannot be so simply eliminated" (p. 15). In other words, while we deny the existence of objective truth, we acknowledge its necessary function (its fictional function?) in discourse. The denial of its actual existence is a moral and political imperative. Truth is a function in the logic of domination. Our knowledge then can be contingent on the future only. Johnson claims that a deconstructive reading proceeds from an attitude in which readers set themselves up to be "surprised by otherness," an attitude that directs us to our ignorance. Every knowing contains its own ignorance.

Soshana Felman (1982) argues that a critical pedagogy directs its attention to ignorance. Ignorance is not a lack of knowledge. It is neither empty space waiting to be filled nor misconception requiring correction. Ignorance is not opposed to knowledge, ignorance in a sense makes possible knowledge. It is not passive, inert, or waiting. Ignorance is dynamic. It is resistance to knowledge. Ignorance is the "desire to ignore," and as Freud and Lacan have taught us, ignorance is instructive and dynamically present in all that we know. An investigation of ignorance creates a new condition for knowledge.

It seems to me that fiction can be used to probe our ignorances and to create new conditions for knowledge. I think my students have been able to use it in that way. The advantage of fiction writing over autobiography is that the writer can claim a greater distance, and, consequently, the desire for ignorance is more readily exposed. The codes of narrative fiction require ignorance on the part of characters; misunderstanding is often critical to the plot and interaction. Moreover, as anyone who has ever written fiction can testify, fictional stories and characters acquire minds and lives of their own. Authors are regularly surprised by their tales; they regularly encounter the "surprise of otherness."

Autobiographical writing, particularly in the classroom context, can inhibit that surprise because we are so concerned with the representation of ourselves. When we tell stories with ourselves prominently and self-consciously at the center, we tend to think of others only in relation to ourselves; we tend to reify others. The exclusive preoccupation with our own concerns and motivations annexes the otherness of the other. Fiction cultivates in us the capacity for an imaginative sympathy that prizes the other's otherness. Fiction also helps us to particularize the general and to generalize the particular. Reading books and stories, we find our own lives figured in those of others; we find the place from which to start a conversation with the world.

When we teach we mean to change people. We mean to bring them to new ways of encountering and constructing the world. But we must remember always that the end educational project is *their* world, too. One of the greatest temptations for teachers is the temptation to colonize their students' consciousnesses. Education should bring people to the place from which they can go on alone and make up their own stories.

If teaching is an art, why not employ art to understand our teaching? I continue to use autobiography and journal writing in my seminar, but now we go beyond ourselves. For their final seminar project, student teachers take some journal entry and turn it into a story containing all of the elements of plot, setting, theme, and characterization of a classic fictional narrative. They are not permitted to write stories in the teacher's first-person voice unless that voice is only one among others. So far, most students have chosen third-person narration, although I have read two stories that employ a collage of first-person voices effectively. Using that fiction, they produce a critical meditation on it having reference to general thoughts on education and teaching. Each student reads the other students' stories, and we occupy the final seminar meetings with interpretations of all of the stories.

One student this year wrote a story entitled "Phillip, Ben and Mr. Binkworthy." Phillip is a fat little seventh-grade boy. He blushes easily, can't keep his shirt tucked in, is always rushing to be on time. His passions are science fiction, comic books, and military tactics. Phillip provides enormous amusement by his role as stooge for Ben and other "cool" kids. He describes the school bus as "the yellow ride to hell." He usually responds to his victimization by assuring himself that someday the other kids will come around. He never loses hope. Every day he is the butt of some new joke. In the story, Phillip has a particularly bad day. It begins with his sleeping too late to be able to watch half of "Masters of the Universe" before leaving for school. At school Ben maneuvers him into a position to "accidentally" spray shaving cream on the back of his shirt — right between his shoulder blades where he can't reach it. Ben "accidentally" steps on Phillip's sandwich and makes him drop his history of the comics right on the exposed peanut butter.

Ben and Phillip are in the same English class. Usually Ben is a very good student, but today he tries to disrupt the class by interrupting with pointless questions. Because they are reading a story that Phillip has read before, Phillip really shines on this day. The customary economy of the classroom is disrupted. Ben, who usually gets a great deal of attention from his teachers, finds this intolerable. To regain the upper hand, he humiliates Phillip in front of the rest of the class by pointing to the shaving cream stain on his shirt. The normally pacific Phillip swings at him. Mr. Binkworthy yells at Ben.

Another story explored a failed vocabulary lesson, a failure that surprised the student teacher because she thought she had prepared her students well for the vocabulary test scheduled for the day on which the story took place. This is a multiple-voice story that begins with the teacher feeling confident that she's been doing a good job. The narration then weaves through the room modulating from voice to voice:

"I wonder if we'll have recess . . . "
"I really hate these jeans. I look so gross today . . . "
"His eyes are really blue . . . "
"I'm going to screw up . . . my stomach hurts . . . "
"I can't ever do anything right for her . . . "
"I can see it on my study sheet 'mirthful' . . . why can't I think of it?"
"I think it has something to do with cows . . . "
"I have to write *something* . . . "
"I wonder if I'll be invited to Meghan's party . . . "
"My dad's going to kill me . . . "

The final voice is the teacher's again. "I don't want to care, but I think they hate me."

The authors of both of these stories explored them critically by focusing on what they know about their students in general developmental terms. They recalled what they had learned from John Dewey and considered in a new light questions of democracy and community, of what is owing to whom. Both concluded their critical essays with meditations on the meaning of dialogue and reciprocity and on questions of authority and responsibility. The author of the vocabulary test found new meaning in the claim that context is important and that student motivation has to be attached to intrinsic interest and desire.

Each week I collect student teachers' journals. I respond to them with questions in the margins only. Both of these incidents had been recorded in the journals, but the post fiction interpretations were considerably more perceptive, sympathetic, and attached to knowledge about teaching and learning. The Phillip story when it appeared in the journal focused on the teacher's frustration. The writer was particularly angry with Ben for not being a nicer person and asked how he could get kids to be kinder to each other. In the story he comes to understand Ben and his needs as well as to sympathize with Phillip. He comes to understand that his own response to each of the boys was implicated in Ben's attempt to humiliate Phillip and in Phillip's martial response.

"When Love and Need Are One" was written by an older student, one who prides himself on his feminist consciousness and on his sensitivity to others. His story opens at his house on the morning of the story with a conversation with his wife. The conversation reveals him to be more self-involved and less responsive to his wife than his autobiographical writings represented him to be. In the incident that serves as the center of the story, a white twelfth-grader reads aloud in class her own story about a recent date with her African-American boyfriend during which they were harassed by racist classmates. The assignment had been to produce a piece describing a character. The class is tense, but probably no one is as tense as the student teacher whose concern is solely with avoiding an emotional conflagration in the classroom. He does manage to keep a lid on things by ignoring the story's content and criticizing it for describing a relationship rather than a character.

His supervising teacher at the end of class said that he might have been inclined to tell the student that she had written a brave story. In the parking lot after school, he ran into two of the boys who had been guilty of racist remarks. They also remarked on her bravery. The story ends after that encounter with the student teacher slumped against his car asking himself, "What did I expect?"

In interpreting this story, the student explored two areas. The first involved the ways in which teachers' expectations can cloud their perceptions. At the end of his twelfth-grade class, he had been congratulating himself on avoiding disaster. He thought he had managed beautifully. His journal account of this event conveyed that sense. The second, and perhaps more important, topic was the role of teachers' needs and desires. At the end of his story, he knew that he had failed pedagogically. He knew that he had failed his students morally because he was much too involved with maintaining his own need to be in control — to be a facilitator, to use his own earlier language. Now he asked himself the brutal question, facilitator of what besides his own representation of himself?

Early in Doris Lessing's *The Golden Notebook* (1962), Anna Wulf reveals, to herself and to the reader, the ambition, simultaneously an anxiety, which has led to her artistic paralysis, psychological fragmentation, and political disaffection. Anna says of her unwritten novel that it should be "a book powered with an intellectual or moral passion strong enough to create order, to create a new way of looking at life" (p. 61).

Anna is talking about herself as well as about her stalled novel — about the artistic creation that is her life. Through her work as a writer, she creates and situates herself in the human universe. Her story is one of psychic and political disintegration, human communion, work, and re-integration. It is a work, as is all of Lessing's, exemplifying the projection of the person into the world of human meanings, a projection achieved through the character's self-conscious patterning of experience into story. This projection of self amounts to a production of self, an achievement, the core of which is the writer's relationship to her work. But she does not achieve this alone.

The first line of *The Golden Notebook*, Lessing's novel, is also the first line of Anna Wulf's novel begun in a *Golden Notebook*. It is given to her by Saul Green, a fellow writer and her lodger and lover. This gift is part of an exchange of gifts between Anna and Saul occurring at the end of *The Golden Notebook* and at the end of their affair. Her gift to him is the first sentence of his new short novel.

This seems to me a fine metaphor for education. Only through mean-ingful work reflexively reconstituted can we invent ourselves in stories powered with an intellectual and moral passion strong enough to empower us to appropriate our own lives and to authorize our entry into those of others. In the course of our reflexive reconstructions, we teachers must encounter the otherness of our students in order that they may appropriate their own stories. These are moral fictions.

In moral fictions, teachers test their own certainties in order that students' dependence on those certainties is continually undermined. In moral fictions we never come to the end of questions, the lives are uncom-pleted, and the voices echo even after the final page is turned. Moral fictions teach us our own ignorance and help our students to come to theirs.

REFERENCES

Austin, J. L. (1962). *How to do things with words*. Oxford: Oxford University Press.

Culler, Jonathan. (1982). *On deconstruction*. Ithaca, NY: Cornell University Press.

Derrida, Jacques. (1981). *Dissemination* (Barbara Johnson, Trans.). Chicago: Uni-versity of Chicago Press.

Felman, Shoshana. (1982). Psychoanalysis and education: Teaching terminable and interminable. In Barbara Johnson (Ed.), *The pedagogical imperative: Teaching as a literary genre* (pp. 21–44). New Haven, CT: Yale University.

Fish, Stanley. (1980). "How ordinary is ordinary language?" In *How to do things with words* (pp. 97–111). Cambridge, MA: Harvard University Press.

Johnson, Barbara. (1987). *A world of difference*. Baltimore: Johns Hopkins University Press.

Lessing, Doris. (1962). *The golden notebook*. New York: Bantam Books.

Sarton, May. (1961). *The small room*. Toronto, Canada: Penguin Books.

Williams, Raymond. (1977). *Marxism and literature*. Oxford: Oxford University Press.

12

Teacher Lore
A Basis for Understanding Praxis

WILLIAM H. SCHUBERT

William H. Schubert is professor of education, specializing in curriculum theory and history, at the University of Illinois at Chicago. He is the author of Curriculum Books: The First Eighty Years, *and* Curriculum: Perspective, Paradigm and Possibility. *He is currently at work on books about teacher lore, the arts as a basis for inquiry into curriculum and teaching, and the student's place in curriculum and teaching. A past president of the Society for the Study of Curriculum History, Factotum of Professors of Curriculum, and program chair of the Curriculum Studies Division of the American Educational Research Association, Dr. Schubert has published in numerous journals and serves on the editorial boards of* Educational Theory, Journal of Curriculum Theorizing, Journal of Curriculum and Supervision, Teaching Education, Educational Leadership, *and* Phenomenology and Pedagogy.

In this chapter, I will introduce *teacher lore* as a necessary and neglected construct in educational literature, noting that it has particular relevance to the theory and practice of curriculum, teaching, supervision, and school improvement. I characterize teacher lore as the study of the knowledge, ideas, perspectives, and understandings of teachers. In part, it is inquiry into the beliefs, values, and images that guide teachers' work. In this sense, it constitutes an attempt to learn what teachers learn from their experience. Teachers are continuously in the midst of a blend of theory (their evolving ideas and personal belief systems) and practice (their reflective action); I refer to this blend as *praxis*. To assume that scholarship can focus productively on what teachers learn recognizes teachers as important partners in the creation of knowledge about education.

In the project I describe, teachers are not merely studied in an effort to learn *about* them; indeed, they are *invited to share in the creation of knowledge.* Put another way, teachers are *asked* to reveal the experiential knowledge that informs their teaching. Sometimes teachers can communicate this best when asked to relate it directly, and at other times they reveal it through stories about their practical experiences.

Both a direct approach (asking teachers to interpret their experiential understandings) and an indirect approach (inviting teachers to tell about their stories) are features of the Teacher Lore Project, an ongoing research venture at the University of Illinois at Chicago, funded under the auspices of the Chicago Area School Effectiveness Council (CASEC). An organization of several hundred schools and school districts in the Chicago area, CASEC provides an opportunity for which administrators, supervisors, teachers, professional association and union representatives, and interested others to join together with university faculty members for conferences approximately four times per year.[1]

The purpose of these conferences is for participants to discuss ideas, share practices, present school improvement initiatives to one another, and listen to noted speakers representing scholarly and practitioner communities. The spin-offs from the conferences, perhaps more valuable in the long run than the conferences themselves, consist of ongoing collaborative research and problem-solving projects in which school-based educators and university-based educators share expertise. The Teacher Lore Project is one such collaborative research venture.

Participants at a CASEC conference were given a simple questionnaire, asking them in three different ways to identify teachers whom they considered to be exceptionally good. The three questions were as follows:

1. Who is the best teacher that you know?
2. Do you know a teacher who has received a prestigious award for excellence in teaching? If so, give the name of the teacher.
3. Who is the teacher that best exemplifies [a list of qualities of teachers derived from progressive education literature]?

Approximately 100 nomination forms were received, most listing someone in each of the three categories. We acknowledge the fact that different experts from whom nominations were received differ in their perspective on what constitutes a "best teacher." Drawing upon Elliot Eisner's (1985a, 1985b) notion of educational connoisseurship, we consider those invited to be nominators (CASEC members) as connoisseurs of teaching. We broadly considered educational connoisseurs to be those who have considerable experience in educational situations and who have developed sophisticated levels of perception and discrimination, similar to connoisseurship in the arts. When they are inclined to be writers, their writing is analogous to criticism in the arts. Steeped in the art (in this case the art of education), they observe, describe, evocatively interpret, and evaluate a work (in this case an educational situation or setting). Their writing provides perspective that enhances the interpretation, assessment, and subsequent action of those who read it (see Barone, 1989; Willis, 1981). Although the nominators represent a range of connoisseurship, we believe that tapping the intuitive and experiential insights of leaders in scholarship and practice is one defensible way to locate good teachers. Moreover, doing so is consonant with an initial assumption of the Teacher Lore Project that values the insights of practitioners.

The Teacher Lore Project grew out of an ongoing seminar that I led with doctoral students on the study of historical roots of progressive education, which lasted from January through June of 1985. Gradually, the group began to study self-selected topics, and students began to deal with their own research projects and dissertations. The idea of teacher lore emerged in the summer of 1986 as an organizing center for many of our discussions, and some of us formed a group to focus more thoroughly on the topic (see Schubert et al., 1987). At that point we sought and received CASEC funding, as noted earlier, designed and distributed the questionnaires, and hired two graduate assistants, Norman Weston and Gary Sykes, who conducted some 20 open-ended interviews with nominees. Combined with other doctoral students whose dissertations and research projects (to be discussed later) built upon the teacher lore idea, approximately 100 interviews have been conducted to date. Interviews ranged from 1 to more than 5 hours each, were conducted with teachers from preschool through college levels, and focused on some dimension of the perspectives, values, and experiential knowledge that gives meaning, direction, and understanding to the reflective action or praxis of the teachers interviewed.[2]

ORIGINS OF TEACHER LORE

The conceptual origins of teacher lore are multiple. They traverse literatures in curriculum, supervision, and teaching, and they rely heavily on qualitative research perspectives and methodologies.

Most curriculum books contain at least vague mention of the important role of teachers in the curriculum-development process (Schubert, 1980, 1986). Many authors appear content to treat teachers as central to the curriculum implementation process but rarely note that implementation, when separated from curriculum development, is a construct that leans heavily in the direction of behaviorist orientations. If teachers *implement* that which "wiser" curriculum leaders select and bestow upon them, and if they *implement* that which evaluation experts assess, then the holistic character of their work (that which gives meaning and direction) becomes disconnected and *deskilled* (Apple, 1986). They become akin to participants on assembly lines rather than professionals who conceptualize, act, and reflect on work derived from deep commitment. The union of theory and practice, the praxis that makes them professional, is disembodied.

A few curriculum writers have devoted book length consideration to the teacher's place throughout the curriculum development process (e.g., Brubaker, 1970; Connelly & Clandinin, 1988; Grundy, 1987; Lease, Frasure, & Johnson, 1961; Pinar & Grumet, 1976; Schubert, 1986; Sears & Marshall, 1990; Sharp, 1951; Spears, 1951). Some writers whose writing focuses directly on teachers and teaching acknowledge curriculum as that which is experienced by teachers and students through their interactions (e.g., Ayers, 1989; Clandinin, 1986; Duckworth, 1987; Henderson, 1989; Miller, 1987; Tom, 1984). Such an emphasis on curriculum by scholars whose backgrounds include pragmatism and practical inquiry, phenomenology and existentialism, and critical cultural studies invokes a reexamination of Dewey's view of curriculum.[3] In this view curriculum unfolds in the democratic probing of genuine human interests and concerns of teachers and students, and its value is found in the extent to which it helps participants create and draw upon knowledge that gives meaning and direction to their experience. Thus, two major origins of teacher lore can be found in this perspective of curriculum. First, if curriculum is developed by teachers in their daily interactions with students, then it can be understood better as such teachers are approached for their experiential insights. Second, these experiential insights held by each teacher constitute a repertoire — that is, their personal constructs or theories of action — that remains a virtually unstudied realm of curriculum theory (Schubert, 1982; Schubert & Lopez-Schubert, 1982). Teacher lore explores that realm.

Supervision and staff development, like curriculum, have taken a similar turn in the literature. As in curriculum, the turn is not the dominant one but is rather an initiative that recognizes the need for democratic interaction and acknowledges the expertise and authority of both the supervisor and the supervised, of both the staff developer and the staff (Bolin & Falk, 1987; Garman, 1986; Lieberman, 1986; May & Zimpher, 1986; Popkewitz, 1987; Sergiovanni, 1985; Smyth, 1984, 1987; Wideen & Andrews, 1987). Today, partnership, interactive action research, and collaboration are hallmarks of many different kinds of efforts to improve schools and other educative situations (e.g., Carr & Kemmis, 1986; Griffin, 1983; Lieberman, 1986; Stenhouse, 1975). In no small measure this is due to a greater acceptance of the image of educators as reflective practitioners promoted by Donald Schön (1983, 1987) and others (Cruickshank, 1987; McDonald, 1986; Raphael, 1985). Such an image recognizes those previously viewed as needing help (the supervised, the staff, the whole range of practitioner) as capable of identifying, analyzing, and solving problems related to their practice.

In short, the supervision and staff-development literature increasingly recognizes today the empowerment that accrues when "outside experts" realize the need to share authority with "inside experts," those who can relate their daily practice to a particular set of circumstances, a situationally specific context. No one in the education profession fits the latter as much as teachers. Their *daily inquiry* needs to be seen as a viable form of research, for it potentially makes available insights and understandings unavailable from other sources. Usually, the reflective inquiry of teachers goes unwritten. Teacher lore enables teachers to tell their stories and reveal their understandings—their personally created, experiential knowledge bases.

Literature on teaching, therefore, is perhaps the most diverse domain of origin for teacher lore. The definitive treatment of research on teaching under one cover is the third edition of the *Handbook of Research on Teaching* (Wittrock, 1986). Yet, although the volume's 1,037 double-column pages contain a wealth of information, only one chapter reports research that directly serves as a basis for the central concern of teacher lore, namely, the need to take seriously the guiding precepts that teachers derive from experience. Moreover, in this chapter by Christopher Clark and Penelope Peterson (1986), only about 10 of 40 pages are devoted to what they call "teachers' theories and beliefs," and within this section only a part entitled "teachers' implicit theories of teaching and learning" has direct relevance as a basis for teacher lore. Clearly, other authors in the volume—for example, Lee Shulman (1986) and Maxine Greene (1986)— refer to the need for inquiry that acknowledges the active role of teachers. However, too little has been done to develop research along this line; hence, the need for teacher lore. Indeed, it is curious that researchers can marvel at a fine study that logs 15,000 hours of investigation by researchers in classrooms (Rutter, Maughan, Mortimore, Ouston, & Smith, 1979) but essentially disregard over 30 *years* of inquiry by career teachers.

It occurred to us that if teachers do build implicit theories (as indicated by Clandinin, 1986; Elbaz, 1983; Janesick, 1977; Munby, 1986; Schubert, 1982), it seems worthwhile to study the character and content of such theories rather than let them quietly descend into obscurity as these teachers retire. It is at least a positive feature that the research on teaching literature points to the need to pursue teacher lore, both by its acknowledgment of the existence of implicit theories and experiential knowledge that teachers hold and by the disproportional emphasis of study of this theory and knowledge. The latter garners the supposition that too many researchers on teaching do not grant sufficient credibility to the theories and knowledge that teachers develop from experience. Through teacher lore we want to offer such credibility.

A second body of literature on teaching is biographic; it consists of more categories and subcategories than can be treated adequately in this discussion. However, several should be mentioned ranging from the popular to the scholarly. Perhaps the most widely selling popular literature on education evolved from a number of counterculture educators in the late 1960s. Among them, James Herndon, John Holt, and Herbert Kohl continued writing during the next two decades (see, for example, Herndon, 1968, 1985; Holt, 1964, 1981; Kohl, 1968, 1984). Their writings are first-person accounts of teaching and learning situations, the sales of which indicate that they reached a broad base of educators and interested others. Clearly, these writings are more than descriptions; they are interpretive renditions of each author's viewpoint. Thus they provide, without the prompting of researchers, a glimpse of the knowledge and values of the theory within these teacher-authors. As such, they are foundational examples of teacher lore. The purposes of the Teacher Lore Project would be enhanced, for example, if our interviews with teachers could elicit a depth of articulate reflection exemplified by these authors as well as by others who span a broader period of time and ideological commitment, including educators such as Edward Eggleston (1871/1957), Jesse Stewart (1936, 1949), Julia Weber Gordon (1946/1970), Marie Rasey (1950), A. S. Neill (1960), Sylvia Ashton-Warner (1963, 1972), Bel Kaufman (1964), George Dennison (1969), Joseph Epstein (1981), William Van Til (1983), Vivian Gussin Paley (1984), Ken MacCrorie (1984), Eliot Wigginton (1986), and Patrick Welsh (1986). One can also find numerous briefer accounts of high-quality teacher shop talk about philosophy and methods of teaching and curriculum written by practicing teachers (Gross & Gross, 1974). These writings serve as examples for the Teacher Lore Project and can be interpreted historically as a major strand of teacher lore writ large.

A second kind of biography, less popular and more scholarly, has emerged in recent years with considerable variety. William Pinar's (1980, 1981) phenomenological and existential autobiography and his work along similar lines with Madeleine Grumet (Pinar & Grumet, 1976) constitute one kind of example. Grumet's (1980, 1988) autobiographical method further develops this work pedagogically. Treatments of teacher biography and autobiography have been expanded in the work of Ayers (1989), Butt & Raymond (1987), Goodson (1985), Miller (1990), Raphael (1985), Traver (1987), and others who have all taken steps to interpret the sense of meaning and direction in teachers' lived biographies.

Critical praxis, educational criticism, practical inquiry, and pheno-menological pedagogy all speak to teacher lore indirectly, if not directly through attempts to capture meaning in teachers' lives through evocative portrayal and assessment. In the literature on critical praxis one finds focus on and sensitivity to issues of class, race, ethnicity, gender, place, age, and health. Particularly influential are studies of teachers and students in view of institutional and ideological constraints on their lives (see Apple & Weis, 1983; Bullough, 1989; Connell, 1985; Freire, 1970; Lather, 1986; Lawn & Grace, 1987; McNeil, 1986; Sharp & Green, 1975; Shor, 1980). Although educational criticism began as a form of evaluation patterned after criti-cism in the arts, it is now viewed more pervasively as a special mode of qualitative inquiry. Although it typically does not focus directly on teach-ers, teachers are a major part of educational situations and contexts re-vealed in criticism (Barone, 1987; Eisner, 1985a, 1985b; Lightfoot, 1983; McCutcheon, 1981; Willis, 1978). Practical inquiry stems from a founda-tion in Deweyan pragmatism and action research, treats the new domain of personal practical knowledge (Corey, 1953; Schwab, 1969, 1971, 1973; Clandinin & Connelly, 1987; Connelly & Clandinin, 1988; Dewey, 1910/ 1933, 1938a), and connects with teacher-as-researcher approaches (Carr & Kemmis, 1986; Rudduck & Hopkins, 1985; Stenhouse, 1975, 1980). Phenomenological pedagogy has its intellectual roots in the work of Martin Heidegger, Paul Ricoeur, and Hans-Georg Gadamer, among others, and seeks to reveal shared essences that pertain to teachers and teaching as well as to the contextual dimensions of education (Hultgren, 1987; Parker, 1986; Suransky, 1982; van Manen, 1982a, 1982b, 1986, 1989).

The humanities, too, can be tapped for insight about teachers' lives.[4] Here I especially refer to historical and literary sources. Many authors of plays, short stories, novels, film, and television programs portray teachers. Sometimes whole works are devoted to teaching and teachers, and at other times one needs to look at particular episodes. Effort is being made to bring together some of these sources.[5] A small amount of historical work also exists to reconstruct images of teaching by exemplary teachers over the centuries (Anther, 1987; Broudy & Palmer, 1965; Chamberlin, 1981; Cu-ban, 1984; Highet, 1950, 1976; Snyder, 1972). In addition, a project is under way to bring together popular "literature" that depicts teaching through magazines, art, records, tapes, movies, and television.[6]

PRAXIS: GUIDING THEORY

The most useful body of theory that has helped both to conceptualize the Teacher Lore Project and to interpret its findings derives from the philoso-phy of John Dewey (1900, 1902, 1913, 1916, 1929c, 1938a). Coupled with works of today that are consistent with and extensions of that work, the Deweyan experientialist tradition makes possible two theoretical orientations to teacher lore as a form of praxis. The first stems from Dewey's technical definition of education set forth in *Democracy and Education*: "That reorganization or reconstruction of experience which adds to the meaning of experience, and which increases ability to direct the course of subsequent experience" (1916, p. 76). Dewey's theory of education, stemming from this definition, requires a theory that is more than a mere intellectual construction. It requires the embodiment of theory in action, or *praxis*; for Dewey the very existence of theory necessitates that it be infused with practice. Praxis assumes a continuous process of critical reflection that joins and mediates theory and practice. Otherwise, it would be impossible for a theory of education to be judged in a manner consistent with the pragmatic tenet that holds that the truth value of a proposition be determined in the consequences of its use. Hence, the theory informed in teachers, that is, that which teacher lore attempts to disclose, is that which must be studied if images of praxis that guide teachers' and students' lived experiences are to be understood. A Deweyan perspective thus gives credibility to the notion that educational theory should be conceived as praxis in the lived experience of teachers. At the same time it gives credibility to teachers themselves as creators of knowledge and theory that can illuminate an understanding of curriculum, teaching, and the educative process.

The second orientation of teacher lore made possible by Deweyan philosophy is symbolized in the concluding statements of *The Sources of a Science of Education*:

> The sources of an educational science are any portions of ascertained knowledge that enter into the heart, head, and hands of educators, and which by entering in, render the performance of the educational function more enlightened, more humane, more truly educational than it was before. (1929c, pp. 76–77)

This claim serves as a basis for understanding what good teachers have learned from their experience, that is, that which has given them the meaning and direction to create such an educational environment.

Drawing upon these two central tenets of Dewey's educational philosophy may be enough to provide a rationale for studying teacher lore and for conceptualizing that study as praxis, a union of theory and practice in reflective action. However, the study of teacher lore can also benefit from a larger and more comprehensive theory, both for purposes of justifying the study itself and for explicating findings as the area of study matures. Both, I suggest, may be found in the continued development of the Deweyan position with special attention devoted to the extrapolation and integration of his philosophy writ large, not his educational writings alone. Therefore, I will provide brief excursions into Dewey's metaphysics and ontology, epistemology, axiology and ethics, aesthetics, logic, politics, and theology.

Over the years, since education became a recognized area of scholarly study, debate has prevailed over the issue of whether a comprehensive theory of education exists or is even possible. Often this discourse has taken the form of a lament, indicating that education and even its several subcategories are too complex for any comprehensive theory to incorporate them. No subfield of education better epitomizes this debate and lament than the curriculum field (see McCutcheon, 1982). Perhaps, as Decker Walker observed in 1980, "a rich confusion" is the best place for curriculum discourse; clearly, this assertion rightly points to the need to maintain realization that curriculum theory should be problematic. However, one major contribution of Dewey was his unyielding campaign against dualistic thinking. Applying his antidualistic message, we need not conclude that either a theory must guide curriculum and teaching or it should forever remain chaotic and situational. On the contrary, Dewey offered a theory that must be understood as praxis. His notions of that which is educative experience and his larger vision of human goodness can only be interpreted in the course of reflective action.

Nevertheless, the larger corpus of his work in philosophy provides something close to a comprehensive theory of education, if that theory is conceived of as the continuously reconceptualized constructs of those who *do* education. Given that view, yet another dualism is dissolved (that of educational philosophy and the wider range of philosophy); and given that view, a set of categories emerges that could provide an understanding of praxis that differs greatly from the prevailing notion of what it means to have a guiding theory. Moreover, it is a perspective that makes an understanding of teacher insight and reflection necessary (not just interesting) for the clear understanding of teaching and curriculum.

Dewey's philosophical works deal with each of the perennial domains of philosophy: metaphysics and ontology, epistemology, axiology and ethics, aesthetics, logic, politics, and theology, as well as educational philosophy. I suggest an illustration of the way each of the categories of philosophy just mentioned could serve as the seedbed of tenets of a perspective or theory of praxis germane to teacher lore. (By viewing theory as perspective, disposition, or sense of direction I do not consider it contradictory to refer to a theory of praxis; on the contrary, such a view of theory enables us to maintain a problematic end of inquiry or theorizing that is both tied to practical situations and remains broadly perspectival.) The illustration of each category will note a general sense of direction derived from Deweyan philosophy, point to its relevance for the idea of praxis embedded in teacher lore, and provide an example of current thought that extrapolates the spirit of Deweyan perspective in novel directions.

Metaphysics and Ontology

In both *Experience and Nature* (1929a) and *Human Nature and Conduct* (1922), Dewey characterizes reality as continuously changing and human nature as an individual and social transaction with situations in a quest to discover, pose, and resolve problems. In current metaphysical discourse Prigogine and Stengers (1984) posit the need for human dialogue with nature as a means of understanding a seemingly chaotic reality more fully. Similarly, Richard Rorty (1979) argues for the need to move away from preoccupation with knowledge that mirrors nature toward an ontological grounding that develops conversation that constitutes and continues our culture and edifies those who participate in it. In several of his writings, Max van Manen (1982a, 1982b, 1986, 1989) addresses the pedagogical character of theorizing and conversing and the ways in which such endeavors enable one to become a qualitatively different person. To understand the phenomena of teaching and curriculum, therefore, it is necessary to enter into the reflective conversation of teachers, to grasp something of what the transactions of their teaching experience have done for them, and to learn how their outlooks are being modified. This is a central purpose of the Teacher Lore Project.

Epistemology

In *The Quest for Certainty* (1929b) Dewey shatters the myth of seeking certain knowledge; in *Logic, the Theory of Inquiry* (1938b) and *How We Think* (1910/1933) he characterizes the knowing process as involving social and human science that is embedded in an individual's interactive encounter with a problematic state of affairs that requires seeking meaning, direction, decision, action, and reflection on consequences. In *Knowing and the Known* (Dewey & Bentley, 1949) he refines his characterization to include more emphasis on dialogue, dialectics, and transaction. In epistemological discourse today, Jurgen Habermas (1984, 1988) develops a theory of communicative action that forges a critical praxis and develops images of its social tasks. Such tasks are explored as a variety of discourses on curriculum by a number of authors brought together by William Pinar (1988). Pinar points out that a second wave of curriculum reconceptualization, in addition to the intellectual discourse presented, has to do with the ways in which such discourse makes its way into elementary and secondary schools. In other words, to draw from Maxine Greene (1988), how could the public space of school be informed by a dialectic of freedom? To what extent does the experiential knowledge of teachers already address these questions? To what extent, for instance, do teachers already rely upon epistemologies of caring and intuition (see Noddings, 1984; Noddings & Shore, 1984) as well as upon reason, authority, tradition, revelation, and other dominant epistemologies?

Axiology and Ethics

In his *Ethics* (Dewey & Tufts, 1908) and *Theory of Valuation* (Dewey, 1939), Dewey outlined responses to matters of value and goodness that require individuals to carefully attend to the broad spectrum of consequences of their being and action, their praxis as it were. Moreover, Dewey's ethics assumes a sense of human goodness, one not inconsistent with that advanced by Alasdair MacIntyre in *After Virtue* (1984) and by Matthew Fox in *A Spirituality Named Compassion* (1977). Both of these contemporary theological philosophers exemplify a faith in human beings to make compassionate judgments about their fellow beings.

The extension of this faith into educational practice today requires that, with Alan Tom (1984), we realize teaching is more than a technical enterprise, that it is a moral craft. With Nel Noddings (1984), too, we must begin to see that consequences can be assessed by more than rational propositions pertaining to justification, equity, and fairness (individualistic orientations); she indicates consequences must be considered, as well, by caring—a relational approach to ethics and moral education. To care, to attend responsively to consequences to persons and relationships, requires an understanding that includes the stories and insights of teachers. Further, it requires that the seeking of such insights is done with full attention to the consequences of one's actions, with understanding of implications of teaching as a moral craft, and with caring. We try to incorporate these values in dealing with teachers in teacher lore interviews.

Aesthetics

In *Art as Experience* (1934b) Dewey develops the idea of expressive knowing and the pervasive use of images and patterns in everyday experience. In short, he paints boldly the centrality of aesthetic awareness throughout the lifescape. Artistic and literary criticism serves as a basis for educational criticism and connoisseurship, as developed by Elliot Eisner (1985a, 1985b), Gail McCutcheon (1981), Elizabeth Vallance (1982), Thomas Barone (1989), and others who exemplify the imaginative and aesthetic study of teaching, curriculum, and the educative process and its context. They identify and portray patterns to enhance the understanding of teachers, their lives and perspectives. Writings by these educational critics serve as an example when interpretations are developed and revised by teachers who become active participants in the art of criticism. Furthermore, good teachers will be acknowledged as potential connoisseurs of their experience from inside the schooling process.

Logic

The nature of reason for Dewey, as developed in *Logic, the Theory of Inquiry* (1938b) and *How We Think* (1910/1933), focuses on the ways in which high-quality reasoning occurs in the course of everyday dilemmas. Further, Dewey calls for a logic that goes beyond the reason of individuals to discover a logic of deliberation in democratic interaction. Similarly, today Richard Bernstein (1983) writes of notions of science, hermeneutics, and praxis that reach beyond traditional conceptions of logic when he calls for a "new conversation" or practical tasks of dialogical communities that move beyond archaic dualistic debates between objectivism or relativism. Though small by comparison with the ideal of democratic communities, we have launched the beginnings of a logic of dialogical community in the face-to-face conversational interviews of the Teacher Lore Project. Indeed, it might be viewed as a symbol of the kind of attempts to reason together that should inform the mutual concerns of teachers and researchers.

Politics

In *The Public and Its Problems* (1927) and *Individualism, Old and New* (1930), Dewey writes of the interplay of politics, economics, society, and individual liberty. He raises issues of equity that have been developed further by Paulo Freire (1970), Michael Apple (1982), Henry Giroux (1988), and Elise Boulding (1988) in issues of class, gender, race, and related variables. A Deweyan sense of involvement is reflected today in work by Eliot Wigginton (1986) in the Foxfire Project and George Wood (1987) at the Institute for Democracy in Education. Such efforts enable teachers to become emancipated from the fetters of deskilling. Talk with teachers in teacher lore interviews provides opportunity for insight into impediments faced by teachers who want to be fully involved in conceptualizing, carrying out, and evaluating the educative process with their students, parents, and relevant others. It also sheds insight on how good teachers overcome some of these impediments and engage in praxis as they teach.

Theology

In *A Common Faith* (1934a) Dewey sketches his belief in the goodness of human beings and the democratic process. The development of appreciation for this belief, this democratic faith, lies at the heart of the basic curriculum question: What knowledge and experiences are most worthwhile to pursue? This question is the basis for asking: What is the good life? How can I lead a good life? What is a good society, and how can I contribute to it? So fundamentally woven into the fabric of being human are these questions that their intense pursuit is religious in character. Such an image of religious character, Dwayne Huebner argues, is revealed in religious metaphors in the language of education (1984). The decision to focus on matters of meaning and direction in teachers' lives, and through the images that appear in the stories they tell, is guided by an intent to capture the religious or spiritual character of being a teacher, of being pedagogic with children and youth.

This discussion of guiding theory is intended to be illustrative, not all-inclusive. It is intended to illustrate dimensions of a theoretical framework that could both explicate a justification for engaging in the study of teacher lore and serve as a set of categories through which teachers' sources of meaning and direction might one day be interpreted. For now, let us turn to the preliminary findings of the Teacher Lore Project.

PROJECT FINDINGS

What are the findings? They fall into two large categories: literature reviews and primary studies. The literature reviews have been the subject of much of this chapter. A great deal of initial effort was devoted to accumulating, organizing, and beginning to conceptualize literature from an array of domains that gives insight into teachers' stories, experiential knowledge, modes of everyday inquiry, and sources of meaning and direction. The second category, primary studies, includes direct engagement with teachers through extensive interviews and observations to shed more light on what and how teachers learn as they teach. The results of this are twofold:

1. Portrayals of what teachers say and write about their lives and work, renditions that lose their vigor when summarized
2. Central tendencies that seem to be emerging from our conversations and the narratives they reveal

Although it is too early to offer definitive conclusions, it should be pointed out that tentative conclusions reflect the interpretations of the individual researchers (who are the central instrument of the research variation within the project) and on the intent of the researcher with respect to the aspects of the general topic he or she explores.[7]

We wondered at the outset of the project if themes of progressive education are alive today. It was from this interest that our third questionnaire item, listing progressive teachers' characteristics as noted earlier, was born. We found that teachers were, in fact, nominated as exemplars of characteristics considered central to progressive education in the Deweyan tradition, and the interviews verified that the teachers did indeed embody such characteristics. However, not only did teachers nominated for item 3 exemplify such characteristics, so did those nominated under items 1 and 2. Thus, regardless of the tendencies that push in the direction of behaviorism, management, technocracy, and prespecified treatments (tendencies that dominate today), teachers regarded as particularly good somehow resist pressures to be deskilled, and they

1. Maintain a holistic perspective on situational problem solving
2. Enjoy being with students
3. Draw insights from student experiences outside of school
4. Maintain a sense of mission about the importance of teaching
5. Exhibit love and compassion for students
6. Determine ways to build on student strengths
7. Exhibit a clear sense of meaning and direction and are in the process of revising the same
8. Guide their work with a quest for that which is worthwhile and just
9. Consider the issue of developmental appropriateness as problematic in each new situation
10. Are actively involved in self-education

Five dissertations and two research studies have now been completed on different dimensions of teacher lore. They provide themes of central tendency, rich portrayals of teachers' narratives, and interpretations of these narratives. Carol R. Melnick (1988) was interested in what it means for teachers to build upon the out-of-school experiences in student lives. She discovered that it invoked classroom understanding of life histories of students and teachers alike, an ethos of celebration of the humanness of both teachers and students, and a mutual invitation to share in the lived experience of members of the classroom community. Patricia Hulsebosch (1988) investigated, through interview and observation, the nature of parent-teacher involvement. She identified characteristics that 'distinguished high and low involvement of teachers with parents. Suzanne Millies (1989) explored the nature of teacher reflection in action and planning. She contrasted in depth an experienced teacher and a novice on a typology of dimensions of pedagogical personality, pedagogical assumptions, and pedagogical repertoire. The character and uses of imagination and intuition in teachers was studied by Virginia Jagla (1989) through classroom observation and interviews. Mari Koerner (1989) investigated teachers' images of their work and the teaching process through interviews and the analysis of metaphors used by teachers. Judith Ponticell[8] studied both teachers who have received special awards for excellence and those who are considered at risk for various reasons; such study affords productive opportunity for contrast, and emphasis on at-risk teachers adds a new dimension to teacher lore. Marilee Ewing (1989) investigated teachers' images of supervisors, supervisory ideals, and their own experience as supervisors in a specific research project and internship in supervision.

Work of the first year of the Teacher Lore Project was presented by a panel of those involved at the Bergamo Curriculum Conference (Schubert, Weston, Ponticell, & Melnick, 1987), and teachers associated with the project and CASEC were given a voice at the annual conference of the American Educational Studies Association (Ponticell et al., 1987). Additional presentations in subsequent years were made at the annual meetings of the American Educational Research Association, the Association for Supervision and Curriculum Development, and elsewhere by individuals and small groups of researchers involved with the project. The work of the project is enhanced by several persons who have engaged in discussion with us,[9] and I am editing a book on the first three years of the project.[10]

Mari Koerner, as a research assistant in 1987–88, reanalyzed the project tapes through the conceptual lenses of her experiences as an early childhood educator, an elementary school teacher, and a teacher educator. Her analysis reveals the following themes in the teacher interviews:

1. Deep feelings of responsibility for student learning
2. High expectations for both students and themselves
3. Self-blame if students fail, noting failure to motivate or make content interesting
4. "No-nonsense" academic task orientations
5. Belief in the importance of a warm, supportive environment

6. Belief in the necessity of teacher excitement to inspire student excitement about learning
7. Eagerness to learn from any resource that might be helpful
8. Wariness of the value of theory
9. Extreme dissatisfaction with teacher education courses
10. Importance of student interest as a basis for teaching and learning
11. Seriousness about teaching
12. Attribution of low esteem from community toward teachers
13. Need for school experiences to be part of real-life experiences
14. Desire to respond with stories and anecdotes
15. Perceptions of uniqueness of the teachers' own situations
16. Desire to be autonomous and one's own boss
17. Willingness to take risks, to be intellectual adventurers
18. Eschewing of boredom in the classroom
19. Strong ties to immediate surroundings
20. Worry about issues of controlling students

The two lists just presented in this section that describe qualities or characteristics of good teachers and other shorter lists of themes done by others need to be analyzed for consistencies, for the meanings implicit in them, and they need to be portrayed with the supportive commentaries of teachers that constitute their basis in evidence. Further, the interpretive lenses of the interviewers and of those who studied the tapes subsequently reveal that the teachers interviewed constitute a very rich source of insights about the praxis embedded in teaching. It is, however, interesting to note how differences in perspectives of researchers provide quite different interpretations of the teachers' commentaries. For instance, sometimes the earlier list of 10 themes can be seen to be at odds with some of the themes derived in the list by Mari Koerner. This surely points to the need for dialogue among interpreters, but it also illustrates the powerful insight embedded in the researcher as the real instrument of research. In fact, interpretation seems to lie in an interaction between researchers and teachers studied.

Returning finally to the Deweyan line of theory discussed earlier, it is interesting to consider the tapes in view of six central assumptions of the Deweyan experientialist tradition characterized by Georgiana Zissis (1987) and derived from a historical study of works by Francis Parker, John Dewey, Boyd Bode, Harold Rugg, William H. Kilpatrick, George S. Counts, and L. Thomas Hopkins, among others. Experientialist assumptions may be contrasted with conventionalist assumptions as follows:

Experientialist	*Conventional*
Search for the good life	Prespecified parameters of the good life
Person as creator	Person as receiver
Knowing as multidimensional	Knowing as rational-technical
Knowledge as intersubjective	Knowledge as objective
Education as intrinsic	Education as extrinsic
Democracy as participatory	Democracy as representative

Preliminary investigations of interview data in light of these categories reveal that the teachers studied tend to be characterized much more by the experientialist assumptions as contrasted with the conventionalist assumptions.

CONCLUSION

The idea of teacher lore has been set forth as a valuable and neglected area of study for understanding praxis in education, with special emphasis on insights for teaching, curriculum, teachers, supervision, and school improvement. Origins of teacher lore were noted with respect to related literature; such literature also exemplifies dimensions of a comprehensive image of explorations that might constitute a broad notion of teacher lore. Drawing upon the philosophy of John Dewey and more recent philosophers and educators whose work represents consistent extrapolations of a Deweyan spirit, a theoretical perspective illustrated briefly the kind of theory that might be developed to provide a foundation for teacher lore as the study of educational praxis. Finally, tentative findings of the Teacher Lore Project were presented along with variations on teacher lore currently being explored.

Through these efforts we hope to encourage the continued consideration of both the reflective process and the content of teachers' experiential repertoires of knowledge and values that give meaning and direction to their work. We hope, too, that teacher lore is increasingly acknowledged as a legitimate form of educational inquiry, one that engages collaborative efforts of teachers, scholars, and interested others to interpret praxis in ways that would not be possible without serious dialogue, conversation, and sharing. Through this sharing we have learned increasingly that narratives of teachers and dialogues with them constitute a genuine and neglected form of inquiry. Through interaction with their stories our own stories were more fully revealed to us. As researchers we have lives that are thoroughly embedded in our work. Likewise teachers inquire deeply and their lives and stories cannot be revealed without a sense of the "research" they live but rarely write about. In addition to written documents, the stories of teachers and researchers are most thoroughly written in the collaboration and dialogue that in turn enable them to grow positively with students.

NOTES

1. Gary Griffin, former dean of the College of Education at the University of Illinois at Chicago, is acknowledged as founding director of CASEC. The Teacher Lore Project is one of several research projects funded by CASEC.

2. *Lore*, as used here, pertains to the broad array of knowledge and learning acquired through the experience of a group, as found in many anthropological studies, and as evidenced in Iona Opie and Peter Opie's (1959) classic on school children. However, we use *lore* to specifically delineate that knowledge which has guiding power in teachers' lives and work (Buchmann, 1980). We are moving beyond viewing knowledge as concepts to also include the values, beliefs, and images that guide everyday work of teachers (a pervasive notion of experiential "knowledge"). Research assistants Norm Weston and Mari Koerner are especially thanked for contributions to the literature review on teacher lore.

3. See Schubert, Willis, and Short (1984) and Schubert (1987). Of course, the best source for a Deweyan curriculum is John Dewey's *Democracy and Education* (1916).

4. A broad basis in the humanities and arts is evident in the work of some who write about teachers and teaching. See, for instance, Greene (1973) and Barzun (1945). These two works exemplify an intellectual orientation quite different from such sociological classics on teaching as Waller (1932) and Lortie (1975). The literature on teachers and teaching has been skewed heavily in the direction of the social and behavioral sciences with little emphasis placed on the rich insights available in the humanities and the arts. Landau, Epstein, and Stone's (1976) edited volume represents an attempt to teach about teaching using literary sources.

5. Examples could be extensive, but a few are illustrative: Roberto Athayde's play, *Miss Margarida's Way* (1977); Leo Tolstoi's story, "A Russian Boy's Tutor," from *Childhood*, and other stories in Munroe and Catherwood (1945); Herman Hesse's novel, *Beneath the Wheel* (1906); portrayals of teachers in several of Charles Dickens's novels, for example, Gragrind in *Hard Times* and the depiction of Paul's education in *Dombey and Son*; the portrayal of the growth and life of a teacher in L. M. Montgomery's *Anne of Green Gables*, and other books in that extensive series; film versions of teachers in books, for example, James Hilton's *Goodbye, Mr. Chips*, Jay Presson Allen's adaptation of Muriel Spark's novel in *The Prime of Miss Jean Brodie*, Pat Conroy's *Conrack* and *To Sir With Love*; the Masterpiece Theatre production, *To Serve Them All My Days*; several popular television series, for example, *Our Miss Brooks, Room 222, Welcome Back, Kotter, Fame, Head of the Class, Bronx Zoo, The Wonder Years*.

Moreover, several projects are under way to examine literary and artistic bases for understanding teachers and teaching, for example: Jackson and Haroutunian-Gordon (1989), which interprets teachers in texts and texts in teachers; an ongoing project of Robert Coles, who is focusing on portrayals of teachers in literature, and efforts by Randy Testa to transform some of these theatrically in performances at Harvard called "School Lessons"; a book edited by Willis and Schubert (in press), an attempt to capture what the arts have said to curriculum inquiry and teaching; experimental dramatic performances that interpret teachers' lived experiences by Richard L. Butt, Charles Hart, and Gregory Nixon, of the University of Lethbridge, "Re-presenting Lived Reality Through Drama: Two Plays With Words About Competence," presented at the Bergamo Conference, Dayton, Ohio, October 29, 1987; and Rubin's (1984) work wherein he develops analogies between teaching and the arts.

6. Those involved in this project at National College of Education (recently renamed National Louis University) in Evanston, Illinois, include Kenneth Kantor, J. Dan Marshall, Susan Jungck, Anne Bennison, and Shirley Kessler.

7. See Eisner (1985b) and Lincoln and Guba (1985). Though different in orientation, both argue that the researcher is the instrument of research. This accounts for quite different renditions of similar sets of data.

8. Judith Ponticell had been a consultant and researcher with the Foundation for Excellence in Teaching in Chicago since 1985 and with Project MASTER (Math and Science Teachers' Educational Renewal), a cooperative project between Chicago Public School Districts 31 and 33 and Patricia Charlier, associate professor at the University of Illinois at Chicago.

9. Along with those mentioned above, Ann Lopez Schubert, William Ayers, Janet Miller, James Henderson, Norman Weston, Anne Isaacson, Frederick Klonsky, Jean Erdman, Tom Thomas, Ken Kantor, Dan Marshall, Danielle Raymond, Frances Klein, Noreen Garman, Alan Tom, and Gail McCutcheon are thanked for their helpful ideas.

10. The book will be edited by William H. Schubert and William Ayers. Other contributors include Patricia Hulsebosch, Mari Koerner, Virginia Jagla, Carol Melnick, Suzanne Millies, and Janet Miller.

REFERENCES

Anther, Joyce. (1987). *Lucy Sprague Mitchell*. New Haven, CT: Yale University Press.

Apple, Michael W. (1982). *Education and power*. Boston: Routledge and Kegan Paul.

Apple, Michael W. (1986). *Teachers and texts*. London: Routledge and Kegan Paul.

Apple, Michael W., & Weis, Lois. (Eds.). (1983). *Ideology and practice in schooling*. Philadelphia: Temple University.

Ashton-Warner, Sylvia. (1963). *Teacher*. New York: Simon and Schuster.

Ashton-Warner, Sylvia. (1972). *Spearpoint: 'Teacher' in America*. New York: Vintage.

Athayde, Roberto. (1977). *Miss Margarida's way*. New York: Avon Books.

Ayers, William. (1989). *The good preschool teacher*. New York: Teachers College Press.

Barone, Thomas E. (1987). On equality, visibility, and the fine arts program in a black elementary school: An example of educational criticism. *Curriculum Inquiry, 17*(4), 421–445.

Barone, Thomas E. (1989). Educational connoisseurship and criticism: Curricular implications. In Torsten Husen & T. Neville Pastlethwaite (Eds.), *The international encyclopedia of education* (Supplementary Vol. 1). Oxford, UK: Pergamon.

Barzun, Jacques. (1945). *Teacher in America*. New York: Atlantic-Little Brown.

Bernstein, Richard J. (1983). *Beyond objectivism and relativism*. Philadelphia: University of Pennsylvania.

Bolin, Frances S., & Falk, J. (Eds.). (1987). *Teacher renewal: Professional issues, personal choices*. New York: Teachers College Press.

Boulding, Elise. (1988). *Building a global culture: Education for an interdependent world*. New York: Teachers College Press.

Broudy, Harry S., & Palmer, John R. (1965). *Exemplars of teaching method*. Chicago: Rand McNally.

Brubaker, Dale. (1970). *The teacher as a decision maker*. Dubuque, IA: William C. Brown.

Buchmann, Margret. (1980). *Practitioners' concepts: An inquiry into the wisdom of practice*. East Lansing: Michigan State University, Institute for Research on Teaching. (ERIC Document Reproduction Service No. ED 187 667)

Bullough, Robert V. (1989). *First-year teacher*. New York: Teachers College Press.

Butt, Richard L., & Raymond, Danielle. (1987). Arguments for using qualitative approaches in understanding teacher thinking: The case for biography. *Journal of Curriculum Theorizing, 7*(1), 62–93.

Carr, Wilfred, & Kemmis, Stephen. (1986). *Becoming critical: Education, knowledge and action research*. London: Falmer Press.

Chamberlin, J. Gordon. (1981). *The educating act*. Lanham, MD: University Press of America.

Clandinin, D. Jean. (1986). *Classroom practice: Teacher images in action*. London: Falmer Press.

Clandinin, D. Jean, & Connelly, F. Michael. (1987). Teachers' personal practical knowledge: What counts as 'personal' in studies of the personal. *Journal of Curriculum Studies, 19*(6), 487–500.

Clark, Christopher, & Peterson, Penelope L. (1986). Teachers' thought processes. In Merlin Wittrock (Ed.), *Handbook of Research on Teaching* (pp. 255–296). New York: Macmillan.

Connell, Robert F. (1985). *Teachers' work*. Winchester, MA: Allen and Unwin.

Connelly, F. Michael, & Clandinin, D. Jean. (1988). *Teachers as curriculum planners*. New York: Teachers College Press.

Corey, Steven M. (1953). *Action research to improve school practices*. New York: Teachers College, Columbia University, Bureau of Publications.

Cruickshank, Donald R. (1987). *Reflective teaching*. Reston, VA: Association of Teacher Educators.

Cuban, Larry. (1984). *How teachers taught*. New York: Longman.

Dennison, George. (1969). *The lives of children*. New York: Random House.

Dewey, John. (1900). *The school and society*. Chicago: University of Chicago Press.

Dewey, John. (1902). *The child and the curriculum*. Chicago: University Press.

Dewey, John. (1913). *Interest and effort in education*. Boston: Houghton Mifflin.

Dewey, John. (1916). *Democracy and education*. New York: Macmillan.

Dewey, John. (1922). *Human nature and conduct*. New York: Holt.

Dewey, John. (1927). *The public and its problems*. New York: Holt.

Dewey, John. (1929a). *Experience and nature*. New York: Norton.

Dewey, John. (1929b). *The quest for certainty*. New York: Minton, Balch.

Dewey, John. (1929c). *The sources of a science of education*. New York: Liveright.

Dewey, John. (1930). *Individualism, old and new*. New York: Minton, Balch.

Dewey, John. (1933). *How we think* (rev. ed.). New York: Heath. (Original work published 1910)

Dewey, John. (1934a). *A common faith*. New Haven, CT: Yale University Press.

Dewey, John. (1934b). *Art as experience*. New York: Minton, Balch.

Dewey, John. (1938a). *Experience and education*. New York: Macmillan.

Dewey, John. (1938b). *Logic, the theory of inquiry*. New York: Holt.

Dewey, John. (1939). *Theory of valuation*. Chicago: University of Chicago Press.

Dewey, John, & Tufts, J. H. (1908). *Ethics*. New York: Holt.

Dewey, John, & Bentley, Arthur F. (1949). *Knowing and the known*. Boston: Beacon.

Duckworth, Eleanor. (1987). *The having of wonderful ideas*. New York: Teachers College Press.

Eggleston, Edward E. (1957). *The Hoosier school master*. New York: Hill and Wang. (Original work published 1871)

Eisner, Elliot W. (1985a). *The educational imagination* (2nd ed., chaps. 9–14). New York: Macmillan.

Eisner, Elliot W. (1985b). *The art of educational evaluation: A personal view*. London: Falmer Press.

Elbaz, Freema; Perland, Marc; Munby, Hugh; & Spafford, Charlotte. (1987). Commentaries. *Journal of Curriculum Studies, 19*(6), 501–510.

Elbaz, Freema. (1983). *Teacher thinking: A study of practical knowledge*. London: Croom Helm.

Epstein, Joseph. (Ed.). (1981). *Masters: Portraits of great teachers*. New York: Basic Books.

Ewing, Marilee. (1989). *Understanding supervisory work*. Unpublished internship paper, University of Illinois at Chicago.

Fox, Matthew. (1977). *A spirituality named compassion*. Minneapolis: Winston Press.

Freire, Paulo. (1970). *Pedagogy of the oppressed.* New York: Seabury.

Garman, Noreen. (1986). Clinical supervision: Quackery or remedy for professional development. *Journal of Curriculum and Supervision, 1*(2), 148–157.

Giroux, Henry A. (1988). *Schooling and the struggle for public life.* Minneapolis:
University of Minnesota Press.

Goodson, Ivor F. (1985). *Teachers' lives and careers.* London: Falmer Press.

Gordon, Julia Weber. (1970). *My country school diary.* New York: Dell. (Original
work published 1946)

Greene, Maxine. (1973). *Teacher as stranger.* New York: Wadsworth.

Greene, Maxine. (1986). Philosophy and teaching. In Merlin C. Wittrock (Ed.),
Handbook of research on teaching (pp. 479–501). New York: Macmillan.

Greene, Maxine. (1988). *The dialectics of freedom.* New York: Teachers College
Press.

Griffin, Gary A. (Ed.). (1983). *Staff development.* Eighty-second yearbook of the
National Society for the Study of Education, Part 2. Chicago: University of
Chicago Press.

Gross, Beatrice, & Gross, Ronald. (1974). *Will it grow in a classroom?* New York:
Delta.

Grumet, Madeleine R. (1980). Autobiography and reconceptualization. *Journal of
Curriculum Theorizing, 2*(2), 155–158.

Grumet, Madeleine R. (1988). *Bitter milk: Women and Teaching.* Amherst: University of Massachusetts Press.

Grundy, Shirley. (1987). *Curriculum: Product or praxis.* London: Falmer Press.

Habermas, Jurgen. (1984, 1988). *The theory of communicative action* (Vol. 1, 2).
Boston: Beacon.

Henderson, James G. (1989). Positioned reflective practice: A curriculum discussion. *Journal of Teacher Education, 40*(2), 10–14.

Herndon, James. (1968). *The way it's spozed to be.* New York: Bantam.

Herndon, James. (1985). *Notes for a school teacher.* New York: Simon and Schuster.

Highet, Gilbert. (1950). *The art of teaching.* New York: Knopf.

Highet, Gilbert. (1976). *The immortal profession.* New York: Weybright and Tal-
ley.

Holt, John. (1964). *How children fail.* New York: Delta.

Holt, John. (1981). *Teach your own.* New York: Dell.

Huebner, Dwayne. (1984). The search for religious metaphors in the language of
education. *Phenomenology and Pedagogy, 2*(2), 112–123.

Hulsebosch, Patricia. (1988). *Significant others: Teachers' perspectives on relationships with parents.* Unpublished doctoral dissertation, University of Illinois at
Chicago.

Hultgren, Francine H. (1987). The student teacher as person: Reflections on pedagogy and being. *Phenomenology and Pedagogy, 5*(1), 35–50.

Jackson, Philip, & Haroutunian-Gordon, Sophie. (Eds.). (1989). *From Socrates to
software: The teachers as text and the text as teacher.* Eighty-eighth yearbook
of the National Society of the Study of Education, Part 1. Chicago: University
of Chicago Press.

Jagla, Virginia. (1989). *In pursuit of the elusive image: An inquiry into teachers' everyday use of imagination and intuition.* Unpublished doctoral dissertation, University of Illinois at Chicago.

Janesick, Valerie. (1977). *An ethnographic study of a teacher's classroom perspective.* Unpublished doctoral dissertation, Michigan State University, East Lansing.

Kaufman, Bel. (1964). *Up the down staircase.* Englewood Cliffs, NJ: Prentice-Hall.

Koerner, Mari E. (1989). *Teachers' images of their work: A descriptive study.* Unpublished doctoral dissertation, University of Illinois at Chicago.

Kohl, Herbert. (1968). *36 children.* New York: Signet.

Kohl, Herbert. (1984). *Growing minds: On becoming a teacher.* New York: Harper & Row.

Landau, Elliot D.; Epstein, Sherrie L.; & Stone, Ann P. (1976). *The teaching experience: An introduction to education through literature.* Englewood Cliffs, NJ: Prentice-Hall.

Lather, Patti. (1986). Research as praxis. *Harvard Educational Review, 56*(3), 257–277.

Lawn, Martin, & Grace, G. (Eds.). (1987). *Teachers: The culture and politics of work.* London: Falmer Press.

Lease, Joseph; Frasure, K.; & Johnson, Mauritz. (1961). *The teacher in curriculum making.* New York: Harper & Row.

Lieberman, Ann. (Ed.). (1986). *Rethinking school improvement.* New York: Teachers College Press.

Lightfoot, Sarah Lawrence. (1983). *The good high school.* New York: Basic Books.

Lincoln, Yvonne, & Guba, Egon. (1985). *Naturalistic inquiry.* Beverly Hills, CA: Sage.

Lortie, Dan C. (1975). *Schoolteacher: A sociological study.* Chicago: University of Chicago Press.

MacCrorie, Ken. (1984). *20 teachers.* New York: Oxford University Press.

MacIntyre, Alasdair. (1984). *After virtue* (2nd ed.). Notre Dame, IN: University of Notre Dame.

May, Wanda T., & Zimpher, Nancy L. (1986). An examination of three theoretical perspectives on supervision: Perceptions of preservice field supervision. *Journal of Curriculum and Supervision, 1*(1), 83–99.

McCutcheon, Gail. (1981). On the interpretation of classroom observations. *Educational Researcher, 10*(5), 5–10.

McCutcheon, Gail. (Ed.). (1982). Curriculum theory [Theme issue]. *Theory into Practice, 21*(3).

McDonald, Joseph P. (1986). Raising the teacher's voice and the ironic role of theory. *Harvard Educational Review, 56*(4), 355–378.

McNeil, Linda. (1986). *Contradictions of control.* New York: Routledge and Kegan Paul.

Melnick, Carol R. (1988). *A search for teachers' knowledge of the out-of-school curriculum of students' lives.* Unpublished doctoral dissertation, University of Illinois at Chicago.

Miller, Janet L. (1987). Women as teachers/researchers; gaining a sense of our-
    selves. *Teacher Education Quarterly, 14*(2), 52–58.
Miller, Janet L. (1990). *Creating spaces and finding voices: Teachers collaborating
    for empowerment.* Albany: State University of New York Press.
Millies, Suzanne. (1989). *The mental lives of teachers.* Unpublished doctoral dis-
    sertation, University of Illinois at Chicago.
Munby, Hugh. (1986). Metaphor in the thinking of teachers. *Journal of Curricu-
    lum Studies, 18*(2), 197–209.
Munroe, Kirk, & Catherwood, Mary Hartwell. (Eds.). (1945). *Stories of school
    and college days.* Chicago: Auxiliary Educational League.
Neill, A. S. (1960). *Summerhill: A radical approach to child rearing.* New York:
    Hart.
Noddings, Nel. (1984). *Caring.* Berkeley: University of California Press.
Noddings, Nel, & Shore, Paul. (1984). *Awakening the inner eye: Intuition in
    education.* New York: Teachers College Press.
Opie, Iona, and Opie, Peter. (1959). *The lore and language of school children.*
    Oxford: Oxford University Press.
Paley, Vivian G. (1984). *Boys and girls.* Chicago: University of Chicago Press.
Parker, Walter C. (1986). Dorothy's and Mary's mediation of a curriculum inven-
    tion. *Phenomenology and Pedagogy, 4*(1), 20–31.
Pinar, William F. (1980). Life history and educational experience [Part 1]. *Journal
    of Curriculum Theorizing, 2*(2), 159–212.
Pinar, William F. (1981). Life history and educational experience [Part 2]. *Journal
    of Curriculum Theorizing, 3*(1), 259–286.
Pinar, William F. (1988). The relation between research and pedagogy. In William
    F. Pinar (Ed.), *Contemporary Curriculum Discourses* (pp. 437–452). Scotts-
    dale, AZ: Gorsuch Scarisbrick.
Pinar, William F., & Grumet, Madeleine R. (1976). *Toward a poor curriculum.*
    Dubuque, IA: Kendall/Hunt.
Ponticell, Judith; Griffin, Gary A.; Schubert, William H.; Henderson, James;
    Fowler, Randal; Bacon, Christine; & Richardson, Otis. (1987, November). *A
    voice for teachers: Foundation and policy concerns of teachers in an era of
    educational reform.* Chicago: American Educational Studies Association.
Popkewitz, Thomas S. (1987). *Critical studies in teacher education: Its folklore,
    theory and practice.* London: Falmer Press.
Prigogine, Ilya, & Stengers, Isabelle. (1984). *Order out of chaos.* New York: Ban-
    tam.
Raphael, Ray. (1985). *The teacher's voice: A sense of who we are.* Portsmouth,
    NH: Heinemann.
Rasey, Marie I. (1950). *This is teaching.* New York: Harper and Brothers.
Rorty, Richard. (1979). *Philosophy and the mirror of nature.* Princeton, NJ:
    Princeton University Press.
Rubin, Louis J. (1984). *Artistry in teaching.* New York: Random House.
Rudduck, Jean, & Hopkins, D. (Eds.). (1985). *Research as a basis for teaching:
    Readings from the work of Lawrence Stenhouse.* London: Falmer Press.

Rutter, Michael; Maughan, Barbara; Mortimore, Peter; & Ouston, Janet; with Alan Smith. (1979). *Fifteen thousand hours: Secondary schools and their effects on children.* Cambridge, MA: Harvard University Press.

Schön, Donald A. (1983). *The reflective practitioner: How professionals think in action.* New York: Basic Books.

Schön, Donald A. (1987). *Educating the reflective practitioner: Toward a new design for teaching and learning in the professions.* San Francisco: Jossey-Bass.

Schubert, William H. (1980). *Curriculum books: The first eighty years.* Lanham, MD: University Press of America.

Schubert, William H. (1982). Teacher education as theory development. *Educational Considerations, 12*(2), 8–13.

Schubert, William H. (1986). *Curriculum: Perspective, paradigm, and possibility.* New York: Macmillan.

Schubert, William H. (1987). Educationally recovering Dewey in curriculum. In Chris Eisele (Ed.), *Current issues in education: The teacher and curriculum* (pp. 1–32). Normal, IL: Department of Educational Foundations and Administration at Illinois State University for the John Dewey Society for Education and Culture.

Schubert, William H.; Hulsebasch, Patricia; Koerner, Mari; Millies, Suzanne; Thomas, Thomas P; Wojcik, Jenny; & Zissis, Georgiana. (1987). Teaching about progressive education: From course to study group. *Teaching Education, 1*(2), 77–81.

Schubert, William H., & Lopez-Schubert, Ann Lynn. (1982). Teaching Curriculum Theory. *The Journal of Curriculum Theorizing, 4*(2), 97–111.

Schubert, William H.; Weston, Norman; Ponticell, Judith; & Melnick, Carol R. (1987, October). *Teacher lore project: The first year.* Panel presentation at the Bergamo Curriculum Conference, Dayton, OH.

Schubert, William H.; Willis, George H.; & Short, Edmund C. (1984). Curriculum theorizing: An emergent form of curriculum studies in the United States. *Curriculum Perspectives, 4*(1), 69–74.

Schwab, Joseph J. (1969). The practical: A language for curriculum. *School Review, 78,* 1–23.

Schwab, Joseph J. (1971). The practical: Arts of eclectic. *School Review, 79,* 493–542.

Schwab, Joseph J. (1973). The practical 3: Translation into curriculum. *School Review, 81,* 501–522.

Sears, James T., & Marshall, J. Dan. (Eds.). (1990). *Teaching and thinking about curriculum.* New York: Teachers College Press.

Sergiovanni, Thomas J. (1985). Landscapes, mindscapes, and reflective practice in supervision. *Journal of Curriculum and Supervision, 1*(1), 5–17.

Sharp, George. (1951). *Curriculum development as the reeducation of the teacher.* New York: Teachers College Press.

Sharp, Rachel, & Green, Anthony (with assistance of Jacqueline Lewis). (1975). *Education and Social Control.* London: Routledge and Kegan Paul.

Shor, Ira. (1980). *Critical teaching and everyday life.* Boston: South End Press.

Shulman, Lee. (1986). Paradigms and research programs in the study of teaching: A contemporary perspective. In Merlin C. Wittrock (Ed.), *Handbook of research on teaching* (pp. 3–36). New York: Macmillan.

Sikes, Patricia J.; Measor, Lynda; & Woods, Peter. (1985). *Teacher careers: Crises and continuities.* London: Falmer Press.

Smyth, John. (1984). Toward critical consciousness in the supervision of experienced teachers. *Curriculum Inquiry, 14*(4), 425–436.

Smyth, John. (1987). *Rationale for teachers' critical pedagogy: A handbook.* Victoria, Australia: Deakin University Press.

Snyder, Agnes. (1972). *Dauntless women in childhood education.* Washington, DC: Association for Childhood Education International.

Spears, Harold. (1951). *The teacher and curriculum planning.* Englewood Cliffs, NJ: Prentice-Hall.

Stenhouse, Lawrence. (1975). *Introduction to curriculum research and development.* London: Heinemann.

Stenhouse, Lawrence. (Ed.). (1980). *Curriculum research and development in action.* London: Heinemann.

Stewart, Jesse. (1936). *To teach, to love.* Baltimore: Penguin.

Stewart, Jesse. (1949). *The thread that runs so true.* New York: Charles Scribner's Sons.

Suransky, Valerie Polakow. (1982). *Erosion of childhood.* Chicago: University of Chicago Press.

Tom, Alan R. (1984). *Teaching as a moral craft.* New York: Longman.

Traver, Rob. (1987). Autobiography, feminism, and the study of teaching. *Teachers College Record, 88*(3), 443–452.

Vallance, Elizabeth. (1982). Focus on students in curriculum knowledge: A critique of curriculum criticism. In W. H. Schubert & A. L. Schubert (Eds.), *Conceptions of curriculum knowledge and focus on students and teachers* (pp. 37–44). University Park: College of Education, Pennsylvania State University.

Van Manen, Max. (1982a). Edifying theory: Serving the good. *Theory into Practice, 21*(1), 44–49.

Van Manen, Max. (1982b). Phenomenological pedagogy. *Curriculum Inquiry, 12*(3), 283–299.

Van Manen, Max. (1986). *The tone of teaching.* Richmond Hill, Ontario, Canada: Scholastic.

Van Manen, Max. (1989). *Researching lived experience.* London, Ontario, Canada: Althouse Press.

Van Til, William. (1983). *My way of looking at it.* Terre Haute, IN: Lake Lure Press.

Walker, Decker. (1980). A barnstorming tour of writing on curriculum. In A. W. Foshay (Ed.), *Considered action for curriculum improvement* (pp. 71–81). Washington, DC: Association for Supervision and Curriculum Development.

Waller, Willard. (1932). *The sociology of teaching.* New York: John Wiley and Sons.

Welsh, Patrick. (1986). *Tales out of school*. New York: Viking.

Wideen, Marvin F., & Andrews, Ian. (Eds.). (1987). *Staff development for school improvement*. London: Falmer Press.

Wigginton, Eliot. (1986). *Sometimes a shining moment: The foxfire experience*. Garden City, NY: Anchor Books.

Willis, George. (Ed.). (1978). *Qualitative evaluation*. Berkeley, CA: McCutchan.

Willis, George. (1981). Democratization of curriculum evaluation. *Educational Leadership, 38*(8), 630–632.

Willis, George, & Schubert, William H. (Eds.). (in press). *The arts as a basis for curriculum inquiry*. Albany: State University of New York Press.

Wittrock, Merlin C. (Ed.). (1986). *Handbook of research on teaching* (3rd ed.). New York: Macmillan and the American Educational Research Association.

Wood, George H. (1987). Action for democratic education. In Chris Eisele (Ed.), *Current issues in education: The teacher and curriculum* (pp. 33–53). Normal, IL: John Dewey Society for Education and Culture.

Zissis, Georgiana. (1987). *Value assumptions underlying the experientialist critique of curriculum literature, 1883–1929*. Unpublished doctoral dissertation, University of Illinois at Chicago.

13

Conversation and Narrative in Collaborative Research
An Ethnography of the Written Literacy Forum

SUSAN FLORIO-RUANE

Susan Florio-Ruane received her master's and doctoral degrees from the Harvard Graduate School of Education. Currently professor of education and coordinator of the Learning Community Teacher Education Program at Michigan State University, Dr. Florio-Ruane teaches graduate courses in ethnographic and sociolinguistic research and in theory, research, and teaching of writing. A widely published scholar in these fields, her current research investigates the relationship between literacy learning and teacher-student dialogue. Dr. Florio-Ruane has been an associate editor of Anthropology and Education Quarterly *and a consulting editor for the* Elementary School Journal.

The Written Literacy Forum was a group of teachers from the public schools in East Lansing, Michigan, and researchers from Michigan State University who worked together during the 1980s to investigate how writing instruction could be made more meaningful to educators. During the Forum's deliberations, the following questions were raised: For what audiences and purposes is educational research conducted? What linguistic forms are used to represent research knowledge? What is the relative status of each kind of knowledge? This paper reports the ways in which the Forum's deliberations about educational research encouraged its members to articulate and examine their assumptions about what researchers and

This chapter was originally prepared for presentation at the Meadow Brook Research Symposium: Collaborative Action Research in Education, Oakland University, Rochester, Michigan, January 20–23, 1985. It has been issued by the Institute for Research on Teaching, Michigan State University, as Occasional Paper No. 102.

teachers claim to know, how they express that knowledge, and the views they hold of themselves and each other as professionals.

Until a few years ago, I worked with teachers chiefly in two ways as I researched their practice. Trained as an ethnographer, I knew teachers as informants on classroom life. From that experience, I learned the value of inviting the collaboration of teachers in framing research questions and in collecting and occasionally analyzing classroom data. Typically, however, these close working relationships changed or ended when, like my anthropologist forebears, I left the field to write the reports of my research.

Mentioning that I left the field to write research reports may seem trivial. There is, after all, a division of labor in education whereby teachers teach and researchers theorize about teaching and learning. But, as I hope this chapter will demonstrate, leaving teachers out of the deliberative and expressive phases of research not only creates communication gaps between teachers and researchers but also limits the quality and usefulness of educational research.

In our efforts as members of the Written Literacy Forum to identify and communicate useful insights for teaching writing, we changed our thinking about research. Starting with published reports of research, and then reading, discussing, and transforming them, we came to realize that science is, in Popper's words, "a branch of literature" (cited in Olson, 1980, p. 97). As such, scientific research in education is subject to many of the same questions one can ask about other texts:

1. Who are the *authors* and *audiences* of educational research?
2. For what *purposes* do people speak and write about practice?
3. What are the *topics* about which researchers write? How do they differ from those of concern to teachers?
4. How do *social position* and the *functions of communication* in their professional lives limit and shape teachers' and researchers' communication of what they know?

A PRACTICAL PROBLEM CONCERNING THEORY

Several years ago, after extended fieldwork in two classrooms, my research colleagues and I withdrew to the university to theorize and write about problems of writing instruction. We emerged nearly a year later with the following:

> The researchers held in one hand a two-hundred page technical report titled, "Schooling and the Acquisition of Written Literacy," and in the other, a five-

page Xeroxed report called "Findings of Practical Significance." The researchers stared at these two documents and wondered why their close and careful
research had yielded so few findings of interest to teachers. (Florio-Ruane &
Dohanich, 1984, p. 725)

This situation was both troubling and frustrating. The researchers
had, after all, heeded nearly a decade of calls to make educational research
meaningful by grounding it in everyday classroom realities (Eisner, 1983;
Erickson, 1973). One of our primary goals had been to discover and describe beliefs held by teachers and students about writing in their classrooms. But our close contact with teachers and their daily lives during data
collection and preliminary analysis apparently did not guarantee that our
theoretical accounts would be meaningful to those we had studied or to
other teachers.

One of the features of fieldwork research, or what Glaser and Strauss
(1967) refer to in the title of their book as the "discovery of grounded
theory," is that researchers remain close to the phenomena they study.
Fieldwork involves the gradual framing and testing of working hypotheses
(Geer, 1969). Theory is tentatively formulated and continually open to
revision as the researcher proceeds via a process of "analytic induction"
(Bogdan & Biklen, 1982). This explanation is, however, an idealistic and
partial account of fieldwork that does not fully acknowledge research as
both a social process and a linguistic product.

Our commonsense notion of theorizing is that it is a formal, linguistic
activity undertaken chiefly by experts. Like their colleagues in the other
social sciences, ethnographers are trained to observe special conventions in
their reporting of research findings. Such formal constraints on communication are intended to ensure the validity of theorists' knowledge claims.
Thus the researcher is pressed to report findings in the formal, usually
written, language of theory. To do this, the ethnographer has historically
withdrawn from informants and taken the steamship home to write one or
several monographs for an audience of benefactors and colleagues.

This arrangement is typical in general ethnographies of traditional
societies where, according to Scheper-Hughes (1979),

for the most part anthropologists (as well as the communities studied) have
been shielded from any local repercussions and aftershocks resulting from
publication because we have traditionally worked in what were until recently
"exotic" cultures and among preliterate peoples. In most cases, the "natives"
never knew what had been said about them. . . . The anthropologist might,
as a professional courtesy, send the village headman or a mestizo *mayordomo*
a copy of the published ethnography which was often proudly displayed in the
village. Its contents, however, normally remained as mysterious as the private

life of the "masked" white man, that professional lone stranger, who would periodically reappear (sometimes bearing gifts) and then just as inexplicably vanish (not infrequently at the start of the rainy season). Within this traditional fieldwork paradigm our once colonized subjects remained disempowered and mute. (p. v)

In contemporary educational research, distances and language differences separating researchers from those they study are not so great. Moreover, there is an assumed applicability of research knowledge to the practical problems of the people studied. Yet surprisingly little effort is made to talk with teachers about the adequacy of educational theory. When such conversations do occur, they are typically initiated by third parties who, in the name of teacher education, are charged with "translating" research for practitioners. Very often those studied remain as "disempowered and mute" as the "colonized subjects" Scheper-Hughes (1979) describes.

When the researcher moves from conversations with informants and recording notes in the field to public, formal descriptions of informants' knowledge and culture, the nature of research changes. Although researchers continue to claim that their theories are incomplete and open to challenge, the rendering of those theories in expository prose, graphs, charts, numerical tables, and formulas dramatically alters their presentation and limits their audience. Even in case studies, which may contain large amounts of narrative, researchers' published descriptions are static and frozen in the "ethnographic present." In addition, publication, which Stubbs (1982, p. 42) argues amounts to "full standardization and codification" of written language, confers on the social scientist "expert" status and confers on theory the status of "fixed" rather than tentative knowledge.

Thus when we showed our teacher-informants the technical report we had prepared for our funding agency and the articles we had written for our professional journals, we and our texts were received politely but without enthusiasm. We assumed, with Buchmann (1983), that "for research knowledge to be useful, people must be able to grasp it" (p. 3). But it seemed that our reports were not grasped even by the teachers whose realities they aimed to describe. This does not mean that the teachers did not read and comprehend what we had written. It meant literally that they did not *grasp* it. People grasp things, reach out to appropriate them, because they have intrinsic attraction or apparent value to them. But the teachers did not reach out and appropriate for their use our formal models of writing in their classrooms or the case studies we had written to illustrate them.

The adequacy of ethnographic theorizing rests, at least in part, on the power of the ethnography to resonate with informants' experiences. Again, to quote Scheper-Hughes (1979):

> While it would be implausible to expect that the members of a community would wholeheartedly agree with the outsider's perspective, with his or her rendition of their social, cultural and psychological situation, that rendition should not be *so* foreign or removed from their commonsense interpretation of the meaning of their lives as to do violence to it. Any ethnography ultimately stands or falls on the basis of whether or not it *resonates*: it should ring true, strike a familiar (even if occasionally painful) chord. (p. viii)

The failure of our reports to "ring true" to the experiences of our informants suggested that in our efforts to analyze the structure and function of their everyday activities, we had lost sight of the insiders' perspectives. As the teachers received our reports in polite silence, we wondered why our work lacked vitality, even for those who had a personal stake in it. Did research have anything to say to practice? Had we really talked and listened to our informants while in the field? Did we lose something in the transformation of our experience into formal reports of research? Had we told not-very-good stories about practice, or in our efforts to be rigorous, had we failed to tell any stories at all?

CONVERSATION AND THEORY

The Written Literacy Forum was created to address these questions. In the fall following the completion of our research reports, we invited the teachers in whose classrooms we had worked to participate in a series of conversations about the findings of the research. For several school years, the group met in classrooms, in homes, and at the university. The questions that came to guide our meetings were the following:

1. Of the many potential "findings" of our research, which were of most importance and use to teachers? To student teachers? To administrators? To researchers?
2. What formats for sharing the research would be best suited to the content? The audience? The social setting?
3. What is the nature of communication among various interest groups in education? How are differences in status and role reflected in participants' knowledge and ways of communicating?

Our aim in creating the Forum was not to teach or translate research findings to teachers but rather to talk and listen in a way different from our previous collaboration. Buchmann (1983) has advocated conversation as an alternative to argumentation when researchers and educators meet. This alternative offers a way to transcend status differences that usually separate teachers and researchers. In addition, conversation admits of more and different sources of information about practice. To this end, Buchmann observes that "what makes conversation attractive is its reciprocal quality, the breadth of subject matter and variety of voices compatible with it, and the surprising turns it may take" (p. 3). In conversation, Buchmann argues, theory is forced to share the floor with practitioners' knowledge and all participants are encouraged to address the values implicit in the work they do.

Although the conversational model captures what we hoped to achieve in the Forum, the early going was not smooth. Because of our unspoken assumptions about the status and role of teachers and researchers, conversation — an activity that seems so natural in some situations — was initially halting. When, for example, the researchers attempted to set an open tone for the Forum meetings by urging that all members participate in setting the group's weekly agenda, we were surprised to find that this idea was not welcomed by the teachers. One teacher summarized it this way:

> When you start talking about us handling the agenda, I can think of agenda items, but I think that you have the overall picture and I'm really not sure I want you to abdicate that responsibility, really. (*Transcript of Forum meeting tape, October 14, 1981*)

Later, as I reflected on this situation in my notes, I wrote:

> These feelings of unease get me to thinking. I wonder first about trying to establish a truly open discourse or dialogue between members of the community of research and the community of practice. If our group operated in a social vacuum, where it was not important how the larger society was organized, we might very handily have provided for an open discourse by allowing the agenda to arise in conversation. Unfortunately, we do not operate in such a vacuum. No matter how we look at it, the researchers had the bulk of the power in the previous study, and, in general we have more power than teachers when it comes to deciding what it is important to research in education and why. . . . It strikes me that it may take some more initiative on our part, indeed, more leadership, to encourage discourse within which we can achieve the noncoercive atmosphere we'd hoped for. Put simply, I have come to the realization that in a social world that

is unequal, you don't get a democratic or open conversation simply by saying that everybody's free to talk. What we may have to do is be more thoughtful about how to organize the conversation such that we relieve the teachers from the obligation of trying to say or do the "right" thing to please us. (*Journal entry, November 6, 1981*)

We decided to work toward conversation as a way of confronting problems of socially negotiated nature of knowledge. As ethnographers we hoped to understand and represent teachers' understandings. But we had recently discovered that we missed (or misrepresented) much of what was closest to the heart of the matter for teachers of writing. These problems did not seem to be ones we could repair merely by "translating" our research into less technical language. Instead, they were fundamental problems of interpretation and values. We reasoned that these needed to be addressed by open and extended conversation with the teachers about the research, its reporting, and its potential use to them and their peers. Within the Written Literacy Forum, therefore, conversation was not secondary to our research. It was a critical stage in the inquiry process, essential if our research was to succeed in uncovering and communicating educators' understandings. In this light, Van Manen (1977) writes that conversation

> is a type of dialogue which is not adversative but, as Socrates expressed it, "like friends talking together." This programmatic idea of method as friendly dialogue characterizes all phenomenological social science. (p. 218)

NARRATIVE AND THEORY

Conversation as a research method is very likely to yield stories as data. If we want to understand people's understanding, we are apt to discover meaning in their stories since, in Joan Didion's (1979) words,

> We tell ourselves stories in order to live. We live . . . by the imposition of a narrative line upon disparate images, by the "ideas" with which we have learned to freeze the shifting phantasmagoria which is our actual experience. (p. 11)

The Forum's conversations were opportunities for teachers and researchers to depart from formal recording or reporting of research and tell each other stories of what they knew about the teaching of writing. These discussions were rich and stimulating. They increased our sense that we needed to create better ways to represent knowledge about educational practice than we had done thus far.

Creating compelling, valid accounts of native knowledge is a perennial problem for anthropologists. Historically anthropologists have handled the tension between narrative and expository accounts of cultural knowledge in a number of ways. Some have kept it hidden. Malinowski, for example, kept a vivid and detailed diary of his Trobriand fieldwork and published, instead, his monograph *Argonauts of the Western Pacific* (1961). Malinowski's diary, now read instructively alongside *Argonauts*, was published posthumously by his wife. Similarly, Laura Bohannan (pseud. Bowen, 1964) published a powerful narrative account of her fieldwork among the Tiv of West Africa in the book *Return to Laughter*. In this extended narrative, Bohannan wrote about experiences she was unable to convert into the expository language of the monograph. But she felt it necessary to do so under the pen name Elenore Smith Bowen. Earlier she published scholarly monographs of the same fieldwork under her own name.

More recently, the tension has been brought out in the open. Geertz (1972), for example, published in one text both his narrative account of the Balinese cockfight and an analysis of it. Others, like Carlos Casteneda (1968) and Jean Auel (1980), have written fiction for which they desire the label "ethnography," and controversies about their books have been seen even in the popular press (Randall, 1984, p. 1). Apparently, if science is, in fact, a branch of literature, *presentation* matters. It matters to the quality of the work and to relationships between author and text, audience and text, author and audience. In this light, Hymes (1980) writes,

> Some of what we believe we know about cultural patterns and worlds is interpretable in terms of structure, whether the ingredients of the structure be lines, graphs, numbers, letters, or abstract terms. Some of what we believe we know resists interpretation in terms of structure. It seems to require, instead, *presentation*. (p. 98)

THE ROLE OF NARRATIVE
IN THEORIES OF PRACTICE

Recently, applied social scientists have argued that it is essential to incorporate practitioners' knowledge in explanatory models of their work (Schön, 1984). Kleinman (1983), for example, points out that in applied fields such as teaching and medicine, theories from biology or psychology are typically applied to the solution of practical problems. However, many health or educational problems require additionally knowledge of the meaning systems of practitioner and client as well as the social and cultural factors shaping their communication with one another. Theories that leave out such social and contextual dimensions of healing or teaching risk creating a gap between our theoretical explanations and the problems experienced by practitioners. They also relegate to the status of folk wisdom the meaning systems of both practitioners and clients, leaving their knowledge and their interactions undervalued and unrepresented in our explanatory systems.

The limitations of such theorizing become particularly visible in stubborn or difficult cases (e.g., chronic pain or the chronic difficulties of economically disadvantaged children in learning to read). These cases call for theories that incorporate the dynamic, transactional aspects of processes such as healing or teaching. According to Kleinman, in moving beyond reductionist explanations to contextual ones, we begin not only to derive more adequate explanations of phenomena but to achieve insights more useful to practitioners.

In teacher education, Erickson (1979) further argues that to move toward such theories, practitioners' knowledge and meaning systems must be tapped as part of the explanatory process. Isolated descriptions of classroom procedures or measures of behavioral outcomes of those procedures may miss, to use Kleinman's (1983) phrase, the "very heart" of the process, whether that process be healing as it occurs in the transaction between doctor and patient or conceptual change as it occurs between teacher and student.

To document and analyze these transactions, Erickson (1982) recommends the crafting of "stories of teaching and learning" in which practitioners play key author roles. These stories have a number of advantages. First, primed by research experiences, teachers can add richness and validity to accounts of their work by uncovering and sharing their own "implicit theories" about teaching and learning (Clark & Yinger, 1979). Second, stories are representations of knowledge that do not dodge moral consequences, and to the extent that teaching is a "moral craft" as well as an array of technical skills, stories of teaching may represent that craft more adequately than research monographs (Ryan, 1981; Tom, 1985). Third, teachers' stories are a largely untapped source of information about teaching and an opportunity for teachers to communicate about their work to others. Bringing teachers' stories into the canon of educational literature may confer special status on both the authors and their stories. About this, educator Roland Barth has written,

> A primary motivation is the satisfaction and recognition that comes from seeing one's ideas in print and knowing that others also see them. Writing about practice lends legitimacy to both writer and practice. Most school people feel that education is an important, worthwhile endeavor, but can't

help but be influenced by society's low regard for their profession. In the view of many educators, education is important but not quite important enough. Being a teacher or a principal *and* a writer is more prestigious than being "just" a teacher. (cited in Sugarman, 1984, p. 6)

Persuasive as these arguments may seem, they defy commonly accepted dichotomies drawn between theory and practice, speaking and writing, text and utterance. Olson (1980) summarizes these generally accepted dichotomies by contrasting "explicit written prose statements" (text) with more "informal oral language statements" (utterance):

> Utterance and text may be contrasted at any one of several levels: the linguistic modes themselves — written language versus oral language; their usual usages — conversation, story-telling, verse, and song for the oral mode versus statements, arguments, and essays for the written mode; their summarizing forms — proverbs and aphorisms for the oral mode versus premises for the written mode; and finally, the cultural traditions built around these modes — an oral tradition versus a literate tradition. (p. 85)

Not only are these activities sharply distinguished, but they are also ~~nmonly~~ commonly stratified so that the progress of development, both within the individual and in societies, is thought to be from oral to literate, a movement toward "increasing explicitness with language increasingly able to stand as an unambiguous or autonomous representation of meaning" (Olson, 1977, p. 258).

These sharp demarcations between speech and writing and the clear superiority accorded the essay for the telling of factual truth have had implications for our professional literature. It is not surprising, given these assumptions, that as fields such as anthropology and education have sought "professionalization" and have become more technical in their orientations, they have tended in their reporting to leave out practitioners' stories and silence their voices rather than to feature them (Hale, 1972; Schön, 1984).

THE SOCIAL FUNCTIONS
OF WRITING ABOUT RESEARCH

One of the limitations of taxonomies of oral and literate language is that they fail to acknowledge the powerful connections between language forms and the social functions they accomplish. To this end, taxonomies not only idealize actual speech and writing but can also reinforce the social differences and boundaries separating speech communities. As applied researchers, we need to look beyond static taxonomies of language forms and ask how language functions for its users—whether those users be researchers publishing reports for an audience or their peers or teachers using anecdotes to explain their educational approaches to interested parents. According to Stubbs (1982), be it essay or story, text or utterance,

> More than anything, language is an activity motivated by users' needs to make things known in particular ways for particular purposes and to establish and maintain common understandings with other conversants; the form of a particular text is always determined as much by the conversants' need to function in these situations as it is by whatever it is they wish to describe. (p. 10)

Teachers and researchers communicate differently about the practice of teaching in several ways. First, teachers have relatively less *opportunity* than researchers to communicate about teaching to their peers or other audiences. Second, when teachers engage in talk or writing about teaching, their *audiences* and *purposes* in doing so may be quite different from those of researchers. Third, the *topics* about which teachers choose to speak and write may be quite different from those selected by researchers. Finally, teachers and researchers typically read different kinds of *texts* about teaching and for different purposes.

If, as Foucault (1972, 1977), Kuhn (1970), and others have argued, a professional field is actually a loosely associated collection of communities of discourse (what Gumperz, 1971, called "speech communities"), then it is not surprising that different members of our field would have different purposes for and ways of talking about knowledge concerning teaching and learning. If we further acknowledge that there are not simple dichotomies between oral and literate language or theoretical and practical knowledge, and embrace, instead, the metaphor of multiple speech communities comprising a field, we begin to see that both the knowledge people have and the ways they represent knowledge are to a great extent shaped by their social places and purposes.

Precisely because it was organized as a *forum*, a place for teachers and researchers to talk with one another, our group was a novel speech community. We brought to its membership people heretofore separated in their ways and opportunities to talk about teaching. Gradually we learned how to converse with one another as we talked, read, and wrote together. In the process, we identified new audiences for our research and created new textual formats for reaching them. In altering such givens as author, audience, format, and purpose, we also transformed the content of our theoretical work.

Forum Texts

Table 13.1 is a summary of the oral and written reports of research prepared in the year prior to the Forum and in the first year of its existence. Note that in the year before the creation of the Forum, the major text produced was a long monograph (progress report) whose audience was the agency funding the study. In addition to reporting for the funding agency, the researchers wrote book chapters and journal articles for vaguely defined audiences. About this type of academic writing, Stubbs (1982) observes:

> A peculiar feature of some academic articles is that it is not certain who their audience is going to be. If the articles are on topics of potentially wide, general interest (such as reading and writing), they are likely to be prepared with ill-defined social groups in mind, such as teachers, researchers, or the man in the street. (p. 31)

TABLE 13.1   Texts Reporting Research Before and After Initiation of the Written Literacy Forum

PRE-FORUM (authored by researchers)

Technical report, including theoretical model
    and case studies
"Findings of practical significance"
Journal articles
Book chapters
Notes for conference presentations and colloquia

FORUM (authored by teachers and researchers)

Quarterly progress reports
Simulation game, "Negotiation Entry"
Handouts for roundtable discussions
Displays of children's writing
Journal articles
Revised case studies with study guides
Autobiography

Unlike the articles and chapters, oral presentations given at meetings of research societies or at university colloquia that year were intended for the limited audience of other researchers. These presentations were notable for their textlike quality. The speakers retained control of the floor. Listeners were not permitted to speak except when a brief question-answer period was provided, time was strictly limited, and speakers' remarks were drawn from previously written texts.

The initiation of the forum led to the creation of new forms of text and talk. Although the researchers continued to write academic articles and reports, these articles changed in three ways. First, some of the articles were coauthored by teachers in the Forum. Second, the progress reports and academic articles, which had constituted the bulk of research reporting in Year 1, amounted to only a small part of the reporting undertaken by the Forum. And third, Forum members clarified the intended audiences and purposes for the reporting of research. With the clarification of audience and purpose came a reinterpretation and transformation of the study's major findings.

Identifying Audiences and Purposes

In the course of Forum conversations, the purpose of our group evolved to reflect not only researchers' concerns about the utility and validity of their reporting but practitioners' concerns as well. For teachers, the Forum offered an opportunity to give and receive moral support and to serve others in their profession. The following comment from a Forum teacher illustrates:

> I wonder if it's not so much what we found out, but the whole process we went through. For people to change or to accept what we found out, they have to go through the process, too. And that it's not very easy . . . to become close to people and risk to say that you're a failure, or that you've had failures in these areas. I remember when I taught school in Pennsylvania — it was a small school, there were only about 10 teachers. It took three years before everyone got to know each other in the building well enough to start talking about the problems they had. . . . They were afraid that they were admitting that they couldn't handle it, that there was something wrong with them, when in reality everybody was having the same problems. And what we've done has taken a long time to establish, and no matter what we find here, we're going to have to tell people that you just don't change overnight. (*Transcript of Forum meeting tape, October 14, 1981*)

Trying to communicate this message to other teachers, we adopted the rhetorical tactic of starting with an audience and a purpose for communicating about research. From there we worked back to our study—its raw data, polished reports, the stories they evoked—and began to draft plans for oral and written presentations. Audiences for whom we ultimately wrote and spoke included prospective and experienced teachers, educational researchers, and curriculum specialists in language arts.

Figure 13.1 is a model that rhetorician Himley (cited in Nystrand, 1982) has devised to relate text to social context. All text exists along a continuum of social distance between author and audience. When author and audience are close to one another in social distance, they share a wealth of contextual knowledge. Thus the text they write for one another is *exophoric* in reference. Much of the information needed to interpret the text remains outside it in the store of shared experience of writer and reader/listener.

In contrast, when social distance between author and audience is increased, reference becomes *endophoric*. Here text needs to provide for the lack of shared background knowledge between author and audience. Endophoric text carries much of the contextual knowledge needed for its interpretation and is therefore more self-referencing than exophoric text.

In light of this continuum, one can see how audience and purpose are intimately related to decisions about presentation. Both endophoric and exophoric references have strengths and weaknesses depending on one's audience and purpose when reporting research. Although the essay or the lecture, for example, may be ideal for reporting to a distant or ill-defined audience, it can lose the author's voice. In preparing a text that can stand by itself, the author is rendered virtually anonymous. There is virtually no room in this sort of writing for the nuance, the vivid anecdote, or the telling joke. As Frake (1981) says, "I imagine it is difficult to tell a joke in first-order predicate calculus" (p. 5).

On the other hand, exophoric reference is of limited value in highly technical writing or when communicating with an unknown audience. Its reliance on shared understanding between reader and writer can make it cryptic or uninterpretable when those understandings do not exist. Yet exophoric reference has great power to evoke in the reader who shares its context images of his or her own experiences that resonate with those drawn on by the author. When the writer knows his or her audience and what he or she knows, the writer can craft a text that is evocative. Both writer and reader participate in the creation of such a text's meaning (Rosenblatt, 1978).

When researchers write for ill-defined audiences in their academic reporting of research, their work frequently falls in the endophoric part of the continuum. Because there is great distance between author and audi-

FIGURE 13.1   Relationship of Text to Social Context

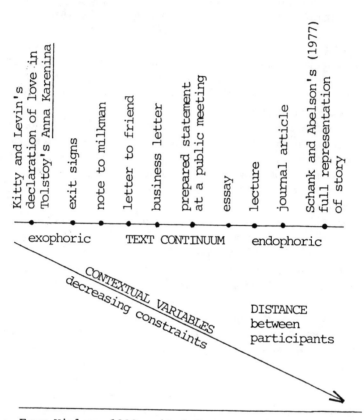

From Himley, 1980, cited in Nystrand, 1982, p.10.
Reprinted with permission.

ence, such contextual information has to be included. In addition, in scientific writing, the rigors of formal research reporting make additional demands. Research texts are quintessential essays in which the author is rendered virtually anonymous, text can stand by itself, and the audience is unknown and distant. But what happens when these texts are expected to bear the burdens of both truthfulness *and* meaningfulness — when they are invoked to instruct *and* move practitioners? They tend to break under the rhetorical burden.

In the Forum, we discovered that as we began to identify and write for more specific audiences, we were better able to consider what these audiences might already know, what they might want to learn more about, or what they could bring to the interpretation of our work. We ventured into genres that were less self-referencing but more vivid, evocative, and immediate. Our communication became less constrained by rules of formal argumentation and, in fact, began to blend oral and written language, narrative and explanation in novel ways. Among the kinds of texts we prepared to share research were simulation games, letters, autobiographies and other personal narratives, and displays of artifacts of children's writing. Most of these texts were open-ended and allowed their audiences to "complete the story." Even in oral presentations, Forum teachers rejected formal presentations to their colleagues. Instead, they created roundtable formats that blended written materials with some oral presentation and considerable discussion.

The Forum teachers also suggested a change in our view of researchers as an audience. Researchers were now not only an audience for other researchers' findings. They were construed by the teachers as an audience in need of continuing education about their own practice. Specifically, the Forum teachers proposed writing to researchers about the process of negotiation of entry into a school site in order to study it successfully. To teach researchers what we had learned about this, the Forum chose to design a simulation game that could be played by fledgling researchers before they ever took a step into the field. In so doing, the Forum members wrote dramatic scenarios, character sketches, and follow-up ideas for discussion. It was left to the researcher audiences to negotiate among themselves the actual plot line for each simulation.

Finally, the Forum revisited the case studies written for the original technical report. In the course of Forum discussions, we sought a clearer audience for these texts. The potential of new texts to offer vivid, vicarious experiences of teaching *and* the opportunity to revisit those experiences suggested they would be useful texts for preservice teachers. Thus the case studies were revised, edited both to make them more richly descriptive and to include a series of open-ended questions to guide their use by teacher educators and students.

TEXT, AUDIENCE, AND VALUES

Figure 13.2 is a model of ordinary societal assumptions about the dichotomies between oral and written language, text and utterance (Stubbs, 1982). Overlaid on the model are Forum texts and activities (from Table

13.1). Note that when we plot the Forum's activities and texts on the model, the bulk of the group's written and oral communication falls on the casual end of a "formal-casual" continuum of standard usage. In addition, Forum talk taking the form of "conversation" rather than "presentation" is further devalued and classified as both "nonstandard" and "casual." As such, that talk is unreproducible as part of a documentary, historical record of teachers' thinking about their practice.

In addition, note that, whether written or spoken, Forum-authored texts tend to fall in the "casual" part of the continuum, research reports in

Figure 13.2   Forum Texts and the Common View of the Relation Between Spoken and Written Language

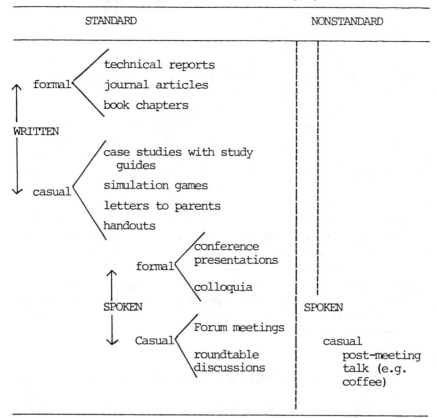

Modified from Stubbs, 1982, p. 40.   Adapted with permission.

the "formal." This formal/casual distinction underscores the status differences between teacher- and researcher-held knowledge and the differential value likely to be attributed to them. Moreover, ranking the expository accounts of research as formal and standard and relegating conversation, narrative — and participants' voices — to the casual and nonstandard domains risks, in Frake's (1981) terms, "making the smart people look dumb." Highly systematic, endophoric accounts of native knowledge, Frake continues, achieve their ends "by framing out of view the contexts within which people display their smartness in their own worlds" (p. 6).

The Forum created the opportunity for several things to change with respect to this formal/casual distinction. First, the Forum provided for the public expression of knowledge from both teacher and researcher sources. Second, to the extent that these rigid boundaries are held in our field, the Forum encouraged teachers and researchers to risk crossing them. It was now possible for teachers to make formal presentations and author articles and chapters (something heretofore not done by them), just as it engaged researchers in more open give-and-take with specific and diverse audiences in education. In this sense, there was movement out of the safety of isolation in the "theoretical" or the "practical," the "formal" or the "casual" domains.

THE KNOWLEDGE WORTH REPORTING

Olson (1980) summarized our ordinary assumptions about theoretical and practical knowledge by observing that "truth in oral utterance has to do with truth as wisdom. . . . Truth in prose text, however, has to do with the correspondence between statements and observations" (p. 104). These distinctions have been called into question recently with some individuals arguing that practitioners often base their knowledge claims on systematic hypothesis testing (Schön, 1984) and others pointing out that research is not value-neutral or disinterested (Eagleton, 1983). Meier (1982) observes that the link between formal written discourse and formal knowledge has served, since the Greeks, to exclude whole classes of knowledge and keep them embedded and preserved in oral tradition. She notes that French scholar Michel Foucault (1977)

> refers to such excluded knowledges as "subjugated knowledges," knowledges whose validity is not dependent on the approval of established regimes of thought, [but which have also] been systematically disqualified from the established hierarchy of knowledges and sciences. (cited in Meier, 1982, p. 21)

It is noteworthy that Foucault also argues that these subjugated knowledges contain most of the "historical knowledge of struggles" within a community. Because they remain outside parameters of scientific discourse, Foucault argues that they "provide society with the only viable source of critical reflection upon its own taken-for-granted assumptions" (Meier, 1982, p. 21). It can be argued that teachers' stories represent subjugated knowledge of this sort. As such their inclusion in research reporting potentially enriches theories about practice and also renders accounts of practice move vivid and moving. In addition, to the extent that teachers' stories are framed outside of the boundaries of scientific knowledge about practice, it is likely that teachers will view research as disconnected from their knowledge and concerns.

In the Forum, teachers' knowledge and researchers' knowledge were brought head to head. There was a great deal to which the researchers had not paid attention while in the field or when writing their reports. Much of what we failed to hear or see or represent can be thought of in terms of the efforts of teachers and students to achieve written literacy in the complex institutional setting of public school. Time and again as we reviewed and revised texts about our research, we realized that in focusing on the "classroom" or "written literacy," researchers had made many tacit assumptions. Our views and depictions of the teaching and learning of writing tended to be telescopic, our portrayals of classroom life and lessons static.

The Forum teachers found most important in our research many details we had overlooked in our initial reporting. They were particularly struck, for example, by the contextual constraints to teaching writing that arise from outside the classroom. They saw in our notes and reports the possibility of powerful presentations about the multiple and conflicting forces that work on them as they teach children to read and write. Many people have a stake in literacy education — teachers, parents, children, administrators, politicians, textbook publishers, and the press. Teachers operate as mediators, making moment-to-moment decisions and long-range plans that aim to balance competing definitions of literacy, competing demands on their time, limited and somewhat ad hoc resources, against their own talents, values, and skills. *This* in many ways was the heart of a story about the teaching or writing that we ultimately came to tell together.

Incorporating the teachers' voices and stories into texts for diverse audiences taught us that not all knowledge can be represented by structural models. Because our initial formal accounts were biased toward the typical, they were unable to capture conflict, compromise, and change. In story and conversation we had access to a great many more of the tensions and contradictions in teachers' work. Whereas a year before we would have waited patiently for teachers to vent their complaints about the district or the principal before getting down to talking about how they teach writing, we now realized that those concerns were intimately tied to teaching writing.

In the Forum we grew to realize that sometimes a story or a conversation is the best way to represent or share some important kinds of knowledge. We also grew to appreciate that such forms of language are not extraneous to inquiry but central to a valid portrayal of teachers' work. We also found, as we met and talked with practitioners, that, to the degree that we admitted and encouraged the voicing of their knowledge, teachers warmed to ideas that research had to offer them as well. One teacher expressed her growing insight as follows:

> I guess I felt really good about getting with the group because my coming to East Lansing was . . . well, I was thinking how valuable all of you were in terms of support people . . . for the first move here. It was like I felt you were friends who cared about me rather than researchers. It just did something really special, and it also opened up some new ways of looking at teaching writing. I had never really thought about it. Perhaps I had done it haphazardly, and then this gave some rhyme and reason. And I think it was a good feeling to be able to talk with other teachers. I had not had the opportunity in my past teaching experience to sit down and talk about the kind of things we'd done in the classroom. And beyond being able to talk with immediate colleagues, we could talk with people out of the university, which was a really good learning experience. I got a balance on both sides. (*Transcript of Forum meeting tape, October 14, 1981*)

Once we began conversations with one another, we learned a great deal more about the processes of teaching and learning writing in school than any of us could have learned in isolation. Insights came from looking at data together and talking about what was there, what was missing, what we had represented, and what we had failed to capture in our reports. That effort productively blurred distinctions between talk and writing, research and practical knowledge, inquiry and teacher education. In the process we believe we created new ways of speaking, writing, and knowing about practice.

Acknowledgments.   Accepting sole responsibility for the chapter, I would like to thank past and present members of the Written Literacy Forum for many conversations that helped to clarify many of the ideas presented here. They are, in alphabetical order, Christopher M. Clark, James Colando, JoAnn B. Dohanich,

Saundra Dunn, Janis Elmore, Wayne Hastings, June Martin, Rhoda Maxwell, William Metheny, Marilyn Peterson, Sylvia Stevens, and Daisy Thomas. I would like to thank one Forum member, Saundra Dunn, for her very helpful comments on an earlier draft of the paper.

REFERENCES

Auel, Jean M. (1980). *The clan of the cave bear*. New York: Crown.

Bogdan, Robert, & Biklen, Sari Kopp. (1982). *Qualitative research for education: An introduction*. New York: Allyn & Bacon.

Bowen, Elenore Smith. (1964). *Return to laughter*. New York: Anchor Press.

Buchmann, Margret. (1983). *Argument and conversation as discourse models of knowledge use* (Occasional Paper No. 68). East Lansing: Michigan State University, Institute for Research on Teaching.

Casteneda, Carlos. (1968). *The teachings of Don Juan: A Yaqui way of knowledge*. Berkeley: University of California Press.

Clark, Christopher M., & Yinger, Robert J. (1979). Teacher thinking. In P. Peterson & H. Walberg (Eds.), *Research on teaching: Concepts, findings and implications* (pp. 231–263). Berkeley, CA: McCutchan.

Didion, Joan. (1979). *The white album*. New York: Simon & Schuster.

Eagleton, Terence. (1983). *Literary theory: An introduction*. Minneapolis: University of Minnesota Press.

Eisner, Elliot. (1983). Can educational research inform education practice? *Phi Delta Kappan, 65*, 447–452.

Erickson, Frederick. (1973). What makes school ethnography "ethnographic"? *Council on Anthropology and Education Newsletter, 4*, 10–19.

Erickson, Frederick. (1979). *On standards of descriptive validity in studies of classroom activity* (Occasional Paper No. 16). East Lansing: Michigan State University, Institute for Research on Teaching.

Erickson, Frederick. (1982). Taught cognitive learning in its immediate environments: A neglected topic in the anthropology of education. *Anthropology and Education Quarterly, 13*, 148–180.

Florio-Ruane, Susan, & Dohanich, JoAnn Burak. (1984). Communicating findings by teacher/researcher deliberations. *Language Arts, 61*, 724–730.

Foucault, Michel. (1972). *The archaeology of knowledge*. New York: Harper & Row.

Foucault, Michel. (1977). What is an author? In *Language, counter-memory, and practice*. Ithaca, NY: Cornell University Press.

Frake, Charles. (1981, March). *Notes toward a cultural analysis of "formal."* Paper presented at the 32nd annual Georgetown University Roundtable on Languages and Linguistics, Washington, DC.

Geer, Blanche. (1969). First days in the field: A chronicle of research in progress. In George J. McCall & J. L. Simmons (Eds.), *Issues in participant observation* (pp. 144–162). Reading, MA: Addison-Wesley.

Geertz, Clifford. (1972). Deep play: Notes on the Balinese cockfight. *Daedalus, 101*, 1–37.

Glaser, Barney, & Strauss, Anselm. (1967). *The discovery of grounded theory.* Chicago: Aldine.

Gumperz, John. (1971). *Language in social groups.* Stanford, CA: Stanford University Press.

Hale, Kenneth. (1972). Some questions about anthropological linguistics: The role of native knowledge. In D. Hymes (Ed.), *Reinventing anthropology* (pp. 383–397). New York: Vintage Books.

Himley, Margaret. (1980). *Text and context: A dynamic interaction.* (ERIC Document Reproduction Service No. ED 193 640)

Hymes, Dell. (1980). *Language in education: Ethnolinguistic essays.* Washington, DC: Center for Applied Linguistics.

Kleinman, Arthur. (1983). The cultural meanings and social uses of illness: A role for medical anthropology and clinically-oriented social science in the development of primary care theory and research. *Journal of Family Practice, 16*, 539–545.

Kuhn, Thomas. (1970). *The structure of scientific revolutions* (2nd ed.). Chicago: University of Chicago Press.

Malinowski, Bronislaw. (1961). *Argonauts of the Western Pacific.* New York: Dutton.

Meier, Terry R. (1982). *Towards a sociolinguistics of writing: A critical assessment of prevailing theory and method in adult basic writing instruction.* Unpublished qualifying paper, Harvard Graduate School of Education, Cambridge, MA.

Nystrand, Martin. (1982). Rhetoric's "audience" and linguistics' "speech community": Implications for understanding writing, reading and text. In M. Nystrand (Ed.), *What writers know: The language process and structure of written discourse* (pp. 1–28). New York: Academic Press.

Olson, David. (1977). From utterance to text: The bias of language in speech and writing. *Harvard Educational Review, 47*(3), 257–281.

Olson, David. (1980). From utterance to text: The bias of language in speech and writing. In Maryanne Wolf, Mark K. McQuillan, and Eugene Radwin (Eds.), *Thought and Language/Language and Reading* (Reprint Series No. 14, pp. 84–108). Cambridge, MA: *Harvard Educational Review*.

Randall, Frederika. (1984, January 29). Why scholars become storytellers. *New York Times*, pp. 1, 25.

Rosenblatt, Louise. (1978). *The reader, the text, the poem.* Carbondale: Southern Illinois University Press.

Ryan, Kevin. (1981, April). *The teacher's story: The oldest and newest form of educational research.* Paper presented at the annual meeting of the American Educational Research Association, Los Angeles.

Schank, Roger, & Abelson, Robert. (1977). *Scripts, Plans, Goals, and Understanding.* Hillsdale, NJ: Lawrence Erlbaum.

Scheper-Hughes, Nancy. (1979). *Saints, scholars and schizophrenics: Mental illness in rural Ireland.* Berkeley: University of California Press.

Schön, Donald. (1984). *The reflective practitioner: How professionals think in action*. New York: Basic Books.

Stubbs, Michael. (1982). Written language and society: Some particular cases and general observations. In M. Nystrand (Ed.), *What writers know: The language, process and structure of written discourse* (pp. 31–55). New York: Academic Press.

Sugarman, Jay. (1984, November). *The production of a school system-based education journal as a means of enhancing professional growth and staff development*. Paper presented at the National Council of States for Inservice Education, Orlando, FL.

Tom, Alan. (1985). Rethinking the relation between research and practice in teaching. *Teaching and Teacher Education, 1*, 139–153.

Van Manen, Max. (1977). Linking ways of knowing with ways of being practical. *Curriculum Inquiry, 6*, 205–228.

14

Story and Voice
in the Education of Professionals

CELESTE M. BRODY and CAROL WITHERELL
with KEN DONALD and RUTH LUNDBLAD

Celeste M. Brody is assistant professor of education at Lewis & Clark College in Portland, Oregon, where she coordinates the Graduate Core Program and the Northwest Cooperative Learning Institute. She earned her Ph.D. from Ohio State University in curriculum and instruction. Her areas of specialization include instructional strategies, adult development, and staff development. An avid whitewater rafter, Dr. Brody focuses on experiential learning activities as a context for understanding the complexities of human learning and growth. She has published on gender studies, community education, and cooperative learning.

Carol Witherell is associate professor of education and director of teacher education at Lewis & Clark College. A former teacher of primary grades, she received her Ph.D. degree in educational psychology from the University of Minnesota. (See also the biographical information at the beginning of Chapter 5.)

Ken Donald, a native Osage-Ponca, holds an M.S.W. degree and an M.S. in school psychology from Lewis & Clark College. He currently serves as a school psychologist for the Beaverton School District in Beaverton, Oregon. His special interests are in working with minority youth and youth with emotional, behavioral, or economic problems.

Ruth Lundblad completed her master's degree in special education for the hearing impaired at Lewis & Clark College. She is a writer, a mother of four children, and a teacher of the hearing impaired.

Stories go in circles. They don't go in straight lines. So it helps if you listen in circles because there are stories inside stories and stories between stories and finding your way through them is as easy and hard as finding your way home. And part of the finding is the getting lost. If you're lost, you really start to look around and listen. (Deena Metzger, "Circles of Stories," p. 104)

The story that follows is actually many stories. It is first the story of how a graduate school of professional studies has created a new vision of what it means to be a professional within a community of inquirers. It is also the story of how we as teachers have responded to the challenge of designing a curriculum and a pedagogy that speak to the special opportunities of teaching adults from five different professional programs. Most importantly, it is the stories and voices of our students themselves as they strive to construct new meaning out of their life experience and offer their teachers our most valuable lessons. It is a story of a shared journey; we are fellow travelers with our students as we attempt to integrate lessons from critical and feminist theory, life-span and social psychology, anthropology, ethics, and the humanities with discourse about our daily lives and the institutions in which we work.

We will describe the origins of our graduate core curriculum, highlight aspects of our team teaching one of the core classes, and offer several of the stories written by our students as they speak to major life-course themes in the adult years. Because it is a story of human connectedness and possibilities, it is a hopeful story. We continue to be humbled in the face of our students' lives and the remarkable intelligence and caring that emerge from a single class experience. Finally, it is an unfinished story because the dialogue continues among the participants. Our understanding of even a single idea or moment in our lives continues to be transformed with each new experience as colleagues, teachers, and friends. We invite our readers to do what we ask our students to do the first day we encounter them on this journey of self-discovery and meaning making: to be willing to listen to your own stories as you hear those of others.

René Girard has observed that the greatest myth of the twentieth century is the myth of our own detachment (cited in Bruner, 1983). Extending this caution, we accept that one of the greatest challenges for professionals today is to guard against their own detachment—from themselves, from their community, and from those with whom they form particular relationships. The tendency of Western cultures to overvalue individualism, autonomy, and competition has deeply defined the character of our nation's higher education and professional programs. These values have structured our social relations, the nature of our inquiry, and the norms that guide our professional lives. Creating a new professional school within a liberal arts college that would guard against such detachment and address the prominent ethical and social concerns of our era was far from a strictly intellectual endeavor. It tested the limits of our ability to create a deeper dialogue among ourselves and with our students, to be creative in our vision of what the curriculum would be, and to practice pedagogy that truly respects our students as adult learners and fellow teachers.

ORIGINS OF THE GRADUATE CORE CURRICULUM

In 1984, the five existing graduate programs at Lewis & Clark College were joined to form a new school, the Graduate School of Professional Studies. These programs included counseling psychology, educational administration, teacher education, public administration, and special education for the hearing impaired. At the time, students and faculty were asked to identify the issues facing them as persons striving to seek satisfying personal and professional lives. Those concerns generally fell into two areas: concern with life-course issues as they affected their ability to maintain a proper balance between personal and professional demands, and concern with the nature of modern organizations as they influence our ability to remain effective in our work or to remain in our work at all. These discussions led to the creation of a common experience for students and faculty across programs. It soon came to be called the Graduate Core Program, identified by three specific elements—one course titled Individual and Societal Perspectives on Adulthood, a second titled Organizational Cultures and Professional Life, and a series of Critical Issues Seminars on important and timely concerns in the professions and society.

We were aware of the importance of educating students with the most advanced knowledge and skills relevant to their current or future professional roles. We were also aware of the limitations of such specialization, since the modern professional works and lives in a complex interpersonal and organizational world. The interdisciplinary core curriculum attempts to speak to common challenges across professions and to address the mission foci of the college in three areas: international studies; gender studies; and science, technology, and human values. Faculty summarized the aims of the core program and the challenge they faced in building curriculum and practicing an inclusive, collaborative pedagogy:

> In the Core, individuals interact with faculty and students in different disciplines. Core pedagogy is collaborative; it fosters inquiry more than providing solutions and understands that knowledge is dynamic and problematic and not static or assured. The Core curriculum engages students and faculty in substantive issues of purpose, meaning and knowing. In particular, it focuses on the influence of culture, gender, age and intellectual assumptions as these factors affect professionals' visions of their work, lives and hopes for the evolution of their community. (*Graduate Catalog*, 1986, p. 10)

TEACHING A CORE CLASS

One of these courses, Individual and Societal Perspectives on Adulthood, was to be designed with regard for the mature adult student, typically a returning professional, a lifelong learner who would be invited to examine major themes of adult development. As team teachers of this course, our first task was to articulate the themes that would guide our inquiry:

1. The expectations individuals have for their lives are based on an interplay of cultural norms, family patterns, and individual choices, commitments, dispositions, and personalities.
2. Individuals develop as adults as these factors interact with individual life experiences. The course of adult development is characterized by both continuity and discontinuity.
3. Throughout the life course, individuals strive to make sense out of their life experiences and choices in a number of domains — intellectual, aesthetic, ethical, psychological, social, and spiritual. In Robert Kegan's words, "the activity of being a person is the activity of meaning making" (1982, p. 11).
4. The effects of life events depend upon how and when they occur within the context of social and cultural expectations. Gender, ethnicity, age, religious values, socioeconomic factors, and social-support networks affect the way we interpret and respond to life events. A major challenge for professionals today is that of building a caring society and a peaceful, interdependent world.
5. The challenge of professional organizations and work environments is to create the conditions for their employees' continued professional and personal development and creativity.
6. Life transitions, relationships and commitments, career choices, and the balancing of one's personal, family, and professional life are persistent life-course challenges (Brody & Witherell, 1987).

We then assumed that adults, as well as children, are natural storytellers, though they have often learned to suppress their urge to tell stories as evidence of knowing (or even experiencing) because of the dominant theory of knowledge as "objectivity and generalizability" within the academic world. Jerome Bruner (1986) has characterized these two ways of knowing as the narrative mode and the paradigmatic (or logico-scientific) mode. Although we acknowledge the distinctive merits of each mode, we designed our course in adult development with the assumption that narrative and story are powerful teachers of the themes and challenges of the adult years.

We regard our curriculum as a dynamic expression of an ethical framework and an instructional method, as we intended to model and foster the values of dialogue and inclusion within the course. We gave careful thought to the practical implications of building an ethic based upon care as well as justice, upon cooperation as well as individual success. We were particularly interested in expanding our ways of knowing as professionals and our capacity to live our lives in caring relation with others, both within our own community called the graduate school and the larger community called our profession.

Connectedness, trust, teamwork—these were easier to talk about in the true, detached academic tradition than they were to actualize as the norms for conducting a weekly 3-hour seminar with 25–35 people from five professions. There was already considerable resistance to this new, additional course requirement for graduate students. What could we do to "break the set" of a typical college class and provide a context for people working creatively and honestly together? As educators, we held the belief that people learn about the life course not through their "seats bolted to the chairs" but by actually living it. One of us had a great deal of experience as a white-water river rafter and had used the river experience to conduct training programs with women. She had used the shared camaraderie, the willingness of participants to "move in and out" of themselves as they reflected on the processes they used to solve problems and "know" what they should or should not do. We knew that the time-honored practices of experiential education were important for adult learners. We wanted to provide a common, intense experience that would require people to solve problems, confront issues of trust when working in groups, explore the meaning of teamwork and examine the implicit understandings about handicaps, gender, culture, and style they each brought to working with people. We needed that common, shared experience from which we could all draw as we moved through the course. We wanted to create a "metaphor for life," much like a theatre is a mirror for life, but one that could be completed within the confines of a weekly course. We instituted a single session "challenge course" offered by the North Portland Youth Service Center as part of the course experience.

The challenge course consists of a series of physical activities and problems requiring group cooperation to be completed. Trained counselor-guides set up physical challenges for the group, including both real limitations and imaginary consequences. Then, our guides step back and observe the antics that follow. Leaping from 6-foot platforms into the arms of one's colleagues and scaling a 10-foot wall successfully may be an awesome physical challenge for some, whereas for others it is not. Challenge may reside in the psychological dimension, where articulating one's own needs or listening carefully to the suggestions of others may be more difficult. Reflective processing of the event is the most important aspect of the experience. Although the challenge course is typically completed in no less than 6 hours, we designed a 3-hour course, offering at the end considerable guidance for self-reflection before the next class meeting. "Processing" was easy because people had more than enough to say about their experience. The week's reflection time worked particularly well with adults, who have developed their self-reflective capabilities. Conducting this event early in the term provided us with a powerful communal experience from which we could consider all the themes of the course. It also served to establish a climate of connectedness, teamwork, and caring toward each other.

The challenge course proved to offer the glue we were seeking. Indeed, the nature of the course themes and the topics we hoped to explore would not be easy to deal with openly with peers unless there was a significant level of trust. Experiential learning coupled with our emphasis upon narrative and the personal story as the thread of the life course proved to be an exhilarating combination.

Another early concern was: How do we organize the major themes from adult development in such a way that they release the participant's own voice through the activities of writing and speaking? How do we frame the issues in the life course in such a way that the professional will integrate these understandings into his or her cognitive framework? We drew heavily upon the Mary Belenky, Blythe Clinchy, Nancy Goldberger, and Jill Tarule's *Women's Ways of Knowing* (1986), Carol Gilligan's *In a Different Voice* (1982), Nel Noddings's *Caring: A Feminine Approach to Ethics and Moral Education* (1984), Tillie Olsen's *Tell Me a Riddle* (1956/ 1976), and anthropologist Barbara Myerhoff's study of an aging Jewish community in *Number Our Days* (1978). Robert Kegan's *The Evolving Self* (1982) provided the pivotal theoretical work, offering a dialectical and constructivist view of human development. Jerome Bruner's *Actual Minds, Possible Worlds* (1986) offered a view of growth as the construction of possibilities, and Mark Pilisuk and Susan Hillier Parks's *The Healing Web* (1986) explored the potency of community and social networks in both individual and societal development. These essays and stories created a set of ideas that we wove together as "braided strands" throughout the course through our written and spoken dialogues with students. We also asked our students to read a piece of fiction or a biography that explored issues of gender, ethnic, or cultural identity within the adult years.

Emphasizing narrative and the personal story as the predominant schema for understanding the life course was a conscious decision about how best to create a context in which professionals can explore the paradoxes of human development. We often elaborated on how dialogue was a particular expression of the narrative mode of thought. Thus, our teaching methodology was guided by two interconnected but slightly different modes of expression: narrative and dialogue.

We were intent on modeling dialogue with our students as we believe that dialogue should be at the heart of a graduate education. We wanted our participants to experience dialogue as Ira Shor and Paulo Freire described: "Dialogue is the moment where humans meet to reflect on their reality as they make it and remake it. It is the quintessential human act, the social moment wherein we establish ties, and where we have authentic recognition of the other" (1987, pp. 98–99). Dialogue is dialectical, in that only through true dialogue, with oneself or the other, can a person be changed or change another. It is the essence of the egalitarian stance in that I have to be able to suspend my self and my constructs in order to receive and hear you, the other, who, at this moment, is me. When we seek to tell our stories, to be heard, it is in dialogue where we create the possibilities to hear and be heard. Again, we continued to create the "braided strand."

We conveyed to our students our belief that the narrative capacity is the way each one of us reorganizes, reassesses, realigns our life experience so that it is continually integrated into our present personal schema, a schema that includes rich cultural and historical features, and ultimately into the schema of the community and the historical context for the culture. Narrative ways of knowing have been devalued in Western science, precisely because of their serendipitous ability to integrate the seemingly paradoxical. The power of narrative is that it allows the individual to continually locate and relocate his or her own voice within a social and cultural context. Narrative and dialogue give each person what Gilligan and Belenky call "voice."

The metaphor of "finding one's voice" soon became common language to the class participants. It was used in several ways in the course. Many students described the experience of "losing their voice" when they returned to school, because of a lack of open dialogue in their classes. They identified and gave new value to the collective efforts of people outside mainstream society attempting to give shape and direction to their world, and they identified those personal, political, and professional dimensions of their lives that had special significance for them.

In concert with Nel Noddings's (1984) and Martin Buber's (1965) claims that dialogue is at the heart of nurturing the ethical ideal, the caring relation, we designed our class around active participant dialogue within discussion groups. Participants were encouraged to release their stories as anecdotes for exploration of the theories we were examining. We explained to them:

> Typically we'd like to begin the class with our own reflections on themes or issues from the readings assigned in preparation for the class. These reflections will be followed or interspersed with comments and questions from class participants. During the second half of the evening, we will break into seminar groups to be led by class members. Each class member will have the opportunity to lead at least one seminar during the term. The seminar leader should prepare, in writing, a five to ten minute reflective essay on an issue from the readings for that evening, to be presented as the topic for the discussion within the group. Following this presentation, the leader shifts to the role of facilitator for a discussion of his or her presentation. (Brody & Witherell, 1987)

Participants were asked to keep a dialogical journal. Our instructions to them provided an opportunity for them to write and think independently yet responsively to the views of the authors we were reading and to other class participants.

> The journal offers you the opportunity to engage in critical and personal reflections on readings, class discussion, field exercises and potential applications of these to your professional life and growth. Think of this writing each week as a continuous process of reflection on both self and community. Try to write when you feel a sense of creative energy, even passion. (Brody & Witherell, 1987)

Students discussed their stories in their seminars and in their journals, relating their personal histories and dramas to those of characters in fiction or biographies that they were reading in the course, to each other's experiences, or to theories of development that we used as conceptual organizers.

We asked students to consider what they were learning from personal narratives about the significance of the life course. Kim Stafford tells us in Chapter 1 that "a story saves life a little at a time." The personal narratives of the participants in our graduate core class, recorded in their journals, autobiographies, and reflective papers, suggest that one of the ways that stories save life is through illuminating the power of connection — a powerful guard against detachment. Connections are forged within lives — that is, across time and context — and between lives — across time, context, persons, generations, cultures, and gender. As the term unfolded, we observed our students with their diverse backgrounds and ages listening to each other with both humility and awe. We noted the respect they felt for the life experiences of each other, and we read in their journals about the quiet yet often profound lessons they were learning from their peers.

STORIES FROM OUR STUDENTS

The story vignettes that follow offer voices that have made such connections within the human drama. They are stories of the human yearning for meaning making. They are also stories of human caring: the memory of caring and being cared for, and the conflicts and yearnings of caring.

We want to suggest that serious writing by students, when shared with class members in this way, can serve both as text and as grounded theory. Students' writing served to organize their concepts and ways of knowing within each seminar group in ways that prepared the groups for their final projects: presentations to the class that described a group action research project, a collective narrative, or a creative synthesis and application of major constructs developed in the course.

These stories join the worlds of thought and feeling. They connect the authors' analyses of self, gender, and culture with their feelings — feelings of joy, sadness, aloneness, anger, and the fullness of relation. They acknowledge the centrality of affect and subjectivity in human ways of knowing. We offer this language and these first-person narratives without apology but rather with the hope that they will convey the power and richness experienced in our study of adult development and social networks.

With Nel Noddings, we feel that there is a great chasm that "divides the masculine and the feminine in all of us" (1984, p. 6). This may be especially true in the academic world, where, as in the rest of our daily life, our aim should be the full expression and reconciliation of these voices, for they are surely the partners in life's dance. Margaret, a 35-year-old counselor in training and a member of a religious order, shows how story and dialogue have helped her find her own voice.

Margaret

Hers is a story of one woman's personal healing through the growth of receptiveness and responsiveness, leading to a confidence in her own voice. Her growth in these areas occurs first through the world of nature, later through her work with a skilled therapist, and most recently through her discovery of female mentors in the case studies of Mary Belenky and her coauthors (1986) and Carol Gilligan (1982) and the fictional writings of Tillie Olsen (1956/1976). She begins her writing with an idea from Mary Belenky with which she personally identifies and continues to explore its meaning for herself in terms of her own history and her future life work as a therapist.

In their book, *Women's Ways of Knowing*, Mary Belenky and her coauthors discuss how one must first begin to hear her own inner voice in order to understand the importance of drawing out the voices of others, whether the other is her child, spouse, student, client or friend (Belenky et al., 1986).

There was a big old tree in the backyard when I grew up. From the moment I was able to climb, that tree was my refuge, my home. I climbed higher each year until by the time I was 17 I would escape and sit in the high branches hidden in the leaves, riding on the eastern Oregon wind. I did a lot of thinking in the tree; the wind in the leaves was my only friend. One time in South Canyon with my dad and brothers I climbed way to the top of a very steep hillside and sat and listened to the wind. I was about 12 at the time. The wind listened to me and required nothing of me.

On warm evenings I would wander around the fields near our house, and a wildness and longing would overcome me and I would think of running. I always knew there was something I wanted very badly, something I needed, someone to listen to me. And always, always there was that Eastern Oregon wind. I let the wind blow through me, calming me, crying for me. I could hear its voice in the trees and wild grasses, moaning and whispering, howling in February. I was so alone, but I had the wind. Yet that wind frightened me, too, because when I heard its cry I would feel things. When you grow up with an alcoholic parent, you do not want to feel things. . . .

There was nothing really dramatic in my home situation. My dad drank, withdrew, and we all kept quiet. The wind was a wonderful friend for many years, as was my journal for a while. The wind allowed me the space to think and feel, the journal helped me to begin to find my voice, and then I found a therapist who let me speak that voice and say aloud the things I'd only thought, felt or written for so long. . . .

That is why I want to be a therapist. There is a lot of beauty hidden in broken lives. There are many voices that have never spoken. Because of their wounds they may never be as strong as they could have been or as lovely, but as Tillie Olsen says, "There is still enough left to live by" (1956/1976, p. 21). In therapy the relationship between the therapist and the client is probably the most essential ingredient for good therapy. The trained therapist must make initial efforts at building that relationship and empathy is the starting point. Empathy is a response that focuses on the other person's feelings in such a way that the person knows they are understood and accepted. It is very difficult to focus on someone else's feelings, thoughts and values if I am not comfortable with my own.

It has always been very important to me that I respond to others in a manner wherein I receive no criticism. This fear has caused me to block my own thoughts and feelings and to become what the listener wants me to be. Most of my life I have had no sense that what I think, feel or value is of any importance, and thus I have been unable to be at ease with myself, to go out of myself to be present to the other. My capacity for empathy is blocked because I have been unable to hear the truth of the inner voice of my own feelings and thoughts.

I now realize that the family situation from which I came was one which actively discouraged me from having my own thoughts and feelings. It was important for me to be quiet, and if I spoke, I was to reflect back what my mother felt and thought. My mother as well stood back from my father, who had the last and ultimately the final word. Mary Belenky describes this as a typical expectation in many women's lives and it was certainly in mine. Conventional feminine goodness means being voiceless as well as selfless (Belenky et al., 1986).

I feel my own voice beginning to be more sure and able to hold its own. At times I can express my feelings and thoughts without too much fear. I used to listen and enjoy, but now I can listen, express myself and enjoy. It's still amazing to me when someone listens to what I say!

Margaret's reflections demonstrate a pattern we found in our participants' writings: When given permission to use personal narratives to discover and reorganize the stories of their lives, adults will invariably explore themes of gender and culture. Certainly the readings of Olsen (1956/1976), Belenky and coauthors (1986), and Gilligan (1982) stimulated the consideration of these themes, as did our emphasis upon caring as the deeply feminine expression Noddings describes (1984).

Ken

It is not a new assertion that telling stories can give an authenticity and power to the writings of a tender author. As teachers we have observed a few students who have a rich background in oral traditions. Although they may be quite competent in the usual college writing discourse, they often excel when given permission to express themselves in the narrative mode. We have included the complete version of Ken Donald's story, "The Ways of My Mother: A Native American Son's Reflection on the Oral Tradi-

tion," because it expresses so fully the significance of the story in constructing "culture." Ken gives us a unique understanding of how the oral tradition provides the theme, symbol, structure, and motivation for the Native
American tradition of connection to the land, to each other, and to a
woman-centered social system (Allen, 1986). Without story there is no
cultural meaning for a people; indeed, culture is a tapestry of stories, as
Barbara Myerhoff (1978) learned from the elderly Jewish men and women
she studied. It is often women who treasure the narrative as a way of
knowing and a way of communicating. Ken shares the story of how a
woman's birth changed the life of a people, bringing new meaning and
wisdom to their culture as they struggled to survive. That Ken is now
carrying on this legacy suggests to us lessons to be learned about connections between cultures and between men and women. This is Ken's story.

The Ways of My Mother: A Native American Son's Reflection on the Oral Tradition

"Sometimes you get so angry. Even worse, you know why you're
angry. And you can't do a thing about it. The more you know, the
more you don't see. The aches and pains of time: it rolls through you
in quivering waves. The human conditions *can* hurt you."

My mom used to tell us this in her oral tales. My mother was
born in the winter of the White-Buffalo. She knew her life was going
to be hard—hard-work, hard-living, hard-luck and hard-to-ignore.
My grandfather, her father, was the last of the Eagle Clan medicine
men. In our tribe, these clans people are privy to the highest forms of
healing arts. My grandmother was the daughter of the chief of our
tribe, the head of the Bear Clan. A joining of the highest, most respected clan, the Eagle Clan (Grandfather), with the deep Earth
symbol, the Bear Mother (Grandmother), produced a blessing: my
mother.

It is January, 1929, in Northeastern Oklahoma, the dream season
of our year. It's a time to open yourself, to open yourself bare to the
wintery Earth and ask for life to begin again. The fruits of our tribe's
dreams allow spring to realize itself. My mother stepped into this
world early that snowy morning. Hundreds of pairs of eyes witnessed
the birth as the tribe gathered around to experience the dream (i.e.,
second coming). The women's eyes misted with joy as a wailing female flung herself into life. The men's eyes blinked rapidly in disbe-
lief. A female? This is the second coming?

This is wrong! Surely the Eagle Clan won't accept her. The

White Buffalo won't come, not yet, not this year. The women reminded the men this blessing brings food to our hearths, "wherever
our fires are lit."

My grandfather felt the eyes, the hopes upon him. He looked
outside. It began to snow and snow. To the sweathouse the elders
trudged. It kept snowing.

When the elders stepped out of the sweathouse into the early
morning sun, before their disbelieving eyes stood a group of white
buffalo. Buffalo are wily and stout, they are big with pride. They
won't stand for any human's touch. They don't even like snow on
their rangy manes. Staring at the elders was a herd of white buffalo,
winter free buffalo; standing without looking; wispy, calm, with
measured breathing. Not one out of breath. Not one was swaying
with pride as does a buffalo. It was as if the buffalo appeared. The
white buffalo showed our tribe what they could not see with their
own eyes. My mom was as special as the second coming! Her birth
called the "White Buffalo."

The White Buffalo brought us to this planet as caretakers of the
Earth. The White Buffalo listens for the call only Mother Nature can
make. When the time is ready, the White Buffalo will return and take
us from this planet. The women of our tribe knew that events happen
when they should. The men knew you live with time—not against it.
The White Buffalo were talking to us.

My mother's birth coupled with the never-before-seen behavior
of the snow-clad buffalo was interpreted by my grandfather as a sign.
Never before in the memories of our people have we had a woman
medicine man. Never before has the breath of the Earth (woman)
been asked to walk where only spirits reside, where the eagles fly, the
home of the medicine ways. The Eagle Clan did accept my mother.
She became Chimi-Chimo, "The Wild Buffalo." Many in the tribe
wondered, was this the direction our Great Spirits wanted us to go? A
woman medicine man could tie us to the Earth preventing us from
ever leaving (being saved). Many eyes watched my mom grow up. My
mom said growing up she didn't feel different, but she saw that people felt different about her.

In retrospect, dropping out of school in the fifth grade freed up
a lot of my mom's time. She spent most of her time learning the medicine ways from my grandfather and the rest of her time, "being wild
with what I learned from Father." Many in the tribe shook their heads
saying, "I told you so!" with their indifference. Many turned away
from the hand reaching out to save them. Through it all, my mom's
sunny disposition kept her detractors at bay, her supporters attentive.

My mother's special calling is her ability to call eagles to appear whenever she feels she needs their presence. She uses her knowledge of the medicine ways to heal sick spirits. Nowadays, tribal members go to clinics and hospitals for direct medical care, but still come to my mom for counselling and spiritual support.

Eight years ago, my mom developed stomach cancer. She went to a hospital in Tulsa, Oklahoma. The doctors wanted to take her to surgery immediately. They told her she wouldn't live one week. My mom said, "Not yet." She went back to her reservation and drove to a special spot she knew. This "spot" was where her father showed her how to step into both worlds — real and unreal, reality and magic. It was at this spot where she received her special calling of the eagles. She sat in her car and thought. She stayed there for days without food or water. My mom had a vision of eagles coming down to her. The eagles sat and watched her for a day. She says they, the eagles, wanted to see what foot she would follow — reality or magic. Eventually she felt a burning peace come over her. As she slept, she felt awakened by a fire in her stomach. She moved out of her body, floating above her car. The eagles were tearing at her stomach with their beaks. Even out of her body she felt the rolling waves of pain flow through her. Finally the eagles stopped, looked up at my mom and then my mom knew it wasn't her time to die yet.

When my mom awakened in the car she felt sick. Her stomach was swollen and the pain was great. She remembered her dreams and thought they were telling her to have the surgery. She drove to the hospital, checked in and was immediately prepped for surgery. When the doctors took x-rays to determine the spread of cancer before opening her up, they were shocked. No cancer was found anywhere. They did every test they could think of, always coming up with the same negative results. The hospital in Tulsa (Oral Roberts' territory) called the papers and told them of this miracle that had occurred. It was described as being done by God. My mom says she agreed it was done. She was a little wary of Oral's god having done it but agreed she had been healed by a power greater than her faith.

This brush with death didn't cause my mom to lead a "one foot in the grave" lifestyle. From her squalid trailer she exudes her special kind of magic. When you talk with her you can hear yourself think. Everyone's her sister or good friend. She pushes on your grips, your pillars of knowledge, your finely-tuned defenses until you can feel her loving acceptance of you. But paradoxically, she does not leave you to drift. Her pointed reminders present you with a way to see yourself while still holding out more possibilities.

My mom just found out she has a hole in her heart. Her heart can't pump enough to keep up sufficient pressure. She's had four heart attacks in the last six months. Doctors predict she won't last another six months. Coming to terms with her life and talking to each of us children will forever be an example of how to die to me. I'll never again be able to forget that significant people die. I'm sad for that. My mom's rich narrative, her stories, her reminder that life goes on, but that each of us has a special way to be *with* life is a "knowing" that is now integrated into my life.

My mom's understanding of her own life resounds with metaphors of the "voice" we all strive to bring forth in ourselves and in our community and culture. Her oral stories were always meant to get us to see, as Native Americans, how to accept yourself. Her narratives were meant to bring us to the cliff, but we had to decide when to jump. Jumping into "a way of knowing" is everyone's journey. I've had the pleasure of a loving guide, the pain of knowing what lay ahead. I am different as a man, as a Native American, and as a counselor because of how I have come to "know" this.

My mom's message is simply, "Find the path to yourself and run to it." I'm still running. Thanks to my mom I have a clearer sense of where I'm running.

We view Ken's story as a wonderful example of the power of story in guiding both the life of an individual and the life of a culture. We are reminded of Cynthia Ozick's allusion to storytelling as a "kind of magic act" (1983, pp. 10–11).

One of the major themes for the course is derived from Robert Kegan's (1982) work on the nature of human psychological development. He creates vivid metaphors to explain the human drive toward competency, increased differentiation, and the making of meaning as we continually strive to "know" the world. Many class participants were drawn to Kegan because of their intuitive sense of the paradoxical nature of life and the complexity of human development. They were relieved that his was not another cognitive-stage theory that somehow did not accommodate their own experiences; rather they were intrigued by the notion that human development is a journey that involves striking balances between the fundamental yearnings of autonomy and inclusion. These "balances" are a kind of "evolutionary truce" where one shifts onto new ground and revisits the old, continually realigning one's constructs while striving to make sense out of one's experiences. Our students appreciated a theory of development that considered their own yearnings not necessarily contradictions but rather expressions of increasing complexity and possibility. Participants wrote and talked, putting their lives in a new order, finding new ways to make sense out of their experiences as they experimented with Kegan's language of meaning making. For example, they connected Pilisuk and Parks's (1986) notion of "the healing web" with Kegan's concept of "embeddedness." Both metaphors speak to a social context that gives support and a "culture of identity" during a particular phase of development.

Ruth

Ruth Lundblad's writing is a particularly dramatic example of the connections students made out of the seemingly paradoxical tensions of the life-course theme. Deeply touched by the fictional account of the old woman, Eva, in Tillie Olsen's story "Tell Me a Riddle" (1956/1976), Ruth applies Kegan's concepts in her analysis of the story as it speaks to her own life, while integrating the religious metaphors so personally meaningful.

A New Song

"Grandaddy, Grandaddy don't cry. She is not there, she promised me. On the last day, she said she would go back to when she first heard music, a little girl on the road of the village where she was born. She promised me. It is a wedding and they dance, while the flutes, so joyous and vibrant, tremble in the air. Leave her there, Grandaddy, it is all right. She promised me. Come back, come back and help her poor body to die" (Olsen, 1956/1976, p. 125).

Sitting here at the computer, trying to harmonize my brain cells into a wedding feast and dance, I resonate with Olsen's story, and with the plight of the dying woman, Eva, who, at her last moment faces point blank life's interplay, and melodious blend of some of their overtures in her life.

Both my song and Eva's song says this: that truth hides in paradox; that it cannot be embodied within either/or parameters, and that personal and sexual individuation serves an even greater purpose — that of renewing relationships between genders and across generations, and of teaching male and female, young and old, to step lively in the streets, in motion together to the trilling of Pan's flute, "so joyous and vibrant, and trembling in the air."

Because life, in its living, tightens the bowstring between radical opposites: between woman and man; between relation and separation; and between community chorus and long, lovely solos in the night. My status as a loner amid a chaotic family life, and Eva's stance in "reconciled solitude" amid America's post-industrial society, become uneasy fortresses against what is instinctively known to be true—that we all swing spiderlike in the winds as members of a tightly knit life network, which begins darkly in the humus nature of our cultural history, continues above ground through the trunk of fierce individuality, and then reaches upward and outward into the sweet, sunlit branches of the Tree of Life; this is our "healing web."

We observe Eva in three life phases: (1) as a Russian peasant girl, drowning in poverty, yet singing about cultural meaning and about hope for a better tomorrow; (2) as a silent American mother, growing bark hard in isolation, and in the lop-sided nurturance of her growing, and then gone, young family; and (3) as a dying grandmother, blowing lonesome as a leaf upon autumn branches, and only just now regaining the power to sing, with the ability to hear her own voice, as she realizes her relationship to the oneness of life. She realizes it only perhaps as she drifts downward in death toward those mossy village roots and intertwining streets where she first heard music, first applauded the wedding, and first participated in the dance.

How could it be that the Old World, so deadly to individual autonomy, had yet harbored a culture which nurtured so well her ability to belong and believe? Because paradoxically, that was where Eva, as she thinks back, can place the feeling of connectedness, that sense of mattering, and of being one with the meaning of life.

But so much has changed. The passion for tending children in the New World has isolated this young mother from adjustment to the new culture, to a new form of inclusion, and to a new life through assimilation of a post-industrial way of belonging and believing. Moreover, her gift for relatedness (granted by virtue of gender) had isolated her from a male-dominated culture which overvalued individuality instead. So, therefore, Eva's very power to connect becomes her prison, a strangely silent prison with parallel bars which look not so unlike strands in social networks, yet lacking intersections.

Eva, then, as an old woman, has been rock dry for a long time. In these later years, life's tree trunk has become barkish, scarred over and defensive. And although she senses a more ancient truth within, authentic living water more powerful than blood, somehow joy, transport, and meaning have yet escaped. The sickness of loneliness invades her; still, it is a sickness she feels comfortable with. Connected in the near past only to babies and to blood, she remained silently aloof. But now, times have changed.

Now, stricken at once with cancer and with cacophony, she finds her voice, and clamors sullenly against the walls of a house she will not part with, a house symbolizing "excluded inclusion," plus a certain domestic detachment from society. Her husband, though, desires a more communal living arrangement instead. And, well, he only makes matters worse. During Eva's last illness he hauls her shrunken body helplessly between the homes of their grown children, as she groans and pleads for solitude instead. As this aged pair continue to roll so merrily along, the wife begins to cry bitterly against her husband in an overture toward dialogue, and toward a kind of understanding so long desired, yet never attempted before.

Bickering like magpies, then, they arrive on the peaceful Southern California coast amid other elderly folk who sit daily upon its shore, content in the gloaming, eyes silent upon the sea. But Eva, now, silent she cannot be. For the first time in a long while she begins to sing, a duet with death now, her new song for morning. I'll never forget Eva on the beach as she suddenly gathers strength and leaps hartlike into the sea; and then, when her long suffering husband gently tries to pull her out, and to wipe her dry with a handkerchief, she grabs the cloth and wraps up some sand to look at later with a strong glass — her womanly way of examining the ordinary for a hint of the eternal, and for the meaning of death, which rages and beats incessantly upon her shore.

Now enter Jeannie, their granddaughter, reality's nurse, yet imagination's artist, who presents the fulfillment of their Old World hopes, who ministers glowingly to her dying grandmother, who calls her lonely grandfather to the old woman's side in an affirmation of life even in confrontation with death, and who forms that healing link which, in balancing life's dichotomies, produces seedlings of promise, and of hope. Through Jeannie's ministrations, the Tree of Life fertilizes itself and the drifting movement downward ultimately becomes the movement up.

One extreme, then, Old World connectedness, represents the traditional female role; while New World individuality represents traditional masculinity. The important point to remember from this story is our need for the healing balance of both extremes; we must orchestrate life's cantata so that both male and female voices sound, and so that both solos and choral pieces flourish, or else harmony and health may be lost.

Whatever life guarantees, it is not the absolute answer. Paradox delivers oxymoronic truth. I desire the realization of this kind of truth in my life, an insight which can be utilized right now without waiting for the emergency of death to graciously point it out. As a college student, wife and as a mother of four, I often feel isolated and overwhelmed. My husband and children are lifesprings to me; yet also life draining. In confrontation with them, I step crazy into the sea, laughing furiously and wrapping up sand to examine later with my looking glass. The sand is my life; the looking glass, my story.

The truth is this: Masculinity and I make interesting music together. Together we cling to the vine, to the Tree of Life, to the ancient of days, so that we need not seek to revolutionize the other, but to harmonize with the other in a tremulous balance, a death defying rejuvenation, and an upward-spiraling flute song into the sky. This is the meaning of balance; and this, of grace.

The stories we have offered demonstrate the power of stories to heal, noted by Sam Keen:

> Stories open you up to the stories of others, as common and singular as your own. That remains the best way we storytelling animals have found to overcome loneliness, develop compassion and create community. Indeed, if the unique stories of individuals are not cherished, a group of people may become a mass, or a collective, but never a healing community. (1988, pp. 46–47)

These writings of graduate students point out the collective power of a class experience and the responsibility of professional education to move beyond the traditional epistemological assumptions about knowledge and ways of knowing. They also attest to the legitimacy of student experience in the shaping of their professional curriculum. And, they demonstrate a way to practice and model an ethic of care.

THE LESSONS WE LEARNED

These early experiences we had as teachers have now become the basis for the curriculum and pedagogy of this course, Individual and Societal Perspectives on Adulthood. What is particularly telling is that over each successive term and with new teams of teachers the course has been highly successful. Student writings and course evaluations indicate that we are doing something right. But what makes this experience so important to us as teachers are just those things that defy smugness and certainty.

Each successive course must be recreated anew, through dialogue between faculty and students. Because the nature of dialogue is to continually rediscover and revisit, we have found that there is no standard and efficient way to teach if the journey each term regards the participants as unique contributors to an evolving curriculum. Hence, a commitment to this kind of pedagogy is a commitment of time and energy, particularly on the part of the faculty. We have learned a lesson we always knew, that team teaching takes time and more time. The ideas brought into the discussions and writings by the students must be considered by both instructors together as part of the "text" of the class, and as material for their own personal and professional growth. Indeed, team teaching offers the teachers the unique opportunity to reflect upon their own teaching, learning, and growth.

One of the challenges we've faced is to communicate the ethos of this course to new faculty. The emphasis on community building, active dialogue, and collegiality among all course participants leads some faculty to question whether there is adequate "content" in the course. We continue to pair a "seasoned" teacher with new faculty to provide a model for the new team member of what is expected. We know that faculty must experience this pedagogy themselves if they are to model it.

We further learned that if we are to come to know our students and understand the power of their ideas to shape the course, then both instructors need to read the major writings of as many students as possible. This is a difficult arrangement to work out because of the numbers of participants in the course, but the benefits in terms of student trust and openness are worth the investment of time. Indeed, our own perceptions of each other's ideas were just as important for the evolving curriculum as our perceptions of our students' thinking.

We value experiential learning with a new level of certainty. The "challenge course" has become a standard part of the curriculum, and we continue to integrate more cooperative learning activities each time we teach the course. The literature on adult learning tells us that adults are most willingly recruited as learners when they feel that their own life experiences will be affirmed and when they have the opportunity to revisit and make sense out of the new in light of the old (Aslanian & Brickell, 1980; Brookfield, 1986; Chickering, 1981; Cross, 1981). Experiential learning builds upon what adults already know about their learning styles, and it creates opportunities for them to integrate new learning in the context of their previous experiences.

Narrative and personal story are powerful modes of knowing, and, although they are not exclusively for adults, we have observed the richness that these ways of knowing and telling have for adults who bring so many anecdotes and examples from life experience. We have seen the sureness with which our students continue to bring their "voices" into their other classes and have observed the benefits of this approach for our students in other classes. Students listen to others with greater interest and use narrative and personal story in their other writing.

It is a pleasure for us to wander through the graduate school at night meeting old friends from these classes and recognizing students from programs other than our own. We sense a camaraderie rooted in caring and take personal pleasure in experiencing a growing sense of community among graduate students and faculty. We are currently working to build better links between the two core courses in adult development and organizational cultures. In response to some students' requests, we also seek more effective means of bridging the course content and method with the challenges and dilemmas our students face daily in their professional lives.

We teach to change lives. Our experience teaching in this program has led to significant changes in our own and our students' ways of thinking and being. In the sharing of life stories and dilemmas of the workplace, we have come closer to understanding the "other" as ourselves, to imagining "the familiar hearts of strangers" (Ozick, 1986, p. 65). We have shared in a learning community that bridged many gaps and explored many paradoxes: feeling and thought; masculine and feminine; teacher and administrator; hearing and deaf; Anglo-Saxon and Native American; teacher and learner; individual and community. It has been a remarkable journey.

REFERENCES

Allen, P. G. (1986). *The sacred hoop: Recovering the feminine in American Indian traditions*. Boston: Beacon Press.

Aslanian, C. B., & Brickell, H. M. (1980). *Americans in transition: Life changes as reasons for adult learning*. New York: College Entrance Examination Board.

Belenky, Mary; Clinchy, Blythe; Goldberger, Nancy; & Tarule, Jill. (1986). *Women's ways of knowing*. New York: Basic Books.

Brody, Celeste, & Witherell, Carol. (1987). Individual and societal perspectives on adulthood. Course syllabus. (Available from the authors at Lewis & Clark College, Graduate School of Professional Studies, Portland, OR)

Brookfield, S. (1986). *Understanding and facilitating adult learning*. San Francisco: Jossey-Bass.

Bruner, Jerome. (1983). *In search of mind: Essays in autobiography*. New York: Harper & Row.

Bruner, Jerome. (1986). *Actual minds, possible worlds*. Cambridge, MA: Harvard University Press.

Buber, Martin. (1965). *Between man and man*. New York: Macmillan.

Chickering, Arthur. (1981). *The modern American college*. San Francisco: Jossey-Bass.

Cross, Patricia. (1981). *Adults as learners: Increasing participation and facilitating learning*. San Francisco: Jossey-Bass.

Gilligan, Carol. (1982). *In a different voice: Psychological theory and women's development*. Cambridge, MA: Harvard University Press.

Graduate School of Professional Studies. (1986). *Graduate catalog*. Portland, OR: Lewis & Clark College.

Kegan, Robert. (1982). *The evolving self*. Cambridge, MA: Harvard University Press.

Keen, Sam. (1988). The stories we live by. *Psychology Today, 22*(12), 46–47.

Metzger, Deena. (1986). Circles of stories. *Parabola, IV*(4). (Original work published 1969)

Myerhoff, Barbara. (1978). *Number our days*. New York: Simon and Schuster.

Noddings, Nel. (1984). *Caring: A feminine approach to ethics and moral education*. Berkeley: University of California Press.

Olsen, Tillie. (1976). Tell me a riddle; I stand here ironing. In *Tell me a riddle*. New York: Dell Books. (Original work published 1956)

Ozick, Cynthia. (1983). Usurpation (Other People's Stories). In *Bloodshed and three novellas*. New York: E. P. Dutton/Obelisk. (Original work published 1976)

Ozick, Cynthia. (1986, May). The moral necessity of metaphor. *Harper's Magazine*, pp. 64–65.

Pilisuk, Mark, & Parks, Susan H. (1986). *The healing web*. Hanover, NH: University Press of New England.

Shor, Ira, & Freire, Paulo. (1987). *A pedagogy for liberation: Dialogues for transforming education*. South Hadley, MA: Bergin and Garvey.

Stafford, Kim. (1987). *Having everything right: Essays of place*. New York: Penguin Books.

EPILOGUE

Themes Remembered and Foreseen

NEL NODDINGS and CAROL WITHERELL

Does everything then come over again a little differently? . . . Is there a pattern, a theme, recurring like music; half remembered, half foreseen? (Virginia Woolf, *The Years*, p. 269)

Our authors have laid out a tantalizing array of uses of narrative and dialogue in education. We have learned much from each other, and we hope that readers, too, have found the project worthwhile.

We learn from stories. More important, we come to understand—ourselves, others, and even the subjects we teach and learn. Stories engage us. Every lecture and after-dinner speaker knows the value of an opening story or two. Sometimes stories introduce us in an entertaining way to new material, and sometimes they just introduce us to the speaker. Engaging storytellers grab our attention and are likely to keep it as they move into more abstract material.

Stories are tools of enchantment. Barry Lopez reminds his readers in *Arctic Dreams* (1987) that the most cherished places in a culture are often not visible to the eye but are rather brought into view through the drama of narrative, song, and performance. Some of these invisible places have been captured in our authors' narratives.

We use stories to explain. In brief or sustained metaphor, we explain to our students by beginning, "It is like this. . . . " Our stories serve an interpretive function, acquainting our students with difficult new concepts by relating them to familiar ideas and personal interests.

Stories can help us to understand by making the abstract concrete and accessible. What is only dimly perceived at the level of principle may become vivid and affectively powerful in the concrete. Further, stories motivate us. Even that which we understand at the abstract level may not move us to action, whereas a story often does.

There are inductive and phenomenological uses for stories. Interpretive theorists use variation upon variation to get at the essences of phenomena. Working case by case, we can build impressive arguments to convince each other that something is wrong, or that something works, or that something comes in infinite varieties. Sometimes we try to carry the day with one dramatic story, and our students should understand this too.

We learn by both hearing and telling stories. Telling our own stories can be cathartic and liberating. But it is more than that. We discover as we tell and come closer to wisdom. Even in the dread domain of mathematical story problems, we are beginning to realize that people learn from making up such stories. Getting into the mind of the story writer untangles some of the mystery.

Finally, stories are powerful research tools. They provide us with a picture of real people in real situations, struggling with real problems. They banish the indifference often generated by samples, treatments, and faceless subjects. They invite us to speculate on what might be changed and with what effect. And, of course, they remind us of our persistent fallibility. Most important, they invite us to remember that we are in the business of teaching, learning, and researching to improve the human condition. Telling and listening to stories can be a powerful sign of re-gard — of caring — for one another.

REFERENCES

Lopez, Barry. (1987). *Arctic dreams*. New York: Bantam Books.
Woolf, Virginia. (1965). *The years*. New York: Harcourt, Brace, & World.

Index